THEY DON'T KISS IN THE MOVIES

THEY DON'T KISS IN THE MOVIES

GURDIP SIDHU

To order additional copies of this book, contact:
Xlibris Corporation
1-888-795-4274
www.Xlibris.com
Orders@Xlibris.com
27126

This book is dedicated to:
My wife, Jagdish and
My two daughters, Nikki and Vinita

I

Hoisting skis to shoulders, we walked back the five hundred odd yards to the inn. Yesterday's storm and today's warm sun had conjured up a skier's dream. Two tired bodies now reveled in the most desirable languor. Showered, dressed, they sat an hour later in a dimly lit, hospitable, warm dining room. Outside, the neon sign glowed in the lowering fog. "The Inn At Whiteface Mountain," it said. Red, green, empty wine bottles shone dimly along the windows, logs crackled in the fireplace, and soft voices drifted across from the other tables. Love and magic hung in the air. My gaze moved past red liquid in wine glasses, losing itself in limpid, brown womanly eyes casting irresistible spells from across the table. She was an apsara, I was sure, one of those heavenly nymphs that entertain the gods, or a houri straight from Paradise. I had chased her all day down the snowy slopes, and would follow her again soon to the room. But she had other plans. Slowly, hypnotically, such are the ways of apsaras and houris, and the cruel lure of the past, I was drawn ever back in time, back, back, back, tumbling through memories long forgotten, to a time when life was melancholy, and I was just a boy in India. Red wine, evening magic, limpid brown eyes, crackling fire-logs, drifting voices, they all conspired, and I yielded. Memories arose from the depths, unfolding relentlessly. More wine, more eyes, more magic, and I was revisiting history.

It was a hot, dry afternoon, as had been all previous afternoons this month of May, the temperature steadily rising day by day, nature stricken with typhoid. If this state of affairs continued much longer, delirium would surely set in—my mother the doctor had said so. In deference to the heat, the chirping of the sparrows had long since ceased; the only sign of activity was the hot, desiccating, life-draining *loo* blowing across the land, driving man and insect, birds and flies, dogs and mosquitoes, to shelter in the shade. Towards evening, an ominous orange glow blossomed in the western sky, a child of the desert, pressing eastwards. Premature darkness enveloped the streets, and an eerie silence gripped the city; even the raucous crows were mute.

And then it hit: dust swooping down, small grain, big grain, newspapers, rubbish, pummeling the metropolis and the unlucky few caught outdoors. Nostrils filled, sneezed; grit blew into, rattled eyes; white clothes turned dull grayish-brown; people, dogs, ran for cover; and the heavens thundered, a fitting counterpoint to the urgent rattling of ten thousand doors and windows. But no rain fell, only dust; yet it was relief. The temperature fell a full fifteen degrees, and a blanket of dust, soothing dust, covered everything, hiding both the beautiful and the ugly. "Dust into dust, and under dust . . ." but no, not quite. Men lived; brooms in hand, they fought back. Painfully, slowly, life returned to the streets of Karole Bagh, a lower middle class neighborhood of New Delhi and home to the street I lived on, the street of the date palms—Khajoor Road.

At the time of partition, 1947, when we were transposed, courtesy of religious zeal beyond our control, of ambitious plans to create a land of the pure, Pakistan, to Delhi from Lahore, the road had the Muslim name of Mohammed Hussain; but the prevailing animosity towards anything Muslim at the time—a reaction to the drive towards purity—was guaranteed to eliminate this commemorative, however illustrious Mohammed Hussain may have been. It hurt me to see wanton destruction of things and names historical, but it could not be denied that the substitute was both appropriate and atune with Nature.

At the time of the name change, I had been away in Shimla (written and pronounced Simla by those of Anglican persuasion, and by those who, willy-nilly like me, were imbibing an English education), a town seven thousand feet up in the Himalayas of the Punjab. This penchant of the British for mispronouncing everything Indian was surely a disease, of the ears may be, or the larynx, or both. Look at Delhi—the spelling is a travesty. Admittedly, it is not the cleanest, nicest-smelling city in the world, but why take it out on its name? It is ancient and historical; it has outlived thousands, may be millions; it will surely outlive us. Then why this petty meanness? My fellow Punjabis and I pronounce it Dilli, the 'd' soft like in many European tongues. For the natives, which for us Punjabis implies the local city-*waalahs* who had slept their way through all the vicissitudes and turmoil of recent North Indian history, it was Dehli. But only the British called it Delhi. What was it with them anyway, that they had to, still continue to, make nonsense of all words Indian? Was there a method to their madness, or wasn't there? No one knew. Their spelling and pronunciation of all Indian names was a continuing comedy of errors, still aped and perpetuated by their Indian protégés. The well-known city of Kahnpur was pronounced and written Cawnpore. Ridiculous, you say; but wait; hold judgment.

Even I was not immune. In deference to British ways, my aunt had registered me in the Sacred Heart School, Lahore, as Amrik Singh Randhawa. It is really Amreek. You could, of course, spell it Umreek, but such are the ways of the English language that, without a doubt, both would be mispronounced here in the New World, my beloved, adopted land, the United States. Greater men than I have shortened their names, cut, slashed, misspelled, simplified, so that what was once Greek, Polish, Russian, is now American. But there is more to a name than a sequence of letters; it is a sound that is familiar, soothing, belonging, loved, intimately a part of one's emotions and being; it is the sound of a mother's voice, and that of a lover beckoning; so I must attempt, at least once, to defend it. Now try this: if you pronounce 'Am' as 'Um' in umbrella, and 'rik' as 'reek', you will have earned my blessings. Randhawa is quite another matter. 'Ran' sounds like 'run', and 'awa' as 'ah-wa'. Now try my name. There you have it; you are now talking like a true, blue-blooded Punjabi.

We Punjabis, as you know, or should if you don't, pride ourselves on the blueness of our blood. It often runs hot, but what blue blood does not? Incidentally, 'Pun' is like the word 'pun', and 'jabi' is 'jaa-bi'. 'Punj', in Punjabi, is, of course, not a misspelled pun, but the number five. 'Aab' is water, river; Punjab is hence the land of the five aabs . . . waters . . . rivers. From northwest to southeast, they are the Jhelum, Chenab (pronounce Chinaab), Ravi (pronounce Raavi), Beas (say Bey-ahs) and Sutlej ('Sut' as in 'Sutcliffe' and 'lej' as 'ludge' in 'sludge'). Each is the size of the Hudson, or bigger, and each bursts its banks every July or August, barring a drought, as monsoon rains swell the waters, spreading destruction, life-giving silt, woe and happiness, happiness and woe, to the surrounding countryside. The aab giveth and the aab taketh away.

Now for him with the misspelled name. I am in my seventeenth year, home from boarding school in Shimla, celebrating an extended leave from studies after successfully completing the Senior School Certificate examination, the high school exam given by Cambridge University, the English one, the prior December. Pre-medical does not begin till mid-July. My parents both work. My father's a lawyer, and my mother a physician. Both seldom have much time for me except to remind me to study, particularly my father, even now when I have no pressing need to, and no exams to take. My mother, an obstetrician, is much too busy, and disinclined by nature, to try to regulate my life; particularly, as of late, the Indian population transposed to Delhi, which includes most of her Lahore patients, has been breeding fast, trying to make up for losses incurred in the birth-pangs of independence. Babies are being born everywhere; no one objects; all celebrate. My father, being simply a lawyer who runs a practice of sorts, has time on his hands, and he insists on spending it plotting my education. So, during this vacation, I have learned, under duress, typing at the

Pitman Academy, a small, ramshackle, little room with heavy, antiquated typewriters in the building opposite Madras hotel (that is 'Mud' with a soft 'd' and 'raas', so Mudraas hotel. I am sorry, but there is just no way out of this spelling mess) in Connaught Circus. Incidentally, but for that period of hammering the keys, I never would have written this book and you would not be reading it, since I have a complete aversion to writing longhand. In hindsight, this is the one time I must concede that my father's heavy-handed manner of dealing with his offspring demonstrated foresight, something often conspicuously lacking. Also in this period, I partook of a college-level course in Punjabi called the *Gyani*, the only thing I ever failed in my life. Why? You will soon see as I tell you about my school. Fortunately, I am free again, though only so long as I stay out of father's sight.

The fact that I went to the all-boys Bishop Cotton School in Shimla instead of some local institution in Delhi would suggest to most people that my family was rich. My next-door neighbors certainly think so. But we are not rich, merely middle class. Most of the money mother earns is consumed supporting relatives, close and not-so-close, who insist on making our house an inn. They drop in from the Punjab invariably unannounced; the first sign that someone has arrived is the pile of baggage lying on the front steps of the verandah. Because of this hospitality function, my family has never seen fit for me to have a room to myself. My activities are carried out in the living room, which in the evenings doubles as a dining room; or in my parents' bedroom, which not surprisingly is the only bedroom. Sleeping arrangements vary with the season. In summer, all of us, including my parents, sleep on string beds laid out on the small lawn in front of the house. Lest you get the wrong idea, there is a high, plastered, brick wall separating the lawn from the street, so there is privacy from the general public. But there is no privacy within the family, or from the neighbors' family, who live in one-third of the house, and also sleep in the same lawn. Not that I object.

You see, India is a country crowded with people, but social contact, particularly that between the sexes, is strictly limited. Any forced togetherness can only help, not hinder, at least for us teenagers. But circumstances have not been on my side. For the past five years, the only times at home have been the annual winter vacations from December to March. In that season, the beds are placed in the verandah, and there is less opportunity to casually talk with others not of my family. This is my first summer at home. So far, though, my neighbors' beautiful daughter has not seen fit to risk showing me affection. "Risk?" you ask. Yes, for the enterprise is fraught with danger. Her family is Hindu, quite opposed to affairs of the heart outside of marriage, and most certainly not with a Sikh, so she has to be careful. I keep hoping that that is the explanation for her diffidence to my advances, because I'd rather not dwell on more depressing possibilities.

Life is indeed dull. All my school friends live far away in posher areas of New Delhi, in bungalows, with membership in clubs where they swim and play tennis, or meet girls who are equally accomplished. I have no such luck, being mired in Karole Bagh with those who would not understand my kind; who go to schools where teachers enforce discipline by beating them in the classroom with the edge of a ruler on outstretched hands, not like BCS where the housemaster called you to his office after school hours to cane you on your behind, and then expected you to thank him for it like any good, 'English-style, public school' lad.

Trying to live in two such totally unrelated worlds was enough to drive any self-respecting Sikh boy to schizophrenia, but all it did for me was to cause a listlessness, and a feeling of despair born of the knowledge that everything was all wrong. For instance, what was a middle-class boy like me pretending to do in a rich boys' school, and then, how was I supposed to fit into a lower middle class neighborhood every winter vacation, a place where almost no one could speak English? Heaven knows how, each year, I made valiant efforts to return to my native tongue, but sadly with only woefully partial success. I cannot express anything even remotely sophisticated without liberally sprinkling every Punjabi sentence with English words. I probably murder the syntax and grammar too. The result is a language that is almost pidgin. Even the most kindly souls would have to label me an outcast, or at best a snob; but I try. Alas, attempting to romance a beautiful girl without the gift of language is not easy, not till you've grown close; but you need language to do that too. Once, in a cinema, I had held her hand, bypassing speech, but we have not been alone again, and I have begun to despair.

When I entered BCS in March 1948, the first two weeks were surely the worst of the eleven years of my life. Though I could read and write English well, I could hardly speak it; and lo and behold, the very first thing I learned was that we were permitted to speak only English, even among ourselves. Speaking Indian, which included Punjabi, was strictly forbidden, on pain of pain by caning; on your behind, like I said before, because that was the only way a gentleman was supposed to be punished. The whole scheme was sadistic: first, forcible separation from home and parents; then from your mother tongue. The mind sputtered and frothed in darkness, unable to find words, ultimately falling silent. To my tender neurons, this was a most diabolical plot. I was not at the time well versed in the niceties of the Hindu, and incidentally also Sikh, theory of reincarnation and the function of *karma* (pronounced 'cur' as in 'curry'; and 'm'), which means acts in a previous lifetime that determine your fate in the present. Like my father says: what is written is written (in your fate, of course) and there is nothing you can do about it. Being unaware, at the time, of this protective fatalism, I could not accept my sorrow with equanimity, and became acutely homesick. "*Beeji* (mother)", I cried in my sleep. I wanted soft comforts, maternal and womanly.

The plot thickens. The train on which we set off for Shimla was much too late arriving at its destination. Unbeknownest to us, there was white powder, later recognized as snow, on the tracks, forcing the engine wheels to slip and skid all the fifty-six miles of narrow-gauge track from Kaalka in the foothills to Shimla. It was eight o'clock, pitch dark by this time, so there was no question of going the remaining three-plus miles to the school. Bedrolls were taken out of the carriage where they were stored, and distributed to us, with the instructions to open and sleep in them. Later, next morning, we were told to re-roll them and tie them up in the original way. But how? Having always lived with servants in the house, and having never been taken on a vacation by my parents, I had never learned to do anything other than play and study. But BCS was a place where you learned, even when you were still three miles and a night away; so we did it, somehow.

Morning saw us loaded into cattle trucks (well, may be not that, but they were at least trucks for carrying bricks; however, let us suppose they were cattle trucks for emotional reasons) and driven off on the Cart Road to school in the subfreezing temperature. We stood because we were too packed to sit; besides, cattle don't sit when being transported, and we were no exception. By the time we arrived at our destination, my hands were blue from hanging on to the bars overhead, which were the only visible means of support, and my back was cold from the snow that had fallen off a deodar (an Indian cedar tree) down my neck on the way. School was hard, stony, frozen ground with a long, two-floored building shaped like en E, the open arms looking south, and with a sloping red roof. There were lists on bulletin boards, and I was informed by an older boy, a prefect, who had read them, that I was to go upstairs to Curzon house. After settling in, we were instructed to go down, line up outside the dining hall, and await in the cold till the call came to march in house by house, Rivaz and Ibbetson on the west, Curzon and Lefroy on the east. We kept standing at our seats until 'grace' was said. Suddenly, from the mouth of the pink-skinned schoolmaster on duty, who was standing at the northern end of the hall, came out a most solemn string of words: "For what we are about to receive, we thank thee, our Lord." "Amen", everybody responded (pronounced Ah-men in the English fashion). Who was the 'Lord?' What was 'Amen?' I wondered, but my mind was not up to formulating the English necessary to find out. Anyway, now we could sit.

Sheepishly, I sat down. The house captain at the head of the table and the house prefect at the tail served everybody a toast and a fried egg, the plates being passed down to the center of the long wooden tables at which we sat, simultaneously from both ends. Knives, forks, spoons were set on each seat, but I had never seen the clawed weapons, and had no idea of their use. So I just sat there and watched, afraid to ask how because I would then have to speak that foreign English. Next came porridge, another novelty that I had never seen before. There were no *paraunthas*, no yogurt with salt and pepper, no *makkhan* (white butter), no *malai* (cream) . . . what kind of a breakfast was this? Somehow, without the slightest understanding of the food or the weapons, I blundered my way through the meal and even got to eat the egg and toast.

The first two weeks were a baptism by fire, but by the time they were over, I had learned to speak English and had made some friends. I was now familiar with essential BCS slang like "bogs' for the lavatories, and 'boff paper' for toilet paper. This last was a real surprise; you see, Indians use water, not paper, to clean themselves. Then there was the fact that there were no doors to the johns, so that you sat there in full view of anyone who walked into the room. My parents would have been horrified to hear that, even though it was obvious to me that this legacy was left to us by the children of our former rulers; and if it was good enough for English sons, surely it must be good enough for us, unless they were really less civilized. Given that they used paper instead of water, there was good reason to believe them inferior. Anyway, I was not going to debate that with my parents.

When it came to general behavior, you were never supposed to 'tit', which means complain, to anyone, not just a teacher or prefect, about being mistreated by some bully. There was to be no putting-of-hands-in-pockets, no matter how cold, because it was sissy-like behavior. My parents, having no idea that there would be snow and bitter cold in the Himalayas, since they had never been there (my mother had actually been there several times, but only in summer, and my father never), had failed to provide me with gloves. Accordingly, by the end of the week, my hands and fingers were swollen, painful and cracked from not-being-put-into-pockets. The condition, I was told, was only chilblains, something that I would get over eventually; but, reassurance or not, it still hurt.

On Sunday, we were all required to write letters home. I wrote to my mother, painfully, with chilblained hands. I was simply too scared to write to my father; besides, I had nothing in common with him, and did not remember ever initiating a conversation between us. Every time we talked, he originated the discussion and I listened, scared, knowing that it was some task he was proposing, and his tasks were never pleasant. He really did not believe in fun and happiness; he believed in contentment, which is not quite the same thing, but which is of the same genre as being resigned to one's fate. He never joked; in fact, he viewed humor as a kind of sadistic exercise, seeing as it was always at the expense of another. He made it abundantly clear that he could see nothing funny in such activity, admonishing us to be 'good' boys, my brother and I, and play when it was time to play, and study when it was time to study. However, if something had to be sacrificed for want of time— you guessed it—it was always play. Out of fear of my father, I had become so skillful at my studies that I never was second in the exams. The conviction was strong that if I ever failed to come first, there would be hell to pay, like losing my playing privileges, and corporal punishment to boot. So, like the proverbial Jack, I had become a studious boy, though I had a natural ability for sports, acquired—you guessed it again—from my father himself. During his days in college, he had been a champion athlete.

The dutiful letter that I wrote made no mention of cold, chilblains, boff paper, door-less Johns, homesickness, or English instead of Punjabi. If I complained, my father might try to help and, knowing from past experience, I could well imagine that the help would be infinitely worse than any complaint I harbored; besides, I was getting used to my problems and even learning to solve them a little. There was another problem I could not mention, and that was about the arrangements for bathing. All they had here was a common hall-like bathroom with ten showers all in a row. The prefect on duty turned them on, and he decided how hot the water was to be, which was nearly always close to boiling, much too hot for my tender skin. After being in that water, we looked as pink as Englishmen, and just as boiled; but that was nothing. The worst was that you had to strip stark naked to have a bath, and that too in front of everyone. Now this was a major problem to all the uninitiated newcomers. Let me explain.

Since there is no privacy in Indian homes, you bathe with your underdrawers on. I was not aware of what happened in homes with daughters, because I had no sisters. Anyway, I had no idea what girls looked like except that grownup girls had breasts. Indeed, I had never seen a naked girl of any age. Be that as it may, hardiness is inculcated into Sikh boys from birth, so I hesitated a little the first time, then decided to plunge in stark naked like the rest of the boys. Other newcomers were not as fortunate; one of them forsook bathing for an entire two weeks, and that in a country where everyone is expected to bathe at least once a day, water shortage or no water shortage. Of course, I made no mention of the bathing problem in my letter, nor the fact that we bathed only twice a week, spring, summer or autumn, not every day as Indians should. The European climate of the Himalayas required European ways. The three-day intervals helped to keep us deliciously odorous, just like Englishmen, until the swimming season opened in June. In those days, deodorants did not exist, certainly not in India. But India is an odorous country, with open sewers, and public defecation by both man and animals, so the nose adjusts easily. These are outdoor smells, but the pink people were willing to smell indoors too. At eleven, I mused, you have much to learn, so I simply shrugged my shoulders; after all, our parents sent us here to learn, and if this is what they teach, this is what we'll learn.

Then there was something even worse, we all had to go to chapel every morning; Christians, non-Christians, everybody. There we learned psalms and hymns, and listened to the headmaster, who doubled as the reverend, preach sermons every Sunday evening. In many ways, he was a strange man. For instance, he used a tie in place of a belt; yes, around his waist; and he had a reputation for caning crooked, meaning that he was likely to hit the back of your thighs when he aimed for your buttocks. Anyway, I looked with favor on psalms and hymns because I had always loved singing. As for the sermons, I think they helped convert me to atheism. Even at that age, listening to those few I did not sleep through, I could see the senselessness and contradictions with which they were riddled. There was scarcely a pleasure in life that was not sinful, and staying away from such things was what earned you God's love. I could not believe my ears, because even my father was more liberal. "How could anybody believe such nonsense?" I wondered. I could not compare it to the Sikh religion because, since the latter was much less organized, it did not submit its hapless members to weekly brainwashing—though attempts are being made in the United States now to make amends— and I had been mercifully spared any sermonizing. I daresay, though, that my father's concept of how to raise a child more than made up for it. To this day, I cannot understand what the devout see in worship. There was no question of telling my parents that I went to church every morning. It would have been like saying that I had become a Christian, something which all Punjabis, not just Sikhs, would be horrified to hear. I have also never told any of my relatives or friends in India. I still am not sure whether my parents know or not, and I am not about to try finding out. Imagine what their reaction would have been if I revealed to them that this best of schools they were sending me to, this school that was modeled on the British public schools, this school that was draining all their hard-earned wealth, was trying to turn us all into little brown Englishmen.

II

BCS imparted independence and integrity, twin virtues prized by the British. It was a Spartan existence with much discipline and honor, akin to a school-boys military academy. There was marching daily through the portals of the dining hall. Then there was marching into Irwin Hall for the movies on Saturday evenings, and once a year to receive the results of the final exams. Those who passed learned here that they would be forever parted by a year from those who failed. There was no second chance; for the failed a year it was, and nothing less; no makeup classes, remedial reading or math; no one to bend over backwards and unearth insurmountable emotional stress, bed-wetting or the like, even though all of these did actually occur. Those who failed were destined to pay for their mistakes, without a doubt; they with their time, and their parents with a year's fees.

But failure was not entirely joyless. Housemates of the flunk-ee looked up at him the coming March because he would be bigger, by a year, and likely adept at sports, a trait always cherished. Highly prized was an ace sportsman who flunked in the final year, because he would have the whole school salivating in anticipatory rejoicing. With a stronger eleven, be it in cricket, hockey, or soccer, it mattered little, the school could now show those Sanawarians, brethren and arch-enemies from the school lower down the hills, who they had to contend with. There would be victories to celebrate; the flunk-ee's house might even win the Cockhouse Shield, that hallowed turtle shell which symbolized the ultimate in physical achievement, namely supremacy in sports, something everyone could crow about.

There was one more marching activity, the daily march into chapel, a march that was periodically sorrowful. The latter was on Sunday evenings, when our imagined iniquities were exposed from the reverend's exalted pulpit; and another study-free weekend announced its demise.

Discipline was the key word. It distinguished us from the undistinguished and indistinguishable 'rabble' inhabiting the outside world, the kind of people who shoved and jostled for seats in cinemas, did not wear suits with handkerchiefs neatly folded into the breast pocket, nor turbans with a ribbon and a badge. We were an elite group, destined to set an example for the country. Our thoughts were elevated; even the air was rarefied, the school being almost seven thousand feet up in the Himalayas, thus closer to God, and hence so much closer to perfection.

Karole Bagh was a far cry from all this. Here we spoke Punjabi, I in a pidgin, my seasonal friends in a street version a notch above mine because it was unsullied by stray English words. The enterprise lacked style, but BCS could scarcely be blamed. I felt guilty for this inability to square the reality of my existence with expensively learned ideals. Steeped in all things Western, British teachers, ubiquitous Hollywood movies every Saturday, marching, honor, discipline, chapel, Protestant good and evil, elevated heights, pocket-less hands, chilblains, and not-titting, I found myself here in my father's universe where to let a child visit the cinema was to corrupt him. Movies were frivolous, almost 'sinful', even though Papaji's (father's) concept of sin was scarcely as damning as the Christian version hurled at us from the pulpit every Sunday evening. 'Shameful' is closer to the mark. The activity in English movies that caught my father's eye and fired his disapproving imagination was the blatant kissing, something which he felt was improper and certainly unhygienic.

Oh Lord, how was I ever conceived, given his notions of romance? I could hazard a guess, but the thought is too disturbing, so let me proceed with the matter at hand. Hollywood pleads guilty, but why object to Indian movies? Kissing is banned here courtesy of the Indian Board of Film Censors. "It is not done in our culture," say the culture-soaked, self-proclaimed, pious sponsors. But we kids have all read 'Pondis' in school. One even brought in a book pilfered from his parents, and kept very safely hidden under his mattress. It was filled with snapshots of stone statues of naked men and women from Khajuraho in poses depicting all the possible and impossible—requiring feats of acrobatics beyond the abilities of human anatomy, whose limitations we were still unaware of—ways of making love.

Ironically, this was the ancient Indian culture of which our government boasted to the outside world, and to which I presume the censors were trying to conform; but then, whence the Puritanism? Censorship clearly was no harking to the past. What was it then? Hypocrisy, insidiously sullying our silver screen. It reeked of evil, prurient thoughts, ideas nurtured in the supposedly self-sacrificing, cess-minds of the censors, voyeurish impulses conveniently hidden in the guise of concern for our moral welfare. The censorial powers presented it as the lesser of two evils: better lust confined to a happy few—they themselves—than an entire nation besotted with it.

There is more in Indian movies. They are all musicals, each boasting at least six or seven songs, which I love, despite my schooling, but which are almost never sung by the stars, but by background singers. For reasons unknown, through a dire quirk of fate operative only in India, those with looks lack the voices, and vice versa. Strange indeed!

After five years of BCS and Hollywood, the musical soap operas that are the Indian movies, with their total divorce from reality, seem hilarious at the very least, but certainly quite harmless unless you are bent on cultivating the soul. Papaji, however, views them differently, even though I doubt that he has ever seen any of these travesties of culture that he so dislikes. His views, I suspect, were probably formed from cinema posters intruding willy-nilly into his field of vision on his daily drive to and back from work.

As for the songs, he knows of them from the neighborhood weddings. These are very public affairs in which the bridegroom and his party, often numbering a hundred to several hundred, come tromping down the street in a procession accompanied by a brass or, among the richer, a bagpipe band blaring away at umpteen decibels. From the bride's parents' house, not to be outdone by the groom's side, loudspeakers competitively spout out popular film songs from the highest corners, loud enough to carry for many streets in all directions. It is an occasion for gaiety and merriment, so why deprive the hapless neighbors of the fun? No fool, nor wise man, dares to object, and the authorities never interfere.

My father is concerned. He believes Indian movies are vulgar. The women, for example, wear makeup and jewelry, an obvious attempt to attract men, and that he feels is something which should not be done in public. As for the weddings, he feels that scarcely anything exceeds them in vulgarity. He would prefer severely abbreviated, simple, oath-taking religious ceremonies divorced from any display of wealth, for expensive clothes and jewelry are expressions of vanity, leading people astray into irresponsible, lustful behavior. My mother, unfortunately, is a sensitive woman ahead of her time, and I wonder how she has managed all these years. Though I sometimes feel sorry for her, my real feeling is of anger at his 'true believer' attitude that has taken a spark out of her life.

It is indeed trying being a woman in father's world. Our family is respected all over the city thanks to my mother. Women, both middle class and rich, seek her out as an obstetrician and a confidante. They, and even all my relatives, ask her advice on family problems; but look at the cruel reality: she who would solve others' problems has unsolvable problems of her own.

One day, about a month back, Beeji and I were standing talking in the drawing room. My father walked in, angrily demanding something from her. She tried to explain that she had been much too busy to take care of whatever it was that he was upset about—quite true, of course, as always. She promised to rectify the problem, but he ignored her. Words flew, and he grew furious, raising his hand threateningly at her.

"No, Papaji," 1 said, placing myself between the two, "You cannot hit her."

He was taken aback. Faced with the sudden realization that he had a grown son, he backed away. I was scared too, but I had stood up to him and, from then on, I grew in stature and in pride.

Don't come away with the idea that my father is a bad man. Quite the contrary: he never drinks, or swears, or lies, or is lazy. He is, as I said earlier, a true believer, in the process excluding from his mind those subtle insights acquired as one grows up, insights that reveal the secret of what makes people tick. His Puritanism lacks poetry and charm. There is no lighter side to life; all is duty and obedience; for him, obedience to what he believes are God's wishes, and for us to him; and his will brooks no resistance.

Not surprisingly, his shuttered mind has an amazing capacity for unwittingly twisting everything to fit his sense of life. Once, I am not quite sure how, perhaps it was at the behest of a caring friend of the family, we convinced him to accompany us to a movie. The locale of the story was a beautiful, mountainous ranchland in America, with the lead played by Spencer Tracy. The story had to do with an industrialist engaged in copper mining or refining, who was discarding blue copper wastes into a stream. These had poisoned the water, and many cattle belonging to the ranchers downstream had died. There was ultimately an armed showdown between Tracy and the industrialist's henchmen and, of course, Tracy's side won. It was good, solid entertainment and Papaji liked it. But we were made to feel sorry for our efforts because, for months thereafter, he reminded us of the *moral* of the story. I am delighted to say though that his enjoyment of the movie has not induced him to try another again, and we are not about to suggest that he do.

Then there is the question of novels and comic books. The latter were strictly forbidden, to the point that we hid them, while novels were read only out of his sight. He felt that both took us away from studies, meaning textbooks, and textbooks only. The idea that novels are among the greatest achievements of man's mind was totally alien to his thought process. They were, at the very least, distractions and, as was obvious from many of their covers, often 'immoral' since they dealt with romantic love and similar tales which tempted readers away from what they 'ought' to be doing. Never having read a novel himself, he felt that stories that were not true, meaning that they had not actually happened in real life, should not be used to waste our time. Fiction was unacceptable because it was fiction, a figment of someone's imagination—a lie. Fortunately, Beeji read novels, and he knew it but kept his peace. It was obvious, even to him, that she could not be required to study any longer; or perhaps he felt intellectually inferior to her, which he was. Beeji's reading gave us courage and by now my elder brother was reading novels openly in my father's presence.

This past spring and into the summer, I read voraciously; secretly and invisibly, of course. I lapped up *Madame Bovary*, short stories by Guy de Maupassant, several novels by Daphne du Maurier, *Pygmalion* and *The Doctor's Dilemma* by George Bernard Shaw, and countless others. There was little else to do but read, and these novels now filled my waking hours and even my dreams. Fantasies replaced the void in real life. But a break was in the offing, for into this desultory life of mine there now entered a visitor, Uncle Harbaksh.

The circumstances were unusual: a letter had preceded him, violating all the precedence set by my relatives. He arrived one morning in a jeep and the servant brought in his bags and placed them in the verandah, awaiting further instructions from my mother. Following the servant and the bags through the gate

was an imposing man, six feet tall compared to my five feet
eight, well built, maroon turban on head, and sporting an
impressive, well-groomed black beard and long mustache. The
beard was tucked-in in the stylish Sikh army fashion under a
woven, black woolen thread that went under his chin much as a
tight hat-strap and was tied over the head under the turban. He
wore a captain's uniform. But this was no dandy; he exuded
confidence, and his manner, as I soon discovered, was affable
and charming.

"So you are Amrik?" he said, shaking my hand and looking
me up and down with approval. "And all grown up, I see."

I smiled in acknowledgment, but recognition did not click
right away. Being away for five years at BCS, I could barely
remember all our relatives and friends. My mother had greeted
him with a warm hug, so I figured he was special.

She made the introductions: "This is your uncle Harbaksh."

He was not really an uncle. 'Uncle' is a ubiquitous,
multipurpose word used in India to address any friend of the
family older than you by a few years or a generation, whether
he is a blood relative or not. Addressing your elders by name is
frowned upon, so it is not surprising that all women in a like
position are referred to as 'aunties.' India, small wonder, is the
land of uncles and aunties.

Harbaksh was around thirty, and rich, having some very
fertile agricultural land in the Faridkot (pronounced Fareedkote)
district of Punjab. His father and my maternal grandfather had
been buddies in England, and our families had been close ever
since. Harbaksh was now in the process of building a house in
Chandigarh, the Punjab capital, and had driven down the
hundred and fifty odd miles to Delhi to buy supplies for the
new home.

Breakfast was served on a little table in the verandah. It
was still early in the day, but the beddings had been rolled up,
and the beds taken away and placed by the side of the house in
the lane leading to the kitchen. The "chicks', those heavy
curtains of cane and cloth made to keep out the heat, had yet to

be lowered in front of the verandah, allowing one to see out into the small lawn whose grass was parched by the summer heat. Everyone had bathed early, which was fortunate, for the taps were already dry. It was only nine in the morning, but we'd be lucky if the water returned by five in the evening. Papaji had left for work early, at seven o'clock, as usual, and Beeji was preparing to leave.

Harbaksh had many chores in Delhi and, since I was essentially free, I went along. We had lunch in Kwality restaurant, in Connaught Circus. There he asked me about my plans for the future. He must have noticed a reluctance in my manner when I mentioned the idea of becoming a doctor, so he bluntly asked me whether I was having second thoughts. I pleaded guilty, explaining that what I really wanted was to become a writer.

"If you ask my opinion," he said, "forget about premed. You're one of those lucky few who know what they want. If you truly care for writing, well then, you should become a writer. You'll starve, of course, but you never know, may be one day you'll be rich and famous. Either way, there is little happiness in work that is not of your choosing, for you've got to love what you do."

It was a big decision, I explained. Papaji would not countenance any change in my plans, in fact his plans, because it was his idea that I should become a doctor. My elder brother had deeply disappointed him by becoming an engineer despite Papaji's desire to make him a physician. I was his last resort and, now that I had agreed, his favorite son. There would be a furor because his apple-cart of contentment would be upset, and he might unwittingly resort to shaming me into a retraction with pleas to my filial obligations, failing which he would bemoan the thanklessness of today's children, and how little they cared for the very considerable expense incurred on their schooling, not to mention the countless sacrifices of their parents. He would fail to see that this had no bearing on my becoming a doctor or a writer; it was merely a question of his wishes over mine, of whose putative design of the future prevailed, a question obscured behind a self-righteous curtain. of obedience, obligations and responsibility. Seeing my obvious discomfort, Harbaksh dropped the subject.

"So what are you doing nowadays?" he asked.

"Nothing," I replied, "simply passing the time till college opens in mid-July."

"A young man like you should be out having fun, not moping around the house," he admonished. "In a couple of days, I'm going up to Solan; you know, the place in the hills. I'll be glad to take you along, if you wish."

When it was made clear that my mother favored the trip, and that she afterwards would tell Papaji, thus bypassing his probable objections, it was settled. I would go to Solan for a much-needed vacation, thus escaping the stiflingly oppressive heat.

We talked awhile some more about my life here, which was not much. I was not about to tell him of the problem of inviting my BCS friends over to the house, and how embarrassing that would be, what with the small house, no room to myself, and a father as strict as mine. Who knew what he might say to me, and to my friends. Bets were that he would tell us to quit wasting time and start studying. The little that I did tell Harbaksh made my life sound dull indeed.

"Surely you have a girlfriend?" he said. "How about the lovely little thing I saw this morning in your neighbor's part of the verandah?"

So he had seen. My back must have been turned in her direction at the time.

"You should take her out to the movies," he suggested.

Who was he kidding? It was obvious that people in the army viewed life differently from us civilians. They were, at the very least, more liberated. But did he not realize that one does not ask a girt out on a date here, not just like that? Even if she agreed, which I doubted given the conflicting social pressures on her, her parents would never let her go. And then there was also her protective brother to contend with.

"She is Hindu," I replied, "my parents and her parents would never permit it."

"Come now, you'll only be taking her out, not marrying her. Even if you did, what is wrong with that? Let me tell you something; and I am talking from experience; women are a breed apart. They are not Hindu or Sikh or Christian or anything else. They are a warm blessing from Heaven and the secret of man's happiness."

I thought he must read the same kind of novels as I, and instantly sensed a kindred spirit, but all I could do was smile back sheepishly, for I was not too proud of my romantic achievements. Not having a girlfriend was like living way below the standards of BCS. But I must have continued to evade the issue, for I told myself how he lived in another world, not the world of Karole Bagh or the Randhawas. However, he did not pass judgment, but let the matter lie.

The chores at the tube-well place in Kashmiri Gate in the old walled part of Delhi, and the stop at the car dealer's where he had to inquire about the possible date of arrival of the new car for which he had placed an order some months ago, were over quickly. We had plenty of time on our hands.

"Look," he said, "why don't we put off the spare parts for the jeep till tomorrow? What do you say we make a trip to Palam (pronounced Paalam)? I have a friend stationed there who I'd like to meet."

I accepted, so we drove over to the cantonment to visit this friend, who lived in the air-force mess. The drive was hot, and the *loo* stung my face in the open jeep. However, towering trees and green, well-watered lawns, an inviting, cool oasis in this hot semidesert that is Delhi, surrounded the Officers' mess at Palam. We settled down at the bar and, while they had beer, I had *nimboo-paani* (lemon juice) with ice. Flight-Lieutenant Karminder, Harbaksh's friend, was younger than him, perhaps twenty-two. A fighter pilot, he currently flew Vampire jets.

For a while, he and Harbaksh made small talk, catching up on recent happenings. Then, looking at my empty glass of *shakanjami,* he asked Harbaksh if it was okay to offer me some beer.

"Well, he's all grown up now, and I'm sure his mother won't mind. Would you like some?" Harbaksh inquired of me.

It was not pleasant being discussed in the third person, and treated like a kid to boot, but I had never drunk alcohol before, so I accepted after extracting a promise from Harbaksh never to tell my father. Then I promptly proceeded to get drunk, which is not difficult with Indian beer since its alcohol content is twice that of its American counterpart. As expected, it tasted awful. Alcohol, as all know, or should, is no culinary delight. The taste has to be acquired, helped along by the psychic elevation generated by a release from one's auto-censor. My attempt at feigning enjoyment fooled no one, and Harbaksh could clearly see how I really felt.

"Look," he said, "you don't have to pretend. Beer is about the most disgusting beverage you can drink. It looks like horse piss, and hardly tastes any better."

Fast as lightning, I hit him with the quick-quip. "How do you know?" I asked.

"How do I know what?"

"That beer tastes like horse piss."

"Holy shit!" he guffawed, "what have we here? And all the while I was thinking you were just a deprived little innocent kid. Touché!"

"Hey Amrik," said Karminder, warming up to me, "come over some time. We have dances at the club every Saturday evening. I'll find you a girl."

"Sure," I said. "I'd love to. But I'm going up to Solan with uncle here."

I had no desire to expose my ignorance of dance steps. BCS, since partition and the coming of Indian Raj, had divorced itself from the gallant, more romantic aspects of English gentlemen's lives; and with them had gone the socials with the girls from Tara Hall, the school on the other side of town.

"I'd prefer you used my name," protested Harbaksh, objecting to my use of 'uncle'.

"It's fine with me, but I doubt that my parents will approve."

"Sure, old boy, they'll learn to live with our modern ways. Change does not come of itself, you have to force it. I'm sick and tired of this uncle business, and I'm sure you are too. 'Uncle' makes a young man like me sound old. Didn't you call your teachers by name in BCS?"

"No, we addressed them as 'Sir'."

"Ah, the British way!"

"Even calling you Harbaksh is something we wouldn't have done in school. Everyone was synonymous with his last name. I was Randy, short for Randhawa. My older brother was Randhawa I, and I Randhawa II—informally, Randy I and Randy II."

"You know," he said, "the British are really the most formal bunch of bastards."

He stopped short as soon as he said that, and turned to me: "You don't object to my colorful language, do you? Being an old Cottonian and all that, you're probably used to 'flavor' in your speech."

"Uh-huh," I replied, "I'm not totally unsophisticated; I only object to stupidity, not color."

Being treated with kid gloves was bothering me, but face it, it was true that I had been sheltered, at least in Delhi, and right now I was living my Delhi-life, not the BCS one.

We spent the hottest three hours of the afternoon at the mess. My second beer was half finished, and I was feeling a trifle light-headed and loose of tongue.

"Harbaksh," I said, "I cannot remember when I last felt so at ease. You two are great company."

"Can it, kid," he said, "it's the beer talking."

"Then here's to the beer," I said, raising my mug; "bottoms up."

"Hold it there," shouted Karminder; playing along with me, "you remember *War and Peace?* We are awfully short of high windows in this single-storeyed temple to the God of liquor? Perhaps the bar will do." He looked at the bartender, who nodded his approval.

I was duly hoisted up on to the bar.

"Bottoms up," they said in unison.

I smiled an adult smile, and then putting the beer mug to my lips, I did not lower it again till it was empty. I felt fine.

"There's nothing to this drinking," I remarked, "except the awful taste."

Harbaksh, Karminder and the bartender gave me a small round of applause. It was now time to go back. We shook hands with Karminder and the bartender, and started walking out.

"Amrik, how would you like to drive the jeep?" Harbaksh asked.

"I don't know how to drive," I answered.

"No problem," he countered.

We got into the jeep, and he showed me how to use the clutch, gears and accelerator. I did as he said, but initially the engine kept stalling, and I was getting irritated with my failure to manage.

"Now, now, don't give up," he said, "try to release the clutch slowly at the end."

I did, and on the fourth attempt, we were moving slowly forward. For about ten minutes thereafter, we circled the parking area in first and second gears. Finally, it was time for us to hit the road. At Karminder's suggestion, we drove over to the airport and practiced some more on the tarmac. I seemed to be doing great.

"Harbaksh," I announced, "I'm ready to drive the jeep back to Karole Bagh."

"Well," he said, pretending to think, "I don't know if I should let you. Not that you can't drive, it's just that you don't even have a learner's license."

"Not to worry," I said, "I'll keep my head about me."

"You will? But you've lost it already. Kid, you are drunk!"

"Nonsense!" I replied, and gave him a demonstration of walking a straight line on the tarmac.

"Well, what do you say, Karminder? Do you think I ought to let the kid risk my neck?"

"In the interests of progress, I would say yes; and I would add . . . his too."

And so it was that we found ourselves driving over the ridge from the cantonment just at the time a dust-storm hit. Visibility fell to zero and I went over the edge of the road, bisecting bushes, bumping over boulders, shaking bones, but with aplomb, for we did come to a stop. I was shaken and embarrassed, and that is an understatement, but the jeep was right side up and all components, inanimate and animate, were still intact.

"I'm sorry," I said to Harbaksh as solemnly as I could; "I should have stopped quicker."

But it was unconvincing, as the beer had divorced my affect from my intellect.

"Nonsense, Amrik, that was a perfect stop," he replied, pretending complete understanding, and trying to buoy up my spirits; "don't let it bother you. Rome wasn't built in a day. We'll sit out the storm, then I'll drive."

With that, he turned thoughtful. "You still have the smell of alcohol on your breath, so let's drive some more in the city before going home?"

He looked at me, a sly expression on his face, "have you ever heard of a red light district?"

"Of course, the place of the prostitutes, but I've never seen one."

"Let me show you then."

"You don't really want to go there, do you?" I pleaded. "Alcohol is bad enough, but if Papaji comes to know of this . . ." I left the rest unsaid.

"Don't worry. A writer needs to learn of the highs and the lows, the good and the bad. The world has to be in your head; you can't write simply sitting at home."

I made it clear that I no longer objected, but extracted another promise not to let leak a single word of this at home, not even to my brother."

"I swear on my loved ones," he promised.

"Oh! And who are they?"

"You obviously don't know much about me," he said. "While you were away in school, I married Mohinder. She and I now have a four-year old daughter, Manveen. We call her Veena. And then there's my sister-in-law Preeti, who stays with us off and on when she's not in Shimla. She was my younger brother's wife, till he died in a motorcycle accident a year ago. Her mother has a house in Shimla where Preeti lives with her and a servant; and when the mother is away, she often comes down to stay with us in Solan. You'll like her, and you'll have a choice of company if you get bored with us older folks. And finally, there is the Labrador, Mackey, a really friendly dog."

The storm abated and, with Harbaksh back at the wheel, we made our way to Kutab Road, Delhi's red light district. It is a dusty canyon lined by two rows of multi-storeyed buildings with ground level balconies, in which sit young women wearing heavy make-up, smiling mockingly and provocatively at all the passersby, and occasionally making lewd remarks, challenging the more adventurous to come sample their wares. What a life! Not afraid to say or do anything; a liberation of sorts, if not a true one. When one of them pouted her mouth at me, and suggestively glanced with her sultry eyes at her substantial, bulging breasts straining to exit her bodice, I was too embarrassed to respond. I simply waved at her in a friendly way, instantly realizing that the gesture was totally inappropriate. Prostitutes were not interested in friendship; they were selling pleasure; quick, commercial, one-shot breaks into manhood. Once over my embarrassment, I asked Harbaksh: "Who are these women, and where do they come from?"

"Oh, I don't know," he replied, "probably mostly from U.P., east of here. In many instances, there's an actual sub-caste in which this is inherited as a family profession, though I daresay most turn to prostitution from poverty, and family and social circumstances. About two-thirds are from villages. Then there are those of a higher class, the dancing girls. I doubt if you'll find them on this road. The ones here are just the poorest.

Sooner or later, they will contract some serious illness like gonorrhea or syphilis, and it's generally downhill after that.

"But it's not all bad. Remember, it's the world's oldest profession, providing something that has been in demand for millennia. Every civilization has had them. In ancient Greece and Rome, some of the high-class ones, the hetaerae, lived in enviable luxury, and maintained large homes. They were accomplished in entertainment, philosophy, rhetoric; you name it. In Byzantine times, one of them, Theodora, even became a queen by marrying the emperor Justinian. In Japan, and also in ancient India, high-class courtesans were much sought after by the rich and powerful. In one famous Sanskrit play set in the fifth century BC, *The Toy Cart* by King Shudraka, one of the main protagonists is a hetaera named Vasantasena who is strikingly beautiful, rich and talented. She falls in love with a Brahmin, and in a typical happy Indian ending, marries him, to the delight of all those who decry the class system of Indian society.

"Even today, in some places in India, prostitution is associated with girls dedicated to temples, often by their parents. It is illegal, but exists anyway. The world's oldest profession may be narrow and mean as you witness here, but it has been colorful too, with ramifications all over history."

How strange it was! Papaji the strict moralist, the prostitutes, and the film censors, all dwelling in the same land, co-citizens existing as multiple but related facets of the human psyche, so different, yet as one; the same flesh and blood, oft with similar longings, but somewhere repressed, elsewhere envied, and still elsewhere flaunted. Which of them was the true Indian culture? All of them, of course, unless you used a selective focus to help claim a phony cultural superiority.

I wondered aloud at Harbaksh's interests.

"Don't let my manners fool you, kid," he replied, "I like the good life, but deep down I am a sober philosopher, just like you."

There was no question he had seen right into me.

"I have read widely," he continued, "and I have a wonderful library of books at my home in Solan. Man, in my view, is primarily a mental creature whose joys and achievements are essentially intellectual. There is much he owes to the physical too, for it enhances, but it does not substitute."

I was delighted. He was a man after my heart.

III

Dinner was at home that evening. The talk was about the Punjab, the harvest, and the prices of foodgrains. Harbaksh told us about his farm; the tractor he had bought, and his efforts at growing grapes; also his modest success with last year's cotton crop. No mention was made of our coming trip to Solan, nor of our visit to Palam; and nothing, of course, about the prostitutes. Harbaksh had promised that tomorrow he would get me a driver's license, but we had both agreed not to mention it before my family.

Papaji excused himself after dinner and went off to his bed in the lawn. His hour of sleep was not subject to changing circumstances, but the rest of us sat around for a long time, listening to episodes of the 1948 Kashmir (pronounced Kushmeer, with the 'u' as in cut) war with Pakistan. Harbaksh was then a second lieutenant in the Sikh regiment, and he was among those who, one wintry night, scaled the rugged heights flanking the 12,000 foot high Zoji La at the head of the Sind river valley north of Srinagar. By morning, when the Kabailis (Pathan tribesmen) holed up in the steep cliffs overlooking the pass realized that they had been outflanked, a feat they foolishly assumed impossible, they abandoned their positions and fled, hastened on in their flight by cannon-fire from the one tank that made it into the rugged, snow-covered passage. By evening, the entire feature was in our hands, and the road to Ladakh was open.

This turned out to be a rare late night, with everybody awake well past midnight. Next morning, Harbaksh and I set off to get the jeep parts and my driver's license. The former we picked up in Pahargunj, and for the latter we proceeded on to the North India Automobile Association office in Connaught Circus where Harbaksh had a friend. A few words with him and, a half-hour later, my driver's license was ready—no learner's license, no test, nothing, just a few words to a friend; that is the way it is in Delhi. Later that afternoon, we took the friend along to lunch at Moti Mahal in Daryagunj, a part of the old walled city of Delhi. This was no payoff, merely an afternoon with a friend. There, over roast chicken, we got to talking again of the Kashmir war. I asked Harbaksh if war was all brave, impossible feats, or if there was more, like fear. Was he scared?

"You bet I was. We soldiers are human, perhaps a little fatalistic; why else would we dare death? And we are trained to have resolve and keep our heads, metaphorically and literally. You keep your nerve under fire and try to plan as carefully as possible; then you have a chance. But in the final analysis, you survive on brains, the brains that tell you that you have better chances if you win than if you lose, and that you take big risks only when there is no other choice, like if it's a matter of life and death."

"But the killing?"

"The killing? Yes, the essence of war, the thing no one talks about. Glory is for fairy tales; killing is the real issue. In his letter to the Emperor Aurangzeb, Guru Gobind Singh proclaimed that when all else fails, and only then, must one resort to the sword. He understood the horror of war, and that one must fight only as a last resort; and that too only to protect what is rightfully yours. You probably take great pride in Maharaja Runjeet Singh as well, but he and the guru are a study in contrasts: the guru fought against injustice, the maharaja for conquest and glory.

"Unfortunately, most Sikh officers today look at a military career as a quest for glory. They are proud that we are fearless and have never run from an enemy, but they forget that we became fearless because right was on our side. When you fight a war for conquest, right is with the defender, irrespective of who wins. Every victory won is another log on the funeral pyre of the moral edifice of the conquerors. For a while they will get by on visions of glory, of feats of valor and achievements that seem unbelievable, but the moral decay will proceed apace so that even as physical victories are won, moral losses mount exponentially. While we try to remember Runjeet Singh for his secular and largely just rule, we hide from our minds the many injustices that must have existed merely to create and maintain his empire, which, after all, was not won at the polling booths.

"Look what followed his death. In one of the battles during the First Sikh War with the British, the one on the Sutlej at Ferozeshahr, we almost had them licked, and then we lost because of treachery. But was that treachery incidental, merely a human failing, an unfortunate happenstance that is all too frequent in history? No. It had been growing like an evil monster, devouring with its weapons of glory and power the innards of the Sikhs, corrupting and decimating those who partook of it the most, their leaders. The treachery was just as ineluctable as the fact that the sun will set today and arise anew tomorrow."

He paused for the effect to sink in, then continued: "But coming back to the question of killing—war is a miserable thing; humanity at its lowest. Everything you and I value is abandoned, and murder has free rein. It is sickening; no wonder soldiers never talk about the people they may have killed. Don't ask me to add up my credits, because they are buried in the darkest recesses of my mind, never to be recalled. To have to kill another human is the ultimate failure, not just for people like you and me who consider ourselves enlightened, but even for the toughened jawaans. Killing haunts soldiers all their lives. You may well wonder why I joined the army in the first place. I was a romantic then; fighting was glory. Now it feels like an affliction. I promised seven years of my life to the army. They will be over two years from now. Then I'll quit and go back to farming, or do something else.

"Amrik, your highest goal should not be to sacrifice your life for your country. It may be a high priority to do it for the ones you love, but still not the highest. The highest should be to live life for them the best you can, as your death is the last thing they want. Value your life, live it to the full, for when you do, whether you like it or not, you will be helping those you love, and yourself too. Happiness is for the living, not the dead. There is no Heaven, nor Hell, nor an afterlife. We live and die right here, in this life; and that is all; so don't throw it away lightly merely for some strangers like your countrymen. Do it only for a moral cause, one that involves those you love, and that too when all else fails. Remember the guru and his words: 'When all avenues have been explored, all means tried, it is rightful to draw the sword out of the scabbard and wield it with your hand.' He knew about right and wrong; and about life."

There was silence for a while. The conversation had become much too profound for an afternoon lunch at a noisy eating establishment. While Harbaksh talked, the restaurant had receded from consciousness. Now it was like coming out of the cool darkness of one's house back into the harsh summer sunlight of the street outside. It was jarring. Harbaksh himself finally broke the spell, ordering tandoori chicken and some tikkas for us to take home for dinner.

Next morning, I awoke to 'happy birthday' greetings from my mother and brother. I had totally forgotten, I was now eighteen. Harbaksh later asked me when the party would be. I explained that I was not one of those who had birthdays celebrated, and the custom, or the lack of it, was unlikely to change now.

"Uh-huh" he said reflectively, "the day is still young."

When we left, my mother gave me two hundred rupees to spend any way I saw fit, and told me to be a good boy. "I don't want you making any trouble for your Uncle Harbaksh and his wife. Give my love to your auntie, and remember to kiss Veena for me."

I assured her I would, hugged her, and then we were off. It was only eight in the morning, but the sun already hurt. By noon, we were at Kaalka, in the foothills. Here we stopped for lunch; and by three we were almost at Solan. The house was about a mile short of the town at a place called Suproon. It was the only house there, set between two spurs of the mountain. The backdrop was a steep mountainside around the right side of which a path led over a ridge at the back into a forest known as the Khildaar jungle.

Thinking back on the events of the day, everything seems unreal, much too good to be true. As we pulled up to the front of the house, the labrador came running out, jumping ecstatically up on to Harbaksh's chest, trying desperately to lick his face. Harbaksh gently pushed him off. Then the dog turned to me, his tail still wagging, and sniffed my ankles. I patted him on the head and rubbed his neck affectionately, and he wagged his tail in approval.

At the door of the house, we were greeted by Mohinder, Harbaksh's wife, who was soon joined by Veena, their daughter. They had come out on hearing the commotion and were now standing there, waiting for us. Harbaksh made the introductions: "Mohini, this is Tejinder Singh and Dr. Harsharan Kaur's (all the 'a's in Harsharan are pronounced as 'u' in hurry) second son, Amrik. He was wasting his time in Delhi with nothing to do, so I invited him over to spend the summer with us here in the cool, quiet comfort of the mountains."

Mohini hugged me warmly, and then I kneeled down and gave a shy kiss to the little girl. I am no good at this kind of thing because girls of any age tangle up my mind with uncertainty. "This is from my mother and me," I said.

Veena shyly put her arms around my neck, and gave me a wet little kiss on the cheek. It was embarrassing, to say the least, for one not used to so much female attention.

"Preeti has gone to Solan," she said, looking up at me, apprising me of what she believed unerringly was the most important piece of information for me to know.

"Preeti is my sister-in-law," explained Mohini. "Veena and she are inseparable. Preeti went out to get groceries. Now that you're here," she continued, turning to Harbaksh, "I do hope they'll be enough because we weren't expecting you so early."

"My chores finished earlier than I thought likely," explained Harbaksh, "so I hurried home."

"I'm glad you did," said Mohini, snuggling closer to her husband, and touching his face with affection; "you have been away three weeks too many, and we have missed you."

It was embarrassing, this mushy husband-wife intimacy, not used as I was to witnessing such affection, so I went back to the jeep to bring in the bags. Soon we were settled down in a small comfortable family room for tea and biscuits.

"I think I'll go over to Solan to give Preeti a hand with the groceries," Harbaksh said after a while. He arose to leave, then turned to me: "Want to come along, Amrik?"

"Sure," I said, and Veena chirped in: "Can I come too, Papa?"

"Why, of course. Preeti will need all the help she can get."

Preeti was a sight for loo-burnt eyes. To say she was beautiful is an injustice, a timid mockery of her charm. My eyes fell in love instantly, feeling her with their sight, defying decorum, shamelessly, greedily soaking in her loveliness; and my mind, it was in ecstatic turmoil, frantically struggling to transcend prose and capture in verse the spell of her presence. But alas, I was no poet, and the quest was doomed. Reluctantly conceding defeat, I stepped down to the prosaic and saw that she was five-five, average for a Jat Sikh girl. She had the fragrance of jasmine and cheeks touched by the blush of dawn; skin smooth as roses and soft as sahtoosh, radiating warmth. And she had eyes, limpid brown eyes that bewitched, sapping my will and stealing my heart away; and they smiled at me.

"Preeti, Preeti," shouted Veena, all excited, jarring me to my senses, "look who we brought for you."

"Sshh," said Preeti, placing a finger on Veena's lips; then she turned to me: "don't pay any attention to her. She's constantly bringing me presents, though this is more than I had bargained for, but . . ." here she smiled at me, "I'm pleased to make your acquaintance. As you must have heard so loudly announced, I am Preetam. And you are?"

"Amrik," I replied, sounding calm. But beneath the facade, I was desperately trying to regain control over my floundering self. By way of explanation, I added: "I just came with Harbaksh from Delhi."

Then, noticing that she was carrying a fair-sized bag of groceries, I offered to help.

"Thank you," she said, handing me the bag, still smiling her magic spell.

"Look," said Harbaksh, "I have some more shopping to do. Why don't you all go back in the car. I'll return in the jeep."

And so it was that Preeti and I, with Veena sitting in my lap, found ourselves driving home together. There had been no shaking of hands. Indian boys and girls don't shake hands when introduced, even if devoured by desire; custom frowns on it. You make the traditional greeting with folded hands, or you do it with the magic of your eyes, like Preeti.

"You are the first girl I've seen driving a car," I said, trying to make conversation.

"Do you drive?" she asked.

"A little. I just learned it two days ago on Harbaksh's jeep."

"What a coincidence," she exclaimed, "I learned driving the same way—on his jeep."

"Were you drunk like I was when you learned to drive?"

Of all the things I could have said, why that? My heart sank, my mind plunged . . . into ignominy, because there was suddenly an edge in her voice.

"You know, he takes too many chances. Mohini is always so worried about his ways. How could he let you drive like that?"

"Oh, no," I said, trying desperately to salvage what seemed already lost, "it was not as bad as you think. I was quite aware of everything." But that surely was a lie. "In fact, I proved it to him by walking a straight line." Good try, but too late—'the moving finger writes and having writ, moves on.'

But what was there to do? Pride diminished, honor lost, hopes shattered; yet I could not bear to lose her; not this way on something as trivial as a mug of beer.

"Yes, I'm sure you did. Just like his brother used to. I don't know too many boys your age who drink. How come you were drinking?"

Perhaps she was trying to be kind, giving me a chance to redeem myself. In disarray, I continued, trying valiantly to find a reasonable defense: "Oh no, it was nothing; just a beer. We were visiting Karminder, Harbaksh's friend at Palam. He insisted that I have a beer, so I couldn't say no. It was nothing, just one beer."

I could hear my captive heart, sunk in gloom, skeptically pointing an accusing finger at me: 'Indeed! You really could not say 'no'? Do you expect her to believe that?'

"It's always one beer," she went on, "they always say that."

Yes, it was not getting any better. Next time I would watch my step, but right now the conversation was getting out of hand, and I was mortified at my stupidity; making wisecracks about drinking to a girl I had just met, the loveliest girl I knew. She had taken offense much too quickly, but what did I know about girls? With genuine remorse, and hoping against hope that it would work, I said: "I'm sorry. It was thoughtless of me. I did not mean to upset you."

There must have been pathos in my voice, or the ring of sincerity, because her face softened. She was quiet, tenderness touched her eyes, and I heard her say words I could not believe: "No, it is not you who should be sorry; I have been remiss. You are our guest, and I was unforgivably rude. The mention of drinking touched a raw nerve in me, and I let myself be carried away. I apologize."

What memories? I had been crude and insensitive; she really had nothing to apologize for. But her words were like a gift horse, a ray of hope; and so I answered back, hastening to make up: "Apology accepted; there will be no mention of drinking again."

"Likewise," she said; then, after a long pause, returning to her friendly and winning ways: "You speak excellent English. Where did you go to school?"

My self, that smitten self that was no longer mine, answered, secure in the hope that all was well: "BCS, and you?"

"Jesus and Mary, in Shimla; and then a year at St. Bede's college."

"Oh! That's where we used to start the practice runs for the marathon race every summer."

"I know, we often saw boys from your school ogling at us girls. You boys were the talk of the college."

Boys had ogled her? From BCS? For shame, but I was not feeling shame; it was elation that gripped me, surmounting all that had just happened. I could visualize bridges across to her; things in common; events, times, places, where our fateful lines of destiny had met. It was plain that we had much in common since both had schooled in Shimla, in boarding schools. I could taste success just around the corner. For a while there my prospects had looked grim; dark clouds had robbed the sunshine, but amid all that floundering, I must have done something right. I had unknowingly dared Fate, but it had merely winked at me, and shown itself to be forgiving and kind.

Back at the house, I brought in the groceries, then excused myself to freshen up. I lay down on the bed in my room, and collected my thoughts. Mulling over the day's events, I resolved to win my way back to honor, and then some more; who knows, even into her heart. I would make it up to her, somehow regain lost ground. Seeing where I was and what I was—dusty and grimy from the journey—I determined that, at the very least, I must look my best. And then there were my hosts to think of: they had put me up in their guest room. It was a first for me; imagine a room all to myself. It made me feel grown up. A lot was happening. There was a time when life was desultory and aimless, but now that was over. I now had everything, or potentially so; the rest was up to me. Events were exciting, and moving; and my heart thumped in assent. I was like a character in the novels I lived on, but the setting was Indian, and all was set in reality; even my father could not object to this. I was I, and all the characters were real flesh and blood. Harbaksh would have to be repaid for this one day, else I would be weighed down with obligations, but presently I had little to offer. One day; yes, one day, when I was someone; and so I went on, dreaming happily. But it was getting late; there were things to be done.

Pulling out a new turban, a freshly starched one, I got Mohini to help me with the 'pooni', the complicated way in which the long piece of fine muslin, six yards long and a yard wide, has to be rolled up before it is tied on the head. The turban tied, I appraised myself carefully in the mirror and decided that I looked good, perhaps even charming; and my image gazed back smartly as I smiled, telling myself, asking rhetorically, with no small amount of satisfaction: "You lucky bloke, what did you ever do to deserve all this?"

By the time I walked out the door, dusk had descended, and it was well past seven. The whole family was waiting for me in the dining room. A cake with eighteen candles lay on the table. While I had been scandalizing myself in the car, Harbaksh had stayed back in Solan to get me this; now I was even more indebted.

Mohini lighted the candles and motioned me to my seat. Then they all sang 'Happy Birthday' while I sat there, hopelessly overwhelmed.

"You may now blow out the candles," Mohini said, "and make a wish. Remember, birthday wishes always come true, so don't do it lightly. Wish what is dearest to your heart."

I looked at Preeti, loving her, silently asking her forgiveness, promising that I would never hurt her again. It had never taken much to satisfy me, ever; mostly because I had never been greedy. But what I wished for now was like Heaven and Earth all in one. I had not shown anything to deserve it, but I wished it anyway, and continued wishing as I blew out the candles, and even as their smoke drifted lazily up to the ceiling. For once in my life, I was extravagant, but I was as one possessed. I could lose, which was all too likely, but Old Cottonians don't think that way. They fight the brave fight, so that even in defeat they carry the day. I had visions of myself failing, wandering aimlessly like the smitten knight in Keats' *La Belle Dame Sans Merci,* but even a loss as terrible as that would be sweeter than past victories that had been won, than coming first in school, or even attaining to the school 'blues' in hockey. There was a wish; the wish was a dream; and the dream must come true. I could not prove Mohini wrong.

The smoke from the candles cleared. Harbaksh congratulated me, firmly pressing his hands on my shoulders; Mohini gave me a big hug; and Veena asked me to seat her on my lap, to be closer to the cake. Now it was Preeti's turn. What would she do? What could she do? I was barely an acquaintance. But I could see her bending down, closer and closer, till her lips touched me, searing my cheeks. It was the lightest of kisses, but it burned into the innermost recesses of my mind.

"This is to make up for all the things I said in the car," I heard her say, slowly, deliberately.

Blushing furiously, tears of joy threatening to inundate my eyes, I floundered in her gaze. This could not possibly be! What was happening here? Indian girls don't kiss boys in public, even as innocently, magically, as on their cheeks. Why, why had she done it? And what did she mean by her words? I had already been forgiven my lapse in the car. My mind whirled with impossible possibilities, all wonderful, one of a kind; but I was weak from trying to keep order in my mind. My eyes were moist with happiness; and my thoughts could not keep still as I got up and looked at my newfound friends around me and thanked them for this wonderful gift, the first such gift in my life. I did not know, they did not know, which gift I was talking of, there had been so many. Perhaps, I meant all of them, perhaps just the last one. But there were conflicting loyalties and conflicting obligations, and all I could do was beam my happiness at them, wet, warm and embarrassed. Then we had dinner, with forks and knives, like on my first day at BCS, but different in every other way. All through the meal, all I wanted was to look at Preeti, but I was afraid lest my renegade eyes would fail me again. Instead, I made idle conversation, even ate. I asked about the dog, and said nice things to Veena, and asked her if she was already going to school, which was quite foolish as she was obviously much too small for that; but what was I to do? The dinner was long, blissfully long; and it lasted for ever.

After the meal, Harbaksh asked if I'd like to go for a walk. I said yes because it would give me time to think. The three of us, that is the two of us and my happy, hapless mind, then set off along the road to Barogh, in the direction away from Solan.

"What was all that about what Preeti said in the car? Did you two have a fight . . . already?" asked Harbaksh.

My mind and I exchanged knowing glances, and debated furiously for an answer. We decided he must not know; one mistake was enough for one day, so I said: "No, it was nothing."

"All right," he said with acceptance, "may be another day."

IV

The eighteenth birthday was a watershed in my life. It was celebrated, in a period of anticipatory jubilation, with the invention of a personal calendar commemorating the day I had fallen in love: Anno Preeti . . . AP; what a pleasing sound! Preet, love; preeti, the one with love. In this preeminently human and most secular of calendars, I awakened to the dawn of day 2, month 1, AP 1. A transformation had come to pass: apron strings cut, a boy had matured to manhood; the bird had flown the nest and was on the wing. Embodied was a loss of innocence, and an awakening; an imbuement of all he saw and heard with meaning, a meaning intensely private, creating a world in which he and not someone else determined the events of his life. No longer a passive pliancy to the will of elders or teachers, he would now step out on his own, marching to the beat of a personal drummer.

I brushed my teeth, bathed, changed my clothes, tied my turban, checked in the mirror, and then when I was sure everything was as it should be, stepped out into the yard.

Harbaksh was standing there, wrapped in an expensive silk dressing gown, admiring his dahlias in the flowerbed by the side of the house. He was also chewing a stick that hung at an ungainly angle from the corner of his mouth. I had an inkling of what it was, having seen my grandfather and other relatives from the village use it, but I chose to let him explain. Having turned a new leaf as per plan and resolve, I initiated the conversation.

"Harbaksh," I said, "do you realize how incongruous you look dressed up in a king's ransom, yet chewing a stick like a cow chewing the cud."

"Correction," he answered, "a bull."

"Have it your way," I said, conceding the point. Whatever are you doing chewing that stick, and in such earnest?"

"Aha! Here, just as I thought; a true, anglicized, modern Indian. Amrik, you have the attractive innocence that comes with ignorance. This stick that you unjustly malign is of the finest kikkar (acacia), expressly brought here from Faridkot for the laudable purpose of preserving my teeth and strengthening my gums and, if need be, demonstrating to the uninitiated that there's more to oral splendor than the toothbrush."

I was a little overwhelmed by my host's eloquence, but I played along.

"Pray explain yourself," I pressed.

"There! Just as I thought! I knew you would need help," he proclaimed triumphantly. "There is a thing or two we rustics know that BCS, in its erudition, has never understood."

Pulling out another kikkar stick from the pocket of his gown, he handed it to me. "This is for you." he explained, "it will transcend any toothbrush ever made, and is backed by the wisdom of tradition and the experience of centuries. It has been with us Punjabis since antiquity, though it is a sad commentary on the times that this ethnic gift of the ages is totally lost on you hill school guys and gals."

"What gals? What ethnic wisdom?" I asked,

He smiled indulgently, and continued: "Before you deny yourself the advantages of new knowledge, do me a favor. Just chew on one end of the stick till it softens. Then I'll show you what I mean. Aha! Here comes the gal, the other anglicized inhabitant of this humble dwelling, my esteemed sister-in-law, Preeti. Good morning to you."

"Good morning, everybody," came the lovely, cheerful voice of Preeti. "And how is our guest today?"

That question, of course, was directed at me. My spirits zoomed, attaining orbital velocity in zero seconds flat. I was enjoying myself up here in heaven, so I easily fell into the groove.

"A little bamboozled, perhaps," I replied, "but otherwise sound and unimpaired."

"Oh, I see!" she said, "just as I thought! My esteemed brother-in-law has been giving you the ethnic treatment."

'Right on, Preeti!' I acclaimed silently; 'you're as smart as they come.' But aloud I said: "Quite so, he's got me chewing this piece of wood."

As explanation, I showed her the sorry end of the stick that I had so far chewed.

"He did the same to me when I first visited." she added, "you and I must have a lot in common. First, we both learn to drive on the same jeep from the same chancy instructor, and then we both get dubbed 'anglicized inhabitants.' Did he also mention the 'attractive innocence of the ignorant?'"

She had memorized all his lines. "Uh-huh," I replied, "that's his game. He almost had me fooled for a while. Even in my ignorant innocence, or innocent ignorance . . . whatever . . . methinks I discern in this yonder man a rustic sophistication, a return to nature, if you will. He hath practiced much; might I presume he hath made thee chew the cud likewise?"

"Yes kind sir, he has; I mean . . . hath; she replied.

Harbaksh laughed. "Not bad, not bad," he said. "The ancient art of rhetoric was not entirely lost with the Greeks."

He pulled out another kikkar stick and offered it to Preeti, who accepted it and placed it in her mouth.

"So how are we today, Preeti?" he continued, "you look good."

"Yes, I feel very rested, thank you. Amrik," she continued, turning to me, "I guess I could call you that, couldn't I?"

"Yes, because outside of BCS that is the only name I carry. You must not call me Randy II, the name I bore in school. Too formal, you know; I can't stand it any more."

"No, I meant you won't mind if I call you by your first name, will you?"

"Of course not. I am delighted to hear you speak my name. Surely it is for some good purpose?"

"Precisely, kind sir," she continued, unable to suppress a smile at the silliness of her words, "methinks you are a touch too formally attired for so early in the day. This establishment we maintain here is at best informal. We have no inspections, require no polished shoes except as it may please your fancy; we do not even expect a trimming of the nails. I daresay fleet shoes (sneakers) are quite acceptable. While we go about bestowing our greetings and blessings on you, you will have graced this house with your prolonged presence, forgotten the gentlemanly rigors of BCS, and hopefully acquired a taste for the nicer, laid-back values of life. You must consider this your own home; yours to enjoy as you please. Is that not so, brother-in-law?"

Harbaksh smiled. "You are quite correct, my lady" he replied.

I smiled inwardly at the gentle thread of ambiguity in her statements. They were polite and formal, yet laced with an intimacy that was bold and provocative. She was living dangerously, just at the edge of seduction. I was a little embarrassed at the possibility that Harbaksh may also have read the same meaning into them, but I loved the way she handled herself. Coming to more mundane matters, however, I had not brought any dressing gown; and anyway, I had nothing in silk. And about considering it like my own home, I could not possibly do that. It conjured uncomfortable visions of giving up the one advantage I had here, a room to myself.

"Sure," I said, with as much nonchalance as I could muster, "rest assured that tomorrow I will be as appropriately casual as Harbaksh here."

Tomorrow was a day away. I could figure out something by then. But first I must enjoy the moment, so I chuckled goodheartedly along with the others at our impromptu performance, whereupon Harbaksh returned to the subject of the kikkar stick.

"Now that both of you have had your fun," he began, "let me explain what one does with this stick. First, it is a 'daatan', not just a stick; and the act of cleaning your teeth with it is 'doing a daatan'. Once you've chewed it for the requisite length of time, the ends are soft and frayed enough for you to scrub your teeth with, maybe even clean your tongue. When you finally rinse your mouth, you will taste the difference: freshness and pleasure unknown in the western world; with teeth white as ivory, and gums strong from bathing in the acacia juices. No Kolynos or Binaca smile will ever match yours. But even if you were perverse enough to take an entirely mundane view of the matter, consider it this way: the daatan is disposable, and unlike money, which you must expend to acquire toothbrushes, it grows on trees."

"And," Preeti joined in, "it is the perfect accompaniment to socializing in the morning. You chew it, admire the dahlias, breathe the clean morning air, relax in congenial company, and spend a pleasant time conversing in the most delightful way. Which brings me to the reason I came out here: tea is ready; would you care to come in?"

We finished the daatan and proceeded into the family room where we sat down to tea and biscuits with Mohini. There was more casual conversation, and then everybody went off to bathe and get dressed. I walked around the house, familiarizing myself with it and the surrounding mountainside. When Preeti finally came out, she was dressed in an open-neck peach shirt and black slacks, distinctly un-Indian attire, and with her hair tied in a bun at the back of her neck. There were black pumps on her feet. I complemented her on her looks, my heart in heaven and my mind composing couplets in a fountained garden.

"You look wonderful." I said, and she did. Slim, with full hips and shapely legs, she was ravaging my poise. For a while, I beat about furiously for something more to say; finally remarked: "It's a beautiful day, isn't it?"

"Yes," she agreed, "I wonder what we could do today?"

"I love walking," I replied. "If you'd like, we could explore the woods on the other side of this ridge. Harbaksh told me it's a lovely place."

"That it is," she agreed, "and it's been quite a while since I went there. Let me ask Harbaksh if he would like to come."

Harbaksh had other plans. He had to go down to Kasauli, about twenty miles back down the road towards Kaalka, where he wanted to meet an army friend of his on some personal matter, so he excused himself. Mohini was busy with work around the house, and with taking care of Veena. She suggested we take the dog along, and wondered if we could look for wild dahlias and bring some back—the flowerbeds around the house could certainly use some more. I changed into my fleets, Preeti packed a durree, some egg-and-tomato sandwiches, a few apples and an empty thermos flask in a basket, and then we set off, alone but for the dog.

It was a pleasant walk. The trail went through pinewoods, up for a stretch, then leveled off, passing a spring on the way where we stocked up with cold water. Finally, it ascended again, till about a mile and a half from the house, we came to an open meadow. Here Preeti spread out the cotton durree on the ground, and we settled down to a picnic lunch. The sandwiches were ordinary, but they tasted heavenly. There was the clean smell of pines, mottled shadow and sun, and a beautiful girl beside me; all perforce added to the taste. The only problem was the age-old dilemma of men new to love—I was at a loss for words. Eventually, I decided on the most obvious approach: I figured that I would tell her something about me, then maybe in return she might tell me something about herself, so I said, somewhat casually, but reddening nonetheless: "You know, this is the first time I've ever been out with a beautiful girl by myself—on a picnic, I mean."

"Come now, a strapping, handsome man like you. You don't really expect me to believe that, do you?" she answered, flattered, but pretending surprise at my comment.

"Well, maybe not, but it's true."

"How come?" she asked, "I would have thought any girl would be flattered to have your company."

I knew she was, so I smiled, my spirits soaring at her observation. I decided to press on.

"I believe you really mean that. In that case, I'm going to accept it as a compliment; but I must warn you, appearances can be deceptive."

"There must be a reason you are telling me this," she said, looking straight into my eyes.

Was there a touch of conspiracy in her voice? I wondered. This would bear watching.

She continued: "I think most people would wish to hide such information, particularly if it were true, don't you think so? In the circles I've lived in most of my life, army officers and their families, young men your age spend an enormous amount of time boasting of exploits, some not-so-true and the rest totally untrue."

"Well, what can I say, having never moved in such circles. The fact of the matter is that I feel uncomfortable getting by on false pretenses. I like you; and I want you to like me."

There it was, a little timid, substituting like for love, but I had said it. I continued: "you wouldn't want to like me for the wrong reasons, now would you?"

"Why, of course not," she said. The aroma of sincerity, feeling, reality, hung around her words. She paused deliberately, or so I thought; then she went on: "This is more refreshing than anything I've heard in the past two years. I don't know what other women feel, but I much prefer the real thing to any fantasy."

The conversation was going my way: it was becoming personal; we were birds of a feather. She was daring me, hinting at a romance. I noticed the way she referred to herself as a woman, but had referred to girls when she talked of my life. Was this her way of telling me that she meant business; she was not to be taken as a girl, like any previous others, but as a woman? Her hint was not really necessary since I had taken her for a woman the moment I set eyes on her. This was the big leagues as far as I was concerned. No childish infatuation this, I was really in love; and love needs a woman to set the heart a-beating.

"In BCS," I said, "the only women we ever saw were the housemasters' wives, the headmaster's wife, and the nurse in the little hospital we had for the occasional boy who got sick enough to require looking after and, of course, the one secretary who worked in the school office. Apparently, things were different before India's partition, in the times of the British. There used to be regular dances between BCS boys and the girls from Tara Hall, but none since I joined. We were told that the headmistress at Tara Hall was upset by what happened at the time of the last dance. Their girls apparently got back much too late, and she held the BCS boys responsible. On this pretext, all future dances were canceled. I suspect the real reason was that, after partition, most of the students in both schools were Indian, and the English parents did not like the idea of their daughters mixing with us. The parents of Indian girls would have been even more opposed to the dances than the British parents, considering their cultural attitude to such things. Whatever the reasons, this state of affairs effectively eliminated any social meetings between BCS boys and Tara Hall girls at the school level.

"At home, life is so different that dating girls has the flavor of fairyland. Perhaps, when I get to college, things will change, but as of now my family doesn't move in social circles where a boy is likely to get to know any girl, at least not enough. In fact, I must confess I don't have a girl-friend . . . not yet."

This was not entirely true, because I did have one right here and now, and that was not lost on her. She made no comment, but was quiet for a while, sitting there looking down thoughtfully at her lap.

"Do you know how to dance?" she finally asked, turning to look at me.

I could sense a challenge, an invitation, in her voice.

"A little," I replied. "I learned a few basic steps at one of the commercial dance studios in Delhi, but I'm afraid I've forgotten most of them for lack of practice. No partner, no practice."

I emphasized the point by shrugging my shoulders. Then, trying to involve her in the probability of us dancing, I offered: "I'm sure you're a very good dancer, aren't you?"

"Fair, I'd say," she replied, understating her talents, "I don't dance everything equally well. You could say I am partial to the waltz. My father had this wonderful collection of Viennese waltzes, and I used to dance to them all the time."

"I know what you mean," I said. Being no small lover of the waltz myself, circumstances had perforce restricted me to the audio level. "The Blue Danube and the Emperor Waltz; I have them too."

"Do you know how to dance the waltz?" she asked.

"Not much more than the basic box step, I'm afraid, but I learn fast. Would you like to show me some of the other steps?"

There, in the only way I could, I had asked her for a dance.

"Okay," she said, getting up. "Come over here to this part; it is more level than over there."

I walked over.

"You know how to hold, don't you?" she asked.

I showed her how. She moved my right hand higher on her back, and then placed her right hand in my left. Her warmth suffused into me; it took all I could to keep from pulling her in, claiming her in my embrace.

"Okay," she said, "1 think you have the hold about right. Let me show you some of the really attractive steps of the dance."

So saying, she slid out of my hold, and showed me how her part was done, then mine.

"How did you learn to do the man's part?" I asked, a touch of jealousy arising in my imagination.

"At St. Bede's, we girls used to dance among ourselves. Obviously, we had to alternate with each other for the man's part, so we got pretty good at it. Now," she continued, turning back to me, "let's try some of the moves. Remember the timing: one, two, three. It's an equal interval between beats. The first beat is emphasized, and you have to rise a little on your toes on the second. You go down on the first. Now, I'll count the beats and you lead me."

We started dancing. My excitement was making me tense and, like all novices, I was also afraid of stepping on her toes. After a while, she stopped.

"You've got to learn to relax, enjoy the dancing. Don't worry about stepping on my toes; you won't!"

We resumed dancing.

"That's better," she said, "yes, that's it. You're doing great. You certainly do learn fast."

"No." I pretended humility, when in reality I was all puffed up with pride. "Like I told you, I did take a few lessons."

Anyway, I told myself, it won't do to be too optimistic at this stage: dancing is an art that takes time to learn.

"Now let's try the hesitation steps and some of the turns," she said, and, as I tried them out, "Oh, that was beautiful! Your Delhi girls must be sadly wanting up here," she said, her eyes turning up at her lovely head, "If I'd been there, I'd have gone dancing with you every day."

Me too, I thought.

"Yes, I believe that," I agreed, "shall I hum the tune?" Her remarks had encouraged me to boldness, so I continued: "It might create the right atmosphere. I love to fantasize. We can imagine we're in a 19th century Viennese ballroom?"

"That would be nice; go ahead."

So I started humming the Blue Danube. I have a rich voice and I've always loved to sing, so this was my chance to impress her and maybe enmesh her in my charm. With me humming, we pirouetted around the meadow, and then I took her through the hesitation steps and a series of spins. We did it again and again till I felt I'd got it. Then I stopped, still holding her in my arms, and looked long into her eyes. It was perhaps too early, and I was afraid to embarrass her, yet I had to make my feelings known. Finally, I smiled and said: "Thank you; that was most enjoyable. You are a joy to lead, you respond so effortlessly. Next time we should do it to music. Maybe then I'll dance better."

"Yes, we must;" she said, "but you are too modest. I enjoyed it more than you think."

She must feel something for me; why else would she say such things? Politeness alone did not demand it; she was trying to tell me things the same way I was, safely but surely. Then she turned and walked back to our picnic spot on the grass. The dog came up to her, and she started fondling it, rubbing its neck and then playfully tickling him with her nose. I looked on, knowing that I was falling ever deeper in love. She was older, perhaps twenty or twenty-one, but that and the fact that she was a widow were the furthest things from my mind; they seemed completely irrelevant at the time. All I could see was that she was smart and delicate, and so much in need of love.

Before I could proceed further, there was one thing that had to be cleared up first.

"I've been wanting to ask you something all morning," I said, "but I don't know if I should."

"What is it?" she asked, looking up at me, still fondling the dog, but playing it strictly neutral.

"It's somewhat personal. I'm not sure I have the right to ask."

"Well, if you don't, we'll never know, will we?"

Her mood had changed. It was somber, but her words were defiant; she even seemed to be daring me to try. Perhaps she knew, with some womanly instinct that only those who are loved possess, what I was itching to ask, and secretly wanted me to plunge ahead. Who knows, even the loveliest woman I knew might need to unburden herself of some secret truth that was cruelly oppressive and which she could not conquer.

So I asked, encouraged by what I sensed in her words: "Yesterday, in the car, you were very upset about what I said.

I'm sure there is a very good reason, but I'd feel better if I knew what exactly I said that upset you. I don't want that episode to stay between us."

She was quiet. She kept playing with the dog for a while, not looking at me. Her face was flushed, and she was desperately fighting her way through some emotional experience she had yet to conquer. She finally looked up into my eyes and said: "I don't know why I'm telling you this; I've never told anyone else, and God knows I never will. You probably know that I was married, and you may also know that my husband, Harbaksh's brother, died about nine months ago in a motorcycle accident. What you may not know was that he was drunk at the time. Do you still want to hear the rest of it?"

She was really asking for my support, so I nodded my head, knowing that I just had to know everything about her.

She continued: "Everybody said how stupid it was for him to have done such a thing. Only I knew it wasn't stupid at all. You see . . ." Here her voice fell very low, being barely audible, "our marriage was a failure, from the beginning, from the very first day."

Water came into her eyes, and tears slowly flowed down her cheeks. She was filled with a consuming anger and a sorrow I could not bear to watch. On an impulse, I moved forward, putting my arms around her and pulling her head down on to my chest. "I'm sorry," I said, trying to comfort her, "1 did not realize. I should never have asked you this; you don't have to say any more."

Then I pulled back a little, and wiped the tears from her eyes with my fingers. She held my hand, letting her tears roll. "No, let me tell it all. I'm not strong enough to hold it in much longer anyway. Maybe you were right when you said one should not allow oneself to get by on false pretenses."

"Look," I said, trying to comfort her, "I understand. Things don't always work out in marriage."

"No you don't understand!" she answered with unexpected vehemence. "People said ours was a marriage made in Heaven.

He was young and handsome, a first-lieutenant in the army, and I was an attractive, some even said beautiful, girl, with an English education, cultured and talented. What could possibly go wrong? The sad truth is that nothing went right."

She looked up at me, hiding nothing. Then she put her arms around me, and said: "Hold me in your arms because I am going to cry. I have to; I cannot hold it back any more. Come, hold me; please!"

I hugged her close, as warmly and as tenderly as I could, while she sobbed, her body convulsing with sorrow.

"I could never have told this to Harbaksh, or Mohini, or even to my mother," she continued, driven by something she could no longer stop. "It would destroy them. They could never forgive themselves, seeing that they are the ones who arranged for us to be married."

"It's okay," I said, trying to comfort her the best I could, "cry as much as you like. I'm here with you."

After a while, she stopped sobbing. For some more time, we just stayed there, holding each other in our warmth, she secure in the comfort of my arms. Then she pulled back, and smiled. She had come to terms with her past.

"I've ruined your shirt," she observed ruefully, looking up at me with her lovely, tear-shot eyes.

"A small price to pay for taking a load off your mind," I replied. "Are you sure you're okay now?"

"Yes, I'll be fine. Thanks for lending me your strength to cry on. You do know that I like you? You've been very nice to me, and I've been such a bore, burdening you with my troubles."

"No, you've been nothing of the kind," I said, "I'm the one who owes thanks. You have done more for me than you know, and it was more than I could have asked for."

She held my hand for a little while, then said: "We should be going back now." Then, as an afterthought, "oh! I completely forgot! We haven't gathered any dahlia plants for the house!"

"We'll look for them on the way back," I said.

There was growing in me a feeling of contentment, a rare satisfaction quite alien to my psyche. For the first time in my emotional life, everything was as it should be. There were no regrets, no unfortunate tricks of fate, no loose ends. I felt at home with Preeti, as I was sure she felt with me. This was a love that was destined to be. Even I, who did not believe in destiny, was happy enough to let it take the credit.

At the spring, Preeti washed her face and then asked me if she looked presentable. "I don't want Mohini to know I've been crying," she explained, "she'll think we had a fight, and that would ruin your reputation."

"And what do you think," I asked, trying to press my advantage, "have you ruined my reputation."

"Just a little, maybe," she replied, smiling.

I laughed at that. "You look beautiful," I said, taking her by a hand, "come, let us look for the dahlias."

By the time we got home. I was traipsing in heaven, but Preeti had so composed herself that no one could have known so much had happened. She was treating me with the same bubbly, somewhat motherly manner she had shown yesterday and earlier in the morning. But now I knew what was in her heart.

We planted the dahlias in the beds, and went in for the afternoon cup of tea. Mohini asked how the outing was, and I told her it was wonderful. I waxed eloquent about the fragrance of the pines, and the beauty of the hills, but I was really thinking of Preeti. Then I fondled the dog, glad that the only witness to our acts of affection was so faithfully quiet.

Later that afternoon, Harbaksh returned, accompanied by a young Sikh gentleman. "This is Lieutenant Gurinder Uthwaal," he said, "I managed to persuade him to come have dinner with us."

I had a foreboding that this was not going to be nice, but I was not going to let myself be discouraged, so I introduced myself. "I'm Amrik," I said, and then moving my hand towards Preeti: "This is Preeti Virk. (The 'vir' is pronounced as in virulent). This here is Mohinder; I'm sure you already know her."

"No, he doesn't," said Harbaksh, "Mohini is my wife, Gurinder; and Preeti is my sister-in-law."

The introductions made, we pulled out some cane chairs and a cane table from the family room and arranged them in a small circle in the porch. Harbaksh brought out three bottles of beer. He asked Gurinder and me if we'd like to have some. I declined, with thoughts of Preeti at the back of my mind, saying that I might have some later, but for the present I was going to manage with a coke. Mohini and Preeti also decided to have cokes.

Harbaksh told us about Gurinder, and how he had met him the last time he was down in Kasauli. Gurinder, it turned out, was also from the Faridkot area and his family had known Preeti's family while her father was still alive, before they had moved to their new house in Shimla.

As the curtain of darkness descended on Suproon, we moved inside to the drawing room. Harbaksh opened another bottle of beer, and refilled his own and Gurinder's mugs. I again declined.

"Darling," said Harbaksh to his wife, "why don't we have some fun. Let's dance. Preeti, would you play some foxtrots, please."

Preeti got up, pulled out a long-playing record, and started playing it on the record-player. The floor of the room was wooden, and we had moved all the furniture away from the center, so there was plenty of room to dance. Harbaksh and Mohini were the first to start, then Gurinder got up and asked Preeti if she would like to dance. She accepted.

As they danced, I could feel anger and jealousy welling up in me. He was good, much better than me, and he appeared relaxed. I was trying desperately to hide my disappointment, but why was she looking so happy dancing with him? I was feeling betrayed, yet I had to find some way to fight the feeling that this was the end of the world. I told myself not to blow things out of all proportion; after all, this was just a dance. Besides, it was not as if she and I were lovers. Just because she had cried on my chest did not mean I had exclusive rights to her attentions. But he was holding her close, and she was not resisting.

I just sat there, sulking with my coke. She had not looked at me even once; why was she so cruel? I was getting demoralized, to the point that I would have even accepted all the beer Harbaksh could offer me.

Suddenly, I was awakened out of my despondency. The music had stopped. There was complete silence. Preeti was again back at the record-player, but what was she playing now? I could not believe my ears! It was the Blue Danube; it must be for me, and she was even looking at me. I must go to her before this oaf of a Gurinder messed it up again. So I arose and asked her for the dance. She smiled back softly, and moved into my arms. My heart revived; there was warmth in her eyes and in her hands. Her pupils were big and beautiful, soft, dark pools of magic, and I knew what that meant.

We began to dance. I was back at the meadow, my love in my arms, the music flowing effortlessly, majestically, through the most secret reaches of my mind; and I danced, never taking my eyes off of hers. And she was looking straight back into them. We pirouetted around the room in one turn after another. There were hesitation steps and spins, my entire repertoire. She was in my arms, and that was all that mattered. Once I thought I heard her whisper, softly: "I love you." I whispered back: "I love you too," oblivious of the room and the people. This was our own private world, one we had molded to perfection.

I was unaware of the music stopping; it never did in my mind, till I heard Preeti whispering urgently: "It's over, Amrik; the music is over."

"Oh," I said, stopping, "I'm sorry, I was not paying attention."

"Bravo!" said Harbaksh, "that was some performance. Where did you learn to dance like that, kid?"

"I knew you would ask," I said, regaining my composure, "let us say I had lessons from someone who cared."

"Yes, it must be. You are good, kid; you know, you are really good. For a while there, you were impressive." He meant it.

"Don't pay any attention to him," I told the small group, trying to make light of something which meant the world to me. "It's the beer talking."

"Touché," said Harbaksh, "you have outsmarted me once again."

Gurinder, I could tell, was eating his heart out, stewing with envy. It was all his fault, he should not have butted in. What did he expect me to do, take it lying down?

Soon dinner was served. Harbaksh opened a bottle of red wine and asked me if I wanted some. This time I accepted, and looked at Preeti, imploring with my eyes that she should accept too.

Harbaksh," she said, smiling, "I think I'll have some too."

He was taken by surprise, but not for long. I knew he had sensed something, but he covered it up well. The dinner was delicious, and afterwards I was only too happy to wave a cheerful farewell to Gurinder as Harbaksh drove him back to Kasauli. I could afford to be generous; this was my day and, looking at Preeti, my woman.

Veena had fallen asleep at the dinner table, so Mohini went off to put her to bed. Preeti said she had something to do, but asked me not to go away as she would be back soon. So I just walked around the room, looking at Harbaksh's collection of books and the few wall hangings and other decorations that were scattered around the room. Mohini and Preeti came back about the same time. Mohini asked if the two of us would join her in a cup of coffee. I accepted gladly since I had no desire to go to my room. All I wanted was to stay here as long as I could, with Preeti. After a while, Preeti excused herself, saying goodnight to the two of us. Mohini and I talked a while longer, about my mother, about BCS, and about my plans for the future.

I told her I was thinking of becoming a doctor. There was little enthusiasm in my words, but I don't know if she noticed. Then she too bade me good night.

I had no desire to sleep, so for a while I hung around the room perusing through the books a second time, then went out into the yard. The stars were as bright as ever, but with more of a twinkle. Even Jupiter seemed to wink down at me. I looked up at these jewels of the night and poured my heart out, softly, dreamily: "Preeti, Preeti, I love you." The dog came up to me and I fondled him. "Everything is so beautiful," I told him, "don't you see it? Even the darkness glows and the wind sings as it blows through the trees. How am I to sleep without her, and make it through the night alone?" With canine wisdom, he just licked my hands as I caressed him. He loved me too, he was saying in his own way, but my heart and I would have to manage on our own. I had exhausted all the possibilities. There was nothing more to do but to go to my room.

The bed had been made, and on it there was a silk, man's dressing gown and a maroon muslin wrap for my head. Also present was an unsigned note that read: "I thought you might need these." I changed, put the note under the pillow, laid my head on it and went to sleep, happy to have something of hers with me.

V

The next day dawned wet and cold. Dense clouds shrouded the mountaintops; blowing mist covered their lower reaches and the house sat there in isolation, darkly silhouetted against a white oblivion. It was Nature saying that this little corner of the world was all that mattered. This little corner was my world! I rolled the maroon strip of muslin around my head, and slipped into the silk dressing gown. When I walked out the door, I was suitably dressed; casual, yet presentable. Harbaksh was ensconced comfortably in a chair in the family room, his hands wrapped around a warm cup of tea, and seemingly engrossed in thought. I wished him 'Sut Sri Akaal,' the Sikh greeting, poured myself a cup too and sat down on a chair.

"Sut Sri Akaal," he said, looking up at me, "and how are you today?"

"Couldn't be better,"I replied, "but I cannot say the same for Nature."

"Yes, perhaps Nature wants us to do something better than wander about the mountains. How was your picnic yesterday?"

"Great. I was reminded of childhood summers at Dagshai when I went dahlia hunting with my uncles. I was barely six, but everything is still clear like it was but yesterday."

"It's nostalgia, memories we cherish so much we never forget them. I remember as a child how my father used to take me along on his horse on wintry mornings, showing me his orchards. One vision I still remember vividly is of a morning when there was hoar-frost on the grass, and low mist covered the village pond."

He paused, smiling wistfully as he thought of days long gone. He was silent awhile, then he said that there was something bothering him, something that did not bode well for the intellectual health of the country. He intended no offence, but felt that the well-educated people of today knew everything about England and the United States, yet seemed rather ignorant of their own heritage and culture. In fact, he felt that today's smart kids were substantially fakes."

"I agree, it's true," I replied. "In fact, even I feel foreign. I know the British version of Indian history that was taught to us in school, but I know next to nothing about us; I mean the Sikhs."

"Fortunately," he observed, "it happens to be a favorite of mine, and I'll gladly enlighten you on any aspect of Sikh history that you wish to know."

At this time, Preeti walked in. I stood up as she entered.

"Hello, everybody," she said cheerfully, "looks like we won't be going out today. Amrik, do sit down, you don't have to get up for me."

"We were talking about Sikh history," said Harbaksh. "Amrik tells me that he knows precious little of our Sikh heritage, so I offered to enlighten him."

Turning to me, he continued: "What would you like to know?"

"Well, maybe another time. I don't want Preeti to feel left out."

I turned an inquiring eye at Preeti. "Why not," she said, "I'm no less ignorant myself."

"Okay, then," I said, "how about something more on Guru Gobind Singh? I think of him with pride, but I don't really know much about him other than his courage as a warrior."

"Yes, that is what everyone says about him, a heroic fighter," Harbaksh continued my line of thought, "but there is more. He was a scholar in at least four languages—Sanskrit, Persian, Hindi and Punjabi—besides being a poet and a philosopher. The one thing I like most is his philosophic thought."

He was pleased to see surprise on our faces. He continued: "Over two hundred and fifty years ago, there was a boy named Gobind Rai. His father, Taig Bahadur, was the ninth in a long line of spiritual teachers, or Gurus, of the religious sect known as Sikhs, started over two hundred years earlier by the first guru, Naanak. Sikh literally means a pupil, one who learns. Sikhism's converts had come mostly from the Hindu, but also to some extent the Muslim, population of the Punjab. It was the time of the Mughal emperors.

"During his ninth year, Gobind received news that his father had just been executed by the emperor Aurangzeb, the most ruthless and bigoted of the Mughals, because he had refused conversion to Islam. Taig Bahadur had assured the ruler that if he could persuade him into converting, then he would guarantee that the Hindus of the Punjab, and the Sikhs too, who did not as yet consider themselves very different, would also convert. No force would be necessary. Aurangzeb, however, failed with the guru and, in impotent frustration, beheaded him. The teen-aged Gobind Rai resolved to fight back. He made it known that his mission was to uphold the Right and to destroy Evil; to see to it that tyrants were torn out by their roots. That was a courageous sentiment to express while Aurangzeb, the most powerful and perhaps the most ruthless of the Mughals, still ruled.

"With his stated goal in mind, Gobind began to learn the martial arts, becoming an expert horseman, archer and swordsman. This all happened at Paunta Sahib in the Himalayan foothills, not far to the east of here.

"Gobind was also a genius as an organizer. The problem he faced was to raise an army imbued with his own spirit, one made of soldiers who would have his single-minded vision and the courage to fight even when the odds were hopelessly against them. He could teach them martial skills, but they would always be outnumbered many times over.

"He and his Sikhs had already vanquished a local force of Raajpoots sent against them by the hill chieftains of the Punjab, who were apprehensive that he might sway their subjects into joining him. Intending to nip the evil in the bud, these chieftains successfully bribed his five hundred Muslim Pathan mercenaries to desert and join their forces, but they still lost.

"After this battle, Gobind felt powerful enough to return to his ancestral home in Anandpur, a place in the Punjab foothills. He proclaimed a meeting of all his followers on the first of Baisaakh, the Punjabi New Year's Day, which also commemorates the completion of the winter wheat harvest. An intriguing part of his message was an exhortation to all Sikhs to come with their hair and beards uncut."

Harbaksh stopped here to see if we had any questions, knowing that the subject of hair always brings up some. Uncut hair is one of the unique physical characteristics of Sikhs, and only Sikhs. They are the only people in the world who, as a matter of religious faith, do not cut the hair on their head, or their beard, or anywhere else on the body. The long hair on the head of Sikh men is normally tied in a bun at the top of the head, which is then covered with a turban. However, the problem of why it is necessary to have them long has often been a sore point with Sikh youth, particularly the well-educated Sikhs of today. It certainty was a sore point with me, so I asked:

"I've never been able to figure out why the stricture against cutting the hair is so rigidly enforced? After all, such long hair doesn't serve any purpose, and it is a bit of a nuisance." I was vastly understating the discomfort of long hair in a hot country like India. Preeti stayed silent.

"It does not seem to serve a purpose now," explained Harbaksh, but it served the guru's purpose that Baisaakhi day. Unfortunately, he did not give his reasons but, from time immemorial, unshorn hair on the head and beard have been customary among ascetics in India. All the previous gurus and most of their disciples apparently also wore their hair long. So the custom already existed; the guru was merely making it obligatory. In this way, the army he raised would symbolically represent an army of soldier-saints who would wield arms in a righteous cause. Indeed, saints in India had, in the past, done exactly that under similar circumstances."

"But," I interrupted, "my impression was that Guru Gobind Singh did not expect, or even ask, his Sikhs to become ascetics."

"Quite true. He disapproved of asceticism, and even ridiculed it. But the keeping of hair may also have been politically expedient because the vast majority of Gobind's followers were Jat (pronounced jut) farmers of the Punjab, among whom wearing the hair long was a popular custom."

"So the keeping of hair was essentially a symbolic, or politically savvy, gesture," I said, "not something magical like Samson's hair."

"That's right," he agreed.

"Then why is it of such earthshaking importance today that a father will disown a son who cuts his hair? I actually know of one such instance, and it did not involve a father who was uneducated, but one who was an illustrious professional. I know of another, a brilliant and sensitive college student, who committed suicide by jumping off the roof of his house after he was subjected to a most chilling rejection from his parents when he came home after cutting his hair."

"I can empathize with your view," said Harbaksh. "Perhaps the Sikhs of today fear that this uniqueness of having unshorn hair is the glue that holds them together and, if allowed to dissipate, would diminish the intensity with which the rest of the guru's message is heard. This is admittedly an argument from a position of weakness, for it assumes the vulnerability of the guru's message. I personally disagree with this view, because I believe the guru's strength lay in his moral message, not in the symbolism of hair. His followers were to utterly abandon the system of categorizing themselves into the four castes or classes that the Vedas and the Shastras of the Hindus laid down for them. They were to consider themselves one people who could freely intermix. No one was to be superior merely by virtue of birth. The Guru also asked his followers to abandon the Hindu deities, and the Hindu places of pilgrimage. To reinforce his avowed destruction of the caste system, he devised a baptismal ceremony in which sugared water that had been stirred with a double-edged dagger and named 'Amrit' (nectar) was offered in the same bowl for all to drink.

"Coming from educated families, the two of you may not realize the significance of this. To grasp it, you have to first understand the Hindu concept of 'jooth'. Anything touched by someone of the lower castes is considered polluted by orthodox Hindus, the pollution removable only by a lengthy and rigorous ritual. Even today, many Hindus, particularly Brahmin women, explicitly believe it, and will go to great lengths to rid themselves of imagined ritual pollution. For example, if the shadow of an untouchable person were to accidentally fall on them, they would have to bathe and then perform a variety of rituals to remove the taint inflicted on them. The whole idea may seem ludicrous, but it is a question of achieving, or failing to achieve, salvation."

"But," I objected, "the guru was propagating a religion, no?"

Harbaksh nodded yes.

"Then," I continued, "God has to enter into his teachings, otherwise it would not be a religion. Where did God come m?"

"Ah yes, God! Gobind, like the other gurus before him, believed in the One Supreme Creator. His God was without form, timeless, and beyond human comprehension. He believed God to be omniscient and all-powerful, and he condemned idol worship. Unlike many other so-called prophets, he absolutely and expressly denied any divinity about himself, fearing that his followers might deify him, in which case his message would lose its rational identity and be merged with the enormous volumes of mysticism that had submerged the rational in Hinduism. Because of this, he stated in no uncertain terms that whosoever regarded him as the Lord, or his incarnation or *avtar,* would be damned and destroyed."

"But he did believe that God was behind his message and his actions?"

"Yes, he considered himself merely an agent of God. The justification for his demands came from God, and if at times the message was inscrutable, as with the admonition not to cut the hair, the ways of God were often beyond human understanding."

"I'm sorry, Harbaksh," I interposed, "here you and I must part company. I will accept anything that stands on its own, subject to the full scrutiny and glare of reason, but not if it has to hide behind the coat-tails of a being who is neither accessible, nor understandable, nor for that matter even definable, that is, God. As far as idols are concerned, I can see how the aversion to idol-worship might have originated under Islamic influence, but there is nothing inherently inferior in the concept of idols as compared to that of a nonmaterial, formless, all-powerful, unified God. Both are symbols only. The person worshipping a stone image does not really believe the carved piece of stone is itself a deity; he is merely using it to help his imagination cope with an elusive divinity.

"The totally abstract God of Sikhism is the same as the 'rubb' of the Punjabis, and is superior to the Hindu gods worshipped as statues only to the extent that you view formless abstraction superior to concretized symbolism. But the two are not fundamentally different. Both attempt, in their own way, to deal with something or someone not subject to the laws of Nature; and I for one believe that since everything that exists is within Nature, if you postulate something that is not subject to the laws of Nature, you are postulating something outside of it and hence nonexistent, since there is no outside. Existence encompasses everything that exists, but everything; so there cannot be anything outside of it. If there is, it already is part of existence, and hence part of Nature. There is no escape from this logic.

"You may, of course, state that all existence itself is God, but then you are in danger of becoming meaningless. You are doing away with identities, of differences and similarities, of the levels of discrimination that make our mind the superb entity that it is. If all is One, then the only recourse you have when faced with different entities and events, or even with Time, is to indulge in paradoxes, contradictions and absurdities like: 'He is One and Many; both Here and There; Over and Under; Inside and Out; Black and White; Transparent and Opaque, Lucid and Inscrutable; Good and Evil; Loving and Threatening; Life and Death; Past, Present, and Future, all these at the same time. You are left with nothing but to subscribe to the mystical Hindu concept of Maya, that all is Illusion, arising from and inherent in, God."

My exposition on God amazed even myself. I had been mulling over these thoughts for years, but had never actually formulated them in such a succinct fashion. There was absolute silence. I had done it again, allowing myself to be carried away. All of a sudden, I was feeling lonely among friends. I turned to look at Preeti, trying to hold her eyes with my own, pleading with her to understand. She should know that I could not pretend to be less than I was.

The falseness of the concept of God had been self-evident to me ever since the first few sermons in the BCS chapel. I could never understand how others could make such a fuss over it. Why was everybody so hell-bent on believing something for which there was no evidence whatsoever? What was it that caused their mental block? Was it fear of the unknown? If so, why must the unknown be imagined as malevolent, why not benign and attractive? Why must the unknown be so inhuman, inhuman in the literal sense of having no human attributes, neither of form nor of beauty, neither of reason nor of understanding? Why all-powerful and inscrutable? Perhaps it had to be inscrutable because if it were ever exposed to the full glare of knowledge and reason, it would cease to exist.

Harbaksh broke the uncomfortable silence: "You have made some powerful points, Amrik. I cannot answer you at present because I'm afraid you have entered an area I have not dared explore. I have to admit that I was shocked by your views, but your objections are legitimate and well thought out. Yours is not a frivolous mind. I am sorry for ending the discussion this way, but I have to think it over."

So saying, he got up and left to get dressed. I looked at Preeti, imploring her to say something. She must realize that it was imperative that I know what she felt. I had arisen from my chair when Harbaksh got up to leave, so I was now standing across the room from her, waiting for her to say something. She finally got up and walked over to me. Grasping both my hands in hers, she said quietly: "Don't feel so alone, love. I don't understand everything you said, but I don't want you to feel isolated. It would hurt me if you did. I wish I could say that I agree with you, but the truth is that I don't know what to believe; only that I trust you and admire you and love you, so don't be despondent. Even to me, the world is beginning to make some sense, so don't despair. Be what you must be, because you are likeable as you are."

Then she smiled encouragingly, admiration and affection no longer hidden, and walked out of the room, my eyes longingly following her receding figure.

By noon, we had all bathed and dressed. Mohini and Preeti had made a delicious breakfast for us: 'paraunthas' stuffed with potatoes and ground meat, yogurt with salt and pepper, white butter, and spiced mango and lemon pickle. Veena was there too, sitting in Preeti's lap, and things were beginning to look cheerful again.

"What were you three talking about all morning?" asked Mohini. "It seemed something very serious. I heard no laughing or chuckling whatsoever."

"Oh, we were just talking about Sikh history," I said. "Harbaksh was telling us about Guru Gobind Singh. I'm afraid I got him sidetracked towards the end, so he never got to finish."

"Don't worry, he'll finish it, I assure you," Mohini continued; "it is his favorite subject. You should see the books he has on Sikh history. Maybe you should read some of them."

"I'm sure I will," I added. "If I'm going to be a writer, which I have often thought of, I have to know everything there is to be known about my own people. I daresay we have a heritage to be proud of."

Harbaksh had now come back. I turned to him and explained: "You and I may have had a little difference of opinion, but I don't want you to get the impression that my admiration for Guru Gobind Singh's achievements is any less than yours. It could not possibly be as I'm a born hero-worshipper."

"You don't have to explain; I understand." he replied. "One has to admire someone who could boast that I'll make the sparrow fight the hawk, and one Sikh a legion; and in a sense, he did. He called his army the 'Khaalsa', the pure; pure of purpose, pure of heart, righteous. And his righteousness was not some mystical religious brand, it was simply justice as you and I know it. Fair play was his preeminent obsession; and humanity too. His soldiers were warned to respect the person and sanctity of the women of the vanquished,—which, in this context, meant Muslim women, or else face his wrath. His aim was genuine independence.

"And he was not any less when it came to the question of who ruled. In Sikh circles, resolutions made by the majority of any congregation carried the day. Such resolutions were called the 'gurmata' and treated as the order of the guru. In decisions relating to their own welfare, then, it was a participatory democracy. Though the Punjab was not liberated from the Muslim oppression in his lifetime, he had set the land on an unstoppable path, so that within a few generations of his death, the Mughal yoke had been overthrown."

"Tell me," I asked, "what were his views on marriage? Did the religion permit cross-caste marriage?"

"Well, you already know that the institution of caste was abolished among the Sikhs, so there was no social barrier to inter-caste marriage. But it is a fact that, as far as the gurus are concerned, their own marriages were all within caste. Also, the marriages were not monogamous. Guru Gobind Singh had two wives; actually three, the last being a woman who he had married as a way of taking under his protection, but with whom the marriage was never consummated."

"I take it then that the rights of women were not high on the Sikh agenda," interjected Preeti. "How else could the guru accept the concept of multiple wives? It smacks to me of a harem." She seemed obviously upset.

"Well, it was not quite like that. Those were hard times; survival was not easy. For a woman to be married, it was the equivalent of having a reliable means of support, of survival."

"But they worked, did they not? Looks to me the survival of the men was as dependent on the women as the other way around. Sure the men did all the fighting, but I think they also got a much better deal than the women. The way history is written, it seems almost as if all that the rulers did was to go around carrying away the women of the Hindus for satisfying their own lust. If rape was the order of the day, how was it possible for life to go on? These women certainly became pregnant, so they must have had children. Who was looking after these children, or was the state one vast camp of abandoned children? The way I see it in our country, a woman who has been ravished by a man is not acceptable as a wife to another, and I doubt if it was any different then. What visible means of support did these women have? Abandoned by the rulers and shunned by their own, how did they survive? I think this state of affairs was highly unlikely. The rulers may have been bad, but I think their attitude towards Hindu women must be exaggerated. Besides, look at the Sikhs themselves. I don't think anyone who has more than one wife can treat them both with full favor. Just the fact that a man has to share his time between them makes it impossible."

Harbaksh was flabbergasted. Preeti's intense attack was both rambling and bitter, but there was truth in it, and sincerity; so he managed to smile and answer: "You two are more than a match for me. Preeti, I would not marry another woman so long as I was married to Mohini, but I am not talking of myself; I am talking of a time almost three hundred years ago. It is possible that, for the times, it was the best that could be expected. It is certain that the guru expressly forbade the mistreatment of women; in fact, Sikhs were required to treat women with respect, whether their own or those of the Muslims."

But Preeti was not about to simmer down. "What a woman needs is more than respect; she needs love. I don't see how she can feel loved when she has to sit around and see her husband marry another woman while she is still his wife."

"Preeti, your point is well taken. I agree with you that it is insulting for a woman to have to share her husband with another, but I am only telling you the facts of history, as I know them. Perhaps, I should not accompany the facts with moral judgments, but if I don't, they become sterile, and then one might as well not think of them at all."

Preeti was mollified. In fact, she was a little remorseful because she was very fond of Harbaksh; and she had hurt him. From the way she looked at him, I could tell she thought the world of this man. So I was not surprised to see her extend her hand over the table to grasp his, and say: "I'm sorry, I was not fair to you. You know I was not questioning your views. I was only questioning the views of the Sikhs and their guru."

Harbaksh squeezed her hand back in return. "No, Preeti, you are right. I just had not looked closely enough at the issue. I realize that people have a tendency to glorify the past, and I am no exception. Just look at the way the Hindus have classified the effects of time on morality. The age of absolute virtue, Sutyug, the age of Truth, was the oldest. Then mankind, and all else, were effortlessly and inherently virtuous. No other choice existed, Nature was so created. Like a newborn baby, it had not learned corruption. Then, as the ages progressed, mankind and all life, even the inanimate Earth, became progressively corrupt, morally decrepit as if aging, till we have the fourth and last, Culyug, the one we are in right now. This is the age where virtue is essentially nonexistent. But look around you, look at the five of us sitting at this table, are we not living proof that the concept of Culyug is a lie; and we are not the only ones. There are countless families throughout the land, and elsewhere all over the world, like us. The present has obviously been much maligned, and the past glorified beyond belief. I guess I'll have to be more careful in the future as to how I evaluate the past."

Preeti was now overcome with emotion. She got up from her seat, ran over to him and hugged him tight, completely destroying my stereotypical concept of subdued, non-demonstrative, Indian womanhood. It was wonderful and inspiring to see someone who was not afraid to show her love.

The rain stopped later that afternoon. Harbaksh and Mohini had to go out to a dinner at Colonel Sandhu's house in Dagshai Cantonment, which is about fifteen miles down the road back towards Kaalka. It is a lovely place, situated on the top of a mountain just shy of six thousand feet. The Kaalka-Shimla road skirts around the lower reaches of the north slope of the mountain, and an access road to the cantonment comes off its northwestern end. The summit of the mountain is flat, with a huge parade ground surrounded by officers' messes, and barracks for the regular soldiers and non-commissioned officers.

Mohini had left instructions for Preeti to buy groceries, so she and I set off after lunch for Solan in her little Vauxhall. She offered to let me drive. Mohini had some trepidation, but Harbaksh assured her that I was okay and, after all, I did have a driver's license.

"He's going to be careful, knowing that our most precious possessions are entrusted to his care," he said, smiling at Preeti and Veena. The drive to Solan was only a mile, and I had little difficulty with the gears, because they were a lot easier to change than in the jeep. Shopping was over in less than an hour, so we had plenty of time on our hands. I suggested that we drive over to Dagshai where I could show Preeti some beautiful sights I happened to know about. So, dropping off the food at the house, and taking along some pears, apples and plums, we set off for Dagshai.

The road rises for a while to cross the shoulder of Barogh Mountain. Then there is a prolonged descent for several miles. Here Preeti showed me how to shift to a lower gear to avoid braking too much. I was proud of myself, everything was working so well, and I had the car and two lovely girls entrusted to me.

On the access road to Dagshai, I stopped at the havaa-ghar (wind-shelter), a little open stone structure with a cemented floor, a corrugated tin roof, and a wooden bench against the back wall. A dirt road branched off to the left from there. We walked along it for a while until we came to my grandfather's house. Nobody was there, and the door was locked.

We used to come there regularly from Lahore in the summer, but since I entered BCS I had been here only once. Situated on the sloping north face of the mountain, it opened to a broad vista extending nine miles down a valley all the way to Sabathu Cantonment. The view was beautiful; clearly, my grandfather had chosen the spot wisely. On that entire hillside, there was not another building to be seen.

About fifty yards further up the dirt road was a bauli (spring) from where we got our drinking water. For bathing, however, we collected rainwater that ran off the roof of the house, keeping for this purpose a large metal drum under the drain at the left rear corner of the house. We walked around the hillside for a while, and then went over to the bauli for a drink of water. I showed Preeti the 'cheekni mitti' (clay) from which I used to make little objects and bake them in my grandmother's oven. I was always impatient to see the result, and more than once I burnt my fingers trying to pick up the baked clay too soon after it had been fired.

I told her about the time when I was seven years old and was sitting next to Naaniji (grandma) while she was cutting red chilies for lunch. I offered to help, and she let me. It was a rather hot afternoon, and I was beginning to wilt and feel drowsy. Getting up, I yawned and told Naaniji that I was going upstairs to take a nap. I never did get to nap because just before lying down I made the terrible mistake of rubbing my eyes. My hands were soiled with the chilies, and very soon my eyes were burning. There was no running water facility in the house. The nearest water was the small stream that ran from the bauli down the dirt road, next to the mountainside. I hurried up there and began dousing my eyes with the cold water, and continued this for hours. By the tine I came back down, Grandma had finished cooking, and had been frantically looking for me. Upon seeing my blood-shot eyes, she was very upset.

"What have you done?" she asked.

Not wanting to look foolish, I replied: "Nothing."

The truth never came out.

Then there was another episode I remembered. A troop of monkeys used to inhabit that mountainside and it was not uncommon for them to sneak into the house through some open window to steal our food. One day they stole my uncle Sukhdev's favorite bag of cookies. Infuriated, he lay in wait in the upstairs bathroom with a gun. My Naanaji (Grandpa) was away at the time, so it was safe. Peeking out through the bathroom window, which he had opened a crack, Sukhdev saw the troop of monkeys return, led by the biggest of them all, a male with a strikingly red bottom, obviously the troop leader. The animal sat on a tree with the tattered remains of the biscuit packet, finishing off the last of my uncle's delights, deliberately, as if taunting. In fury, the rifle was raised, aimed, fired. There was a sickening thud as the corpse hit the ground. Sukhdev had been avenged. But there had been a desecration. An enormous shrieking and wailing broke out immediately. We were surrounded by our evolutionary ancestors, perhaps a hundred, screeching at us, jumping on the tin roof, making noise like drumbeaters trying to flush a tiger out of a forest.

Swinging past windows, making threatening gestures, but scampering away every time they saw an enemy with a gun or a stick, they harassed us for hours, well into dusk. Then, as suddenly as it began, the noise subsided—they had gone; the dead leader, comrade, husband, lover, father, had been lamented. My uncle came out, picked up the corpse, walked some distance down the mountainside, and threw it away into thick under-brush. My Naaniji was sworn to secrecy: Naanaji must never know, else there would be hell to pay. My uncles knew full well that monkeys were sacred to the Hindus, and that an unpleasant incident could result if any of the inhabitants of the neighboring town came to know of the killing. Be that as it may, the monkeys did not steal our food again for a long time.

The forecourt of the house was about twenty feet wide, and at its lower end was a retaining wall facing the valley. Preeti and I sat down on it, legs hanging over the edge, while Veena played about the yard. Preeti handed me a pear, and cut one for Veena. While we sat there eating, she asked me if I had any hobbies.

"I read, and I draw and paint," I told her.

"What do you use?"

"Charcoal, and water color." I replied. "Actually, I really don't know how to use the latter. My paintings look more like oil paintings, if you know what I mean. They lack the washed appearance that makes water paintings so attractive."

"What do you like to draw?"

"Faces mostly," I said. "I generally paint sceneries, but I prefer faces. I tried painting a few in water color and they came out pretty good, even though they looked like oils."

"I like painting too," she said, "I could show you how to do water-paints."

"Do you have any paints and paper at the house?" I asked.

"No, they are in Shimla."

"Well, do you think we could drive up there, like tomorrow? We could pick up some charcoal, and paper and paint, and I could even show you my school. And, given time, we might even make it to one of the cinemas on the Ridge."

"Okay," she said, "That would be fun. The house is locked up. My mother is away with my Mamaji (mother's brother) in New Delhi, but I have a key. Tomorrow it is then. I'm sure going to love this."

Our minds were full of romantic escapades, and our amorous appetites were literally watering with imagination. After a while, we got up and walked back down the dirt road to the car, then headed back to Solan, as it was time for Veena's dinner and bedtime.

VI

Back at the house, Preeti gave cooking instructions to the servant, and took Veena off for a bath. Dinner was ready when she came back. After dinner, we were talking of things we enjoyed doing when, on an impulse, she got up and brought something from Harbaksh's bedroom to show me. It was a pastel portrait of him sitting in his favorite chair, wearing his silk dressing gown and a red muslin wrap around his head. The resemblance was striking, and the stroke-play sophisticated, but there was something missing.

"I like that, Preeti," I remarked, "you're an artist."

"Thank you," she replied, "I had thought of pursuing art by joining college, but the marriage finished all that. Many a time I wanted to try again, but every time a creeping depression came over me, and I lost heart. This," she pointed to the portrait, "is the only work I've done since the marriage."

The marriage had taken a lot out of her, like her fire; it was clearly noticeable in the portrait; so I told her: "You ought to give it another try, with more gusto. There is a sadness in Harbaksh's portrait, as if you were thinking, what good is it, I'm never going to achieve anything. I think you have talent, and I'm willing to help any way I can."

"It's nice of you to say that. I'm sure I could use it, help, I mean, but I don't think there is much you can do. I have pretty much ruined my life beyond the point of no return."

This demoralization was a side of her I had not seen before, but there must be something I could do. There had to be, the way I felt about her.

"Preeti," I said as forcefully as I could, deliberately ignoring her statement of despondency, "what you are saying is not true. All cannot be lost. Tell me, how many others before me have you shown this portrait to?"

"None," she answered, "I've never wanted to. Look, I really would like to talk, but first I have to put Veena to bed. After that, I'll be all yours."

If you put it that way, I mused, okay! She had smiled with that last line; maybe she was thinking what I was thinking. Sweeter words no man could ask for. Twenty minutes later, she was back and a lot more cheerful. Perhaps my words of encouragement had been taken to heart. The servant had washed the dishes and the cooking utensils, and had just left for his house, which was in a village somewhere down the road to Solan. We were now alone.

"You were going to tell me something," said Preeti, walking up to me, "now here I am."

"Perhaps we should first have some music," I suggested.

"A capital idea. What would you like?"

"Something to warm the heart, bring back memories, like the Blue Danube?"

"You have taken a cue right out of my heart," she said, smiling conspiratorially as she complied with my request.

The room, even the music, was now different. No one was lookinq over our shoulders, no Gurinder, not even Harbaksh or Mohini. The depths of her eyes, those windows to her soul, were there for me to fathom at my leisure, for as long as I wished. Her heart was here too, hanging on my every word, eagerly waiting to be touched. There was no need to dance, the music was enchantment enough; so I just stood there, holding her, gazing into her magical eyes.

"Preeti," I said, "we're all alone. There is no one here but us."

"Yes, no one," she answered softly.

Slowly, I pulled her close and kissed her softly on the lips. It was my first kiss. She kissed back, a little stronger, her eyes closed. I pulled her closer still, enclosing her in my arms, feeling her incredible warmth. Her arms were wrapped around my neck.

The melody kept playing, taking its toll on her resistance, uniting us in a crescendo of pleasure. Somewhere through that waltz, I must have lost myself. When she finally pulled back, I realized the music had stopped a while ago. Thinking back on that day, I wonder how many of you have kissed to music. In dreams, I have kissed floating in air or gliding through water; but awake, there is no match for music. It plays with you, willy-nilly tightening, loosening, your muscles; moving you in harmony; imbuing your lips and body with its flow and passion; melodious, brave, challenging, daring, the kind of sentiments only it can evoke, and to which you cannot mount any resistance. So it was with us. My mind was in turmoil. She had a captivating, warm fragrance, and a body both soft and strong, inviting me to explore her with my lips, first her neck, then her ears, relishing their perfection, occasionally breathing in a word every now and then. "I love you, Preeti," I said. "I'm crazy about you. I need you even to breathe."

I could feel her smiles of pleasure as I spoke, and I could smell her happiness, but she was a woman, that magical species that never ceases to amaze.

"Take care what you say," she said, teasing me. "I am not an easy woman to please."

But her kisses were hot, and her body shuddered with delight as I held her close.

"I can manage you," I replied.

And so we went on with no end in sight. After a while, she pulled back. "Amrik," she said, hesitating when no hesitation was called for, "I'm afraid; I'm older and a widow. Can anything come of this?"

Even as she spoke, her actions gave her words the lie. Her passion was pleading with me, begging me to tell her she was wrong. Why did she have to do this, I wondered, bringing up the mundane in the midst of triumph? Was there not strength enough in my arms to allay her fears?

"What do you mean?" I asked, still continuing to make love, hoping to sway her back to unconcern.

"What will people say?" she pleaded.

"What can they say? It matters little, and I don't care."

"Perhaps not, because you are a man and this is a man's world, my love, but I am a woman. If you keep loving me, you will have destroyed my reputation, then nobody will want me. I cannot always have everything I want."

"Oh, but you can! Do you know what you want?" I asked.

"You, of course, but I'm afraid to ask. I have never wanted so much before, and I'm afraid. What if you are denied me? Love is something new and terrifying, and I feel helpless. If somebody comes to know of this, what will they say? That the designing widow put her charms on an innocent boy, and entrapped him in her snare?"

She was pleading, I could see, but as much with Fate as with me. She wanted my strength, my reassurance, but she was also crying out to Fate's invisible hand to be gentle with her.

"There is not much you can do, darling," I replied. "I love the beautiful widow, and I will not let her go. In your heart you want me, so I will not deny your wish. Your destiny is my destiny. You can, if you wish, have me and eat me too."

She was reassured, at least for the time. I was beyond myself with ecstasy, touching her in places I'd only dreamed of before; feeling her, down from her slim waist to her hips, and the firm rising of her buttocks. The pleasure was enough to make me cry. I pressed her in, not afraid that she would feel the hardness rising up in me. There was no desire to resist. All I wanted was to surrender to my urges, but it was not to be. With an effort of will much stronger than mine, she pulled herself back, all breathless, then pulled me right back to her again, her head resting on my chest. Oh, what a reprieve!

"Amrik," she implored, "what am I going to do? What will Harbaksh and Mohini think of me? They trust me, and here I am, alone in their house, shamelessly making love to their guest, and I don't even feel guilty. I don't know if I can hide my feelings this time. It's not the same as yesterday."

There had to be an end. With an abruptness that was almost painful, as if at the behest of some malign fate, we tore ourselves apart and walked out the door. The cold air outside was a shock, but I held on to her hand—I needed her touch. I suggested that we go for a walk.

"But what about Veena," she said.

"We won't go far. I promise we'll remain within earshot of the house."

She put her arm around my waist, and I put my arm around her shoulder. In this way we wandered, close together, cheeks touching, murmuring loving sounds now and then, letting our systems wind down. For several minutes, no word was said. Then she spoke: "Amrik, what will you do when the vacation is over?"

"Go to college, I guess."

"To premed?"

"Yes, though why I'm doing it, I don't know. I'm not really interested in becoming a doctor. Maybe I'm doing it to please my father. He says it's a secure profession."

"I married Inder because my mother wanted me to. I would have a secure life, she said."

Preeti's voice was heavy with self-blame and remorse.

"Why did you not say no?" I asked.

"Why did *you* not say no?"

It caught me by surprise. There was an intensity in her question that hit me like a bucket of cold water.

"No to what?" I asked, hoping it was not what I thought it was.

"To becoming a doctor."

It was. She was driving me honest, and she was right. Here I was asking her to explain her motives, when all the time I was just as guilty. Why had I not said 'no' to my father? Because I lacked the guts. It was all coming to me now, clear as a cold spring morning.

"You know what I really want to do?" I asked, addressing the question as much to myself and the heavens as to her.

"Make love to me," she giggled, amused at her cleverness.

"Of course, that too," I said, hugging her close. "I mean in terms of work?"

"Why would you want to work? What could be more important than me?"

"Nothing is more important than you, but I would love to be a writer."

She stopped, turned to stare at me, and in a tone of disbelief and some impatience with my vacillation, gently berated me: "You mean you know what you want to do, and yet you're going ahead with plans to do something else?"

"You don't know my father," I replied, a little embarrassed by her accusation because the truth hurt, "he doesn't even permit the reading of a novel. How do you think he'll react when I tell him I want to become a writer of those infernal things? Can you imagine when he'll say?"

She smiled ruefully. "You are making the same blunder that I made when I got married. I should have had the sense to pay attention to my own misgivings, and then the guts to say 'no'. I had no desire to marry a stranger, that's all Inder was to me."

I stopped. For once in my life, I knew I had to listen, really listen. There are some things in life that outweigh all else, and this was one of them. The more I thought of what she said, the more sense her words made. The confusion in my mind was clearing as her thoughts blew through it like a breath of fresh air. I could see it clearly now: I had to become a writer, father notwithstanding. The connection between my happiness and what I did for a living was so plain that I felt like a fool for not having seen it earlier. No choice remained; I just had to do what was right by me. Slowly but surely, my mind was beginning to follow the dictates of reason. The choice was obvious, there was but one way. I would not go to Hindu College to do premedical; instead, I would go to St. Stephen's to study literature, history, philosophy, and psychology. These were the subjects I had always been fond of, and they were the tools-in-trade of a writer.

I was in love with Preeti, but it was more than that. I was grateful to her. Here I was reading psychology and philosophy, and I had missed the most fundamental truth, that you don't ask others what you must do, you ask yourself. Then you do what your heart most wants to do.

"Preeti," I said, happy and relieved beyond belief, now that the decision was made, "I cannot begin to tell you how much I owe you. You have taken a great burden off my mind; I feel liberated. You are a marvel; you've clinched my career for me. I am going to do what I always wanted. I'll give up premed, and join St. Stephen's to become a writer."

The treasures of the world were spreading themselves before my eyes. There loomed immense possibilities. I knew what I was to be, and no one but I would decide. My confidence grew, coloring every thought, opening new dimensions and vistas for the future. I was happy, satisfied, confident that I would achieve whatever I wished. But there was unfinished business still. Preeti was happy for me, but not as ecstatic as she should have been, now that I was her lover. She must be wondering what would happen when I left for Delhi. I grasped both her hands in mine.

"There is something more, Preeti," I said.

"And what is that?" she asked, quite unaware of the quandary I was conjuring up for her. She sat there innocently, a lovely rose blowing in a fountained garden.

"Will you marry me?" I asked.

She looked at me in disbelief, unable to believe her ears. She was taken by surprise; stunned really. A deep quiet descended over her. She was thinking, desperately. But what could she be thinking? I wanted to help, but I must not. This is one thing she will have to decide for herself. If she loves me as I love her, she will say yes; but if she does not; no, that is impossible. Her eyes, her lips, they do not lie. She loves me, there is no question that she does. But what is she thinking? She could be saying to herself: he offers me a two-day romance, and then he wants to marry me. How dare he! He is but a boy of eighteen, barely able to drive a car. I'm a woman of twenty, married, widowed. He has no visible means of support, but for his parents. I have an officer's widow's pension. But why do I want to take his side? What is there in him that so fills my heart with longing? He is intellectually precocious, no doubt, and attractive in a rugged sort of way. But there is more to marriage than good looks and smart words. He loves me and I love him, oh how much I love him! He makes me feel alive again. And he dares to say and feel what is in his heart, even presumes to tell me what's in mine. He has warmth and tenderness, and that something about him that makes me feel that he can do no wrong. He is clean and honest of heart. He lives in the here and now, and yet has visions of a future. He dares to defy the idea of God, and yet I don't fear for him. I want to mother him, and I want to be his wife. He knows that I love him, and uses that against me; why else would he ask me to marry him? He mocks me, dares me to say 'no'. He knows I'm weak. All he has to offer me is himself, but why can't I refuse? Why do I feel the world ending at the very thought of being without him?'

She was quiet for a long, long time, then she looked up and asked, trying to hide her inner turmoil: "Are you asking me to marry you?"

Her voice belied her calm, laying bare her frantic efforts to find a way out of her dilemma.

"Yes, I want you to be my lover, and my wife."

I was playing with words, perhaps without planning to, but I had to keep her mind from giving up. I had to force her to accept what she felt, because life would be miserable without her.

"But I can't."

"Why not? Why can't you marry me?"

"I don't know, but how can I marry you?"

"If you want to marry me, there is nothing to stop you."

She looked at me, her eyes wet with tears, almost begging for my help.

"I love you, but I don't know what to do. How can we be married?" she implored.

"Preeti," I said, knowing that I had to help. "Look at me. This is your life. No one, but no one can tell you what to do with it, not even I. Most things in life are ours for the asking. All we have to do is take them. But we set up imaginary dilemmas, imaginary obstacles where none exist. We timidly give up what is ours by right, believing that what comes easily cannot have been deserved. Happiness and love should come easy, but we try to value them only if they come with much travail. Why do we concede so much to suffering, and so little to joy? May be I don't know all the answers, but I will one day. Right now, all I can tell you is that you and I have a right to happiness, even if it comes as effortlessly as this."

Preeti grasped my hands a little tighter. I could see resolution coming back into her eyes. Her brow cleared, and confidence replaced the ambivalence there before. She looked straight at me, smiled, and said very slowly: "I'll marry you if it's the last thing I ever do." Then she chuckled, and her face softened: "May I call you 'darling'?"

"Is that all! You can call me anything you wish, even something as alien as husband."

"Darling, darling Amrik, I take you to be my husband if you will take me to be your wife."

"I do," I said.

"You do what?" she teased, pretending not to understand.

"I do take you to be my wife."

We both laughed, and then again, and again for a long, long time. We stopped when it began to hurt. Our eyes were wet with tears, but our hearts were joyous.

"Are we married or are we not?" she asked, still chuckling.

"We must be," I said, "I feel married."

She shook her head. "I cannot believe this. Marriages are supposed to be solemn occasions, with much fanfare, with lots of relatives, with laughing, drinking and crying; with trips to the bazaar to buy jewelry and beautiful clothes; with months of planning. Marriages are supposed to be something you cannot take lightly. They have to be arranged through uncles, aunts and other relatives. The groom's family has to be looked into, their and his credentials checked, his reputation assessed, one's own reputation protected. Who would have believed marriage could be so much fun. Seriously, Amrik, are we really married. This is much too easy. It seems almost flippant."

"Look, darling, if I may call you that, the occasion for solemnity is when you fall in love, not when you marry. Marriage is but a formality, something one should take for granted. Once you have love, there is nothing earthshaking about marriage. In the eyes of the law, of course, we are not married, nor in the eyes of my parents or your mother, or your brother-in-law, but they are not the ones getting married. I am marrying you, and you are marrying me. They can afford to make mistakes, but we cannot because, my love, we are the ones getting married. We must marry because we need to be married. When I asked myself today: 'Can you live without her?' the answer came back: 'No!' Your fate was sealed right then. What else was there to do but to marry you."

"Oh, and I had nothing to say?"

"I guess not," I said, "unless you want to turn the world upside down, and have women proposing to men."

"May be I should," she answered, "it might make the world a better place. Then, after a pause, she continued: "We are married, you know what that means? We could go to bed together. I know I won't feel guilty."

She looked at me invitingly, appropriately shameless.

"What is it like?" I asked.

"What is what like?"

"You know. Making love; all the way."

"I wouldn't know," she replied.

"But you were married," I objected.

She did not answer for a while. Her head was lowered and her smile slowly faded. This was something she could not make light of. I could see it was hard, but she was going to answer the only way it could be answered. She lifted up her hands and cupped my face in them, looking at me with tenderness and pain. She knew it hurt me just as much to hear her say it as for her to tell.

"My love, yes, I was married. I had sex, but I never made love. With you, I will make love, for the first time, like you with me. I am just as innocent of desire as you, so this marriage will be my first in the truest sense of the word. You will know when you make love to me that I have never made love before."

We sat on the protecting wall by the side of the road, and I caressed her cheek with my hand. With one hand behind her back, I let my other hand travel down her front, letting it move over her breasts as it wished. I felt her arms, and her wrists, and her hands, and the round form of her thighs. I knew I wanted to have her right there and then, but it would have to wait.

"We cannot do it in this house, not tonight" I said, knowing in my heart that these were her sentiments too.

"I know," she said, "we'll wait. Life is long."

The night moved along, but we just sat there, unwilling to enter the house. We knew once we went in, we would have to go our separate ways, to separate bedrooms, and sleep separately, and we wanted none of that. But what was this? Preeti had suddenly got up.

"I hear Veena crying," she exclaimed, and ran back to the house.

I followed. The little girl probably had a bad dream, and was standing next to the door of her parents' bedroom, rubbing her eyes and sobbing. Preeti picked her up and put her back to bed, and in less than a minute, she was fast asleep again. Coming back out of the bedroom, Preeti walked up to me, put her arms around my neck, and kissed me. I kissed her back and, in no time, my hands were at it again, feeling her hips and cupping her breasts. It was irresistible. She must have had more resolve than me, for finally she pushed me away, and without looking up, in a manner that seemed almost cruel, went away to her room. That left me nothing to do but go back to mine.

For a long time I lay awake in bed, thinking of her and of being a writer, seeing us together in places that were dear to my heart. I don't remember when I dozed off, because I never heard Harbaksh and Mohini coming back. When I awoke, the sun was streaming in through the window on to the opposite wall, and I could hear the sparrows chirping. I got up, went to the bathroom, dressed up in the usual 'casual' style, and went out. No one was around. They were still fast asleep. I sank down into one of the cane chairs in the porch, and started thinking:

'I now have responsibilities. If Preeti and I are to live together, it could not be at my parents' house; there was not enough space, and no privacy. But we could not live anywhere else unless I began to earn some money. How was I going to do that? I could begin to write, may be short stories for magazines, may be even a novel one day, because there is little money in short stories, but more in novels. Maybe I could teach, tuitions and that sort of thing. I could teach English, and history; whatever anyone wanted. And may be Preeti could sell some paintings. She was good, she had talent. May be she could work for an advertising agency, making drawings and paintings for them. There were a whole lot of may-bes, but that is what the world is made of, and may-bes have an uncanny way of coming true."

Harbaksh was the first to come out. He was carrying a cup of tea. "Mohini's made some tea; why don't you go in and get yourself a cup too," he suggested.

I did.

"How was the party?" I asked.

"You know these army parties," he said, "they are all the same. Still, it was fun. Yes, it was pretty good. So, what did you do?"

"We drove over to Dagshai after the shopping. I showed Preeti my grandfather's house, we had a little picnic there, and then we drove back. I'm really getting good at driving."

"I knew you would have no trouble. Did Preeti show you how to use gears to slow down when going downhill?"

"Yes," I said, "it really works."

"I still remember the time I taught her that. What a day! We were in the jeep coming down the long slope from Summer Hill—you know, the place just this side of Shimla—down to Tara Devi. She was driving and the brakes failed. Fortunately, we were still slow. I somehow managed to get myself into her seat without knocking her out of the jeep, and then, with much banging and bouncing, with sparks flying all over us, I scraped the jeep to a halt against the mountainside. It was a total wreck, but we made it. It was close; boy, was it close! If there had been any traffic, we would have been done for, and I would not be here, nor would Preeti, nor for that matter would you."

"She never told me that!" I said.

"I didn't think she would; but she sure remembered her lesson."

We sat around for a while, not saying very much, then he suddenly got up. "God! I'm losing my discipline. We should have done our daatan before having tea. Let me get one for each of us."

When he returned, he gave me a daatan and started chewing on one himself. But there was no walking up and down the yard. The party must hove been a long one, because he plopped right back into his chair, quite out of character for him, I thought.

"Preeti showed me the pastel portrait she made of you," I said, trying to find a way of telling him about our proposed trip to Shimla. "I think she has a lot of talent. It's a pity she's not doing anything with it."

"Yes, I think she should be doing something too, but ever since Inder's death, she has been moody and, I regret to say, rather fickle of purpose. Do you know that my portrait is the only thing she's done since then. Personally, I think she's taking it much too hard. A young woman like her, she should try to be more outgoing and social. All she wants is to be with us and look after Veena. If I didn't know better, I would think Veena was her daughter, not Mohini's. I'm afraid this excessive caring for the little girl is her way of hiding something from herself." He paused for a while, reflecting inwardly on some thought, then continued: "You know, she has changed since you came. You are a good influence. Being with someone her own age is what she needs. Look at what happened yesterday, the way she plowed into me about the Sikhs and their guru having more than one wife. It was not her at all. She has never shown interest in such matters. To tell you the truth, I never would have suspected there was so much spunk and fire under that pretty exterior."

I waited an appropriate length of time, not offering any comment, then said: "She tells me that all her pastels and paints are in the house in Shimla. I suggested that we drive up there so she could bring them back. Then she could do some more of her sketching and painting. I also thought that may be we could roam a little around the town, perhaps see a movie, and just have a good time. For nostalgia's sake, I mean. I spent the last five years of my life in those hills, you know. What do you think?"

"I think it's a capital idea, but count us out. Mohini and I are too tired from last night's party. I certainly had too much to drink. But I'm all for anything to get Preeti back to her normal self again. She was such a delight when I asked her mother for her hand for Inder."

"I know. She told me."

"She did?" He looked surprised. "You must have some special talent, kid. She hasn't mentioned his name even once since he died; won't talk of him no matter what I do. I have tried to tell her that you cannot keep grief bottled up within you. You have to let go sooner or later, else it will consume you, but she won't listen. I wish I could do something for her. Anyway, if she is willing to bring her paints and paper down here, that is a good beginning. I sure hope it works, because if there is anything that will, it is this. She loves painting."

VII

"**A** mrik, could you come in for a minute?"

That was Preeti calling me from the family room. As I entered, she led me into my room. Then she closed the door and turned around to face me. She looked agitated; signs of an inner conflict, an overworked conscience, guilt, covered her face. But there was no trace of indecision. Whatever it was, she had resolved it. Why then had she called me? Could it be second thoughts, a panicking at the altar, so to say?

"What is it, Preeti?" I asked, trying to hide my misgivings as best I could. "You're not having cold feet, are you?"

"No," she said, "it's nothing like that. I gave myself to you last night; that cannot change. You are my man, and that is that. Remember, we are married—tied hands and feet with bonds of love."

She smiled in amusement at what still seemed to be a little game.

"Then why the troubled look?" I asked.

"It's not what you think," she said, "I was thinking of Harbaksh and Mohini. You know how they are for me. They are my family, not by blood, but more family then my mother. I would not dream of keeping secrets from them. I'm proud of our love, my darling; not telling them makes me feel untrue. They love me as much as you do, only different. I know Harbaksh would give his life for me if he had to, and Mohini would do no less. If we don't tell them, we are implying a fear that they may not approve? An unpalatable thought, don't you think? My happiness has to be a source of joy to all who love me, and they certainly do; so what have we to fear?"

I hugged her close, then cupped her face in my hands. "I don't know what to say, Preeti. You are more wonderful, braver, more loving than I believed possible. I'm like putty in your hands. Just say the word, and it shall be done, whatever you wish. Shall we tell them now?"

"No, let us wait till after breakfast. You go finish your tea while I get ready." She kissed me wetly on the lips, nipped me on the neck, and walked me hand in hand out of the bedroom into the family room. There we parted company, she going to her room and I to my cup of tea.

At breakfast, Harbaksh told Mohini of the trip Preeti and I were planning to Shimla. She offered to make a picnic lunch for us with paraunthas, potatoes and cauliflower; and she would pack some pickle as well. Preeti added that she would take some fruit too. This way we would not have to worry about where we went all day.

"Maybe you two can climb up to Jaakhoo peak and picnic at the top," Mohini suggested.

"Not very likely," I explained; "too big a hike; besides, the monkeys at the Jaakhoo Temple would make small work of our lunch; like the last time I was there with my brother, who just happened to have peanuts in his shirt pocket. Monkeys have an eye for such goodies, so we were soon surrounded. A big one jumped my brother, grabbed the nuts, and made off with them. You can well imagine what happened next. There was no question of fighting for our rights; we knew when we were beaten. Yes sirree, discretion was the better part of valor, so we turned tail and ran down the mountain, terror goading us on, till we broke the land speed record for humans on two feet. Were it not for a fallen tree across our path, we may never have stopped. The Jaakhoo Temple? We never did see it."

"All the more reason why you should see it now," insisted Mohini, "you're a grown man; you wouldn't let any monkey scare you, now would you?"

"I'm not known to be suicidal, Mohini," I replied, "but that aside, what do you think the monkeys would do to a beautiful girl like Preeti? They'd want to carry her off as one of their own. And this time I would have to fight."

"I see your point," said Harbaksh, enjoying my bold and public compliment to Preeti.

Any fool could now tell I was in love with her, and Harbaksh was no fool. So he said to his wife: "Mohini, you had better relent. After all, we are responsible for their welfare."

Harbaksh and Mohini were good folks, and I loved them. Everyone laughed, each for his own reasons; I for the chance to say publicly what I thought of Preeti; Harbaksh because he could see what I was up to; Mohini at my cleverness; and Preeti simply because she loved me. But when we simmered down, Preeti turned serious.

"Harbaksh, Mohini; Amrik and I have something we wish to tell you," she announced.

Her tone was too solemn for them not to know that it must have something to do with affairs of the heart. They looked concerned, probably worrying whether we knew what we were up to; such affairs, they knew, could never be taken lightly.

"Preeti, is something wrong?" asked Mohini.

The question was significant more for what it left unsaid than what it said. In such matters, you never want to say the wrong thing; the easiest way out is a show of concern, even though everyone knows that love is one thing for which no such sentiment is necessary. It is what drives concern away.

"No, nothing's wrong," replied Preeti, "it's just that it is something important. I would much prefer to tell it in the verandah."

Harbaksh and Mohini were a little perplexed by this request, but they went along. So we all moved out into the pleasant morning breeze.

"The first thing I have to say," continued Preeti, "is that I have decided to go to college."

Preeti, I thought, are you trying to play it safe? How smart, starting with the most neutral decision of all! But then, on the other hand, it is always better to work one's way up to the climax; it is a tried and true rule of good theater.

"Oh, that is wonderful," they both chimed in, almost as one, relieved that the news was as simple as that. But surely they were wondering what Preeti had meant when she said "Amrik and I" have something to tell you.

"There is more," Preeti continued, "I am planning to do fine arts. One day I will be an artist with a name, and you will be proud of me."

Their question was still not answered, but Mohini was taken in by Preeti's skills.

"We are already proud of you, love," she said, "but I would be even more so when your paintings grace all the rooms of this house."

"That they will," affirmed Preeti.

Harbaksh was not satisfied, so he tried another approach to placate his curiosity.

"Preeti," he said, "what made you change your mind? You could not have failed to notice that I have hinted for months, gently and diplomatically, of course, that it was high time you stopped moping around and made something of yourself. I'm sure glad to hear this."

Then he made an indication towards me and, with a sly little smile, asked her directly: "Did this young man have anything to do with it?"

He couldn't wait, could he?

"Yes," she said, "he had everything to do."

There, the cat was out of the bag.

"I see," Harbaksh continued, still keeping the same insinuating smile in his eyes, "and what do you have to say to this, Amrik?" he asked, turning his gaze towards me. "You were my charge for the duration of the summer. Now it seems you have decided to take a charge of your own. Do you deny it?"

"No sir, not me." I replied. "How could I? Unless I may be permitted to state that you are wrong to the extent that the young lady has taken charge of me. She has convinced me that I would be wasting my time in premed, and would be much better off, and happier too, if I were to turn my energies towards becoming a writer."

I had improvised the script, but Preeti gave me a winning nod of approval, certifying my statement with her stamp of excellence.

"And is that what you want?" he asked.

"Yes, my father may not be too thrilled, but my life is my own, and I must do what I must do. I am at heart a weaver of tales. My accomplishments cannot grace the walls of your house, but they might help decorate the shelves; perhaps even brighten the glow of the winter fire-place as you sit there reading to Veena, reading tales of love and valor to delight the heart. My stories will be fiction, all untrue; they will not talk of the world as it is, but as it might be; and that, you must agree, is what stories should be all about."

Harbaksh was thrilled.

"Mohini," he said, "is it not wonderful to see how two educated people can look after each other?"

Then he turned to us. "Look, when I spoke of today's anglicized youngsters being a bunch of fakes, you did not really think I was referring to you, did you?"

"Of course not, though the thought did cross my mind," I replied facetiously.

"And mine too," chimed in Preeti, "though I quickly dismissed it."

"Did you hear that, Mohini. Today's youngsters don't even know how to lie well. Remind me to give them a lesson on it one of these days."

There was much mirth and joy, and we hadn't even broken the real news yet. I turned to Preeti.

"What are we going to do?" I asked her softly.

"Don't worry,' she said, "I have an idea."

So saying, she turned to the others, and addressed them: "There is only one thing missing but that can be rectified. Don't any of you move."

So saying, she went in, and in a moment came out leading Veena by the hand. She took her to Mohini and put her in her lap.

"What is this going to be," said Harbaksh, "a picture-taking session? Or are you planning to paint a group portrait? Young lady, have you forgotten that you have no camera and your artistic wherewithal is still in Shimla."

"That is just perfect," said Preeti. "What do you think, Amrik; do you think this is about right?"

"As good as can be expected," I said, "and we have them about where we want them. Come here, Preeti."

I put my arm around her shoulder and addressed them: "Dearly beloved, we are gathered here before Harbaksh, Mohini, Veena and last, but not least, our canine friend from the land of Labrador, Mackey, to announce the most wonderful news, which is . . ."

"That we are in love, and wish to get married!" chimed in Preeti.

Silence. For a long half minute, that is all there was, thunderous silence. Utter disbelief covered Harbaksh and Mohini's faces. Then the dog barked, unnerved by the unnatural quiet. Veena got up and started cuddling him, thinking that he wanted to play. Harbaksh finally broke the lull. He had been suppressing a laugh for a long time, but could not hold himself back any more.

"A stellar performance!" he proclaimed. "Of all the darndest things!" And here he shook his head, as if in disbelief, "you really mean it, don't you?"

"Of course we do," we answered in unison, and then Preeti continued: "we would have told you earlier, but you were gallivanting so late into the night that we innocents were fast asleep by the time you came home."

I liked that added touch; innocents indeed!

"Can you believe it, Mohini, just three days. Hey, kid, it took us a week capturing the Zoji La, and here you have conquered our most precious possession in half that time. And I thought you were not even trained. I should have known.

What else can you expect when you teach a young men to drive a jeep. You sow ideas in his head, only this time they fell on the most fertile soil in the land."

"I appreciate the compliment," I said, smiling proudly back at him.

Then he turned serious. He was about to say something, but Mohini stopped him, got up and kissed us both, hugging us in one common embrace.

"I love you both," she said, "I know you will be very happy."

"What she is trying to say under all that hugging," said Harbaksh, "is that you have kindled in us a touch of nostalgia. We were married under similar circumstances, only it took us about two months longer. Our marriage was a scandal, like yours is bound to be, but it was worth it."

Preeti was taken by surprise.

"I was not aware you had a love marriage!" she exclaimed, her expression incredulous, but also delighted by the news, "no wonder you always look so happy."

Overcome with emotion, she ran forward and kissed them both.

"Why did you not tell me?" she asked,

"What was there to tell?" said Harbaksh, "I thought it was all too obvious."

"Of course it was;' said Preeti. "Forgive me for being so dense. My world has been colored blue for so long, I had thought your happiness was purely fortuitous, thinking as I was that yours was an arranged marriage like all the others."

Preeti was getting much too close to the truth about her own marriage, and I was afraid that it may sadden the occasion. But Harbaksh and Mohini never let on, even though I suspected they had noticed the clue.

"Don't give it a thought, my love," he said, standing up and hugging us both, "but first things first. What are your plans?"

"We will need your help," said Preeti.

Here she hesitated, looking at me a couple of times, wondering whether she should say it. Finally, she did.

"We wish to be together tonight. You must find a way to marry us," she said.

"Consider it done," said Harbaksh. "I will have a magistrate lined up by the time you two love-birds return from Shimla. Just make sure you don't take too long. I want you back by three."

He turned to Mohini and said something into her ear, then turned to me.

"You do drink champagne, don't you?"

"I cannot say I do, but I will. We all will."

"Okay, you two better hurry off to Shimla before I change my mind about the magistrate."

There followed some very emotional good-byes, even though we were going away only for about five hours. Preeti hugged Mohini and told her in front of everyone:

"Mohini, I love him so much, I could not have waited another day."

"Come on, Preeti," I said, "you are embarrassing me."

"And why does a statement of love embarrass you?" asked Mohini.

"I don't know," I said, "maybe because I was a deprived little urchin. I don't wish to tempt my fate."

"Fate has nothing to do with it, kid," advised Harbaksh, "you are not half bad."

So, shedding mushy tears of joy, we mounted our motorized steed, the Vauxhall, and set off to nostalgia, the Himalayan town of Shimla. Trailing us, we could hear Harbaksh's shout: "Don't forget to visit Scandal Point."

"What does he mean by that?" asked Preeti.

"You know, Scandal point, the place at the intersection of the Mall and the Ridge. They say that is the place where the amorous Maharaja of you-know-what princely state in the plains drove away the Viceroy's daughter, right out from amidst a bunch of English dandies. Afterwards, he was forbidden to ever step foot in the town again."

"Oh, what a nice man!" she said, "a true romantic!"

"I don't know about that," I corrected. "He was reputed to have over a hundred wives, and God knows how many sons and daughters from them."

"Aw! Another Sikh polygamist," she said, "and here I thought he was a wonderful man."

"I don't know about that either, but he did right by his children. His kaakaas (sons) were scattered all over the dorms of BCS and Sanawar. Handsome blokes, all of them. There must have been problems, though, because I remember one who used to wet his bed all the time. They had English nicknames like Peter, Andrew, and Dick, and I was told English governesses in the palace."

"He had daughters too, in equal numbers," said Preeti. "They used to grace the halls of our boarding school and St. Bede's. You are right about their looks, they were certainly all attractive. Why do you think princes and princesses are so good-looking?"

"Well, what do you expect? Here is a maharaja roaming the mountains with his roving eye, taking the pick of the womanly crop. And he himself wasn't half bad-looking."

"But how could the parents agree to marry their daughters to him, knowing that he already had a wife?"

"Remember, Preeti, these people here are quite poor. Their daughters may have been just chattel in the palace, and the parents might have had to go in through the back door when they visited, but they did not want for wealth or comfort."

"I still don't like it. The daughters were simply being sold to a high bidder."

"Let me tell you about the alternative, before you completely blow your top. You know this servant of yours. Well, my grandfather used to have a servant at Dagshai just like him, except that he was one of the local hill-people. He had two other brothers, and every other year we used to have a different one of the three working for us. One day while I was down at Dagshai for a ten-day summer vacation from BCS, my naaniji asked me to go with the servant to Kasauli to buy some wool

for a sweater she was knitting. The servant had his family along
with him. His wife was short, like all these hill people are, but
very pretty. She had a three year old son and a two year old
daughter. They were all coming along because they had some
things to buy for themselves too. Kasauli is a long way from
Dagshai, about seven miles, so we had the whole day to
ourselves. There I got talking to Nundi, that was his name. I
asked what he was doing the previous year, when his brother
Bhagwaan was working for us. He explained to me that they
were three brothers, and for every couple of years, two of them
would go down to the plains of the Punjab, or to Delhi, and
work as house servants, because work is plentiful there, whereas
it is nonexistent here.

"'Who looks after your land here?' I asked, "and the cow
while you are away?"

"My wife does; and the brother who stays back at the house,"
he replied.

I did not quite understand the arrangements. Being only
thirteen, and having spent the previous two years cloistered in
BCS, I was not quite sure what to think of a man leaving his
wife and children with his brother for two years. A platonic
relationship, I presumed; or else a lot of trust.

Back at the house that evening; I asked mg naanaji to
explain to me this strange arrangement that Nundi, Bhagwaan,
the third brother, and Nundi's wife had with each other.

"It is quite simple," he explained; 'the three brothers have
the same wife. At any one time, only one brother stays with her
while the other two go down to the plains to make a living."

"But what about the children," I asked, "whose are they?"

"The three brothers don't think in such terms," he answered.
"They think of them simply as children they have in common. It
doesn't really matter; they all belong to the same mother and she
is the one that really counts. It is what we call a matriarchal system."

"But that is polyandry?" Preeti said, horrified.

"So," I said, shrugging my shoulders, "there must be a
shortage of women. Look at it this way: the local rich guys

here, aided and abetted by roving maharajas, corner off most of the pretty women. That leaves very few for small-time peasants like Nundi and Bhagwaan. So what do they do? They could either fight each other for the few women left, or they could agree to share them. Fortunately, they prefer the more peaceful, latter alternative. It seems to work."

Preeti shuddered at the thought.

"Does no one care for love?" she asked, afraid that the answer would be 'yes'. The world around us was enough to convince her that we were a couple of freaks, along with a few others similarly blessed, like Harbaksh and Mohini, somehow misplaced into this society.

"I would not share you with anyone, and heaven help me, I will murder anyone who suggests that I share myself with someone other than you," she asserted.

"Preeti, love is an act of mind. The more mindless one is, the more sex is just sex. As you cultivate your mind, it grows and needs more to nourish it. There comes a point when sex is not enough. I could not do it without love, nor could you. We should feel sorry for the rest of society that they are willing to let themselves be the way they are, but it is their own choice. I had thought education would have changed all that, but what kind of an education do they get in most of the schools? The best teaching is by example, as you know. What can our teachers teach us? They are in the same boat as our parents. No wonder we crave for Hollywood movies. No matter how improbable their stories, or their extravaganzas, at least love is taken for granted. Then turn around and look at our movies. I don't know all that much about them, having been sequestered away at BCS all my teenage years, but I know lots of Indian songs. The best ones are all mostly tragic. Lovers very seldom seem to win out, and almost never in a defiant way. They have to bow to the culture, and always end up compromising. They don't even dare to kiss."

"Oh God, you really crack me up, Amrik! I love your humor! Imagine the two of us in an Indian movie, so brazenly romantic, kissing and touching as and how we felt like. The film would never get past the censors. They would just sit there poring over us with magnifying lenses day after day, claiming that it is so degraded that they need more time; and more scissors, I bet, to keep the juicy snippets all for themselves. And all the time their eyes will be ogling us, trying to will the clothes off our bodies. Oh, those lechers! I wish I could get my hands on them so I could wring their rotting necks!"

We drove along for a while, silently, both reflecting in our own minds on this mixed-up society of ours, a society that constantly hungered for a distant past, but let the present rot. Heaven only knew what the past was really like. If it was in fact as open as they said it was, how come they dreamed up this God-awful caste system and the system of arranged marriages? Rumor had it that even the enforcement of these anachronisms was infinitely worse.

"And look at this system of Suttee! What a fraud!" said Preeti, jockeying herself back into my thoughts. "Could you imagine a wife in an arranged marriage throwing herself alive on the funeral pyre of her husband. It had to be murder, I tell you, it had to be murder! Our elders then have the gall to tell us it was a just society."

I stopped the car at Tara Devi. There is a gap here, a flat very low stretch between the mountains, extending a few hundred yards. We walked over to the railway station, and I showed Preeti the view of my school five miles across the valley to our east. It was situated on a long southerly spur of 'Shimla's tree-crowned hill', to borrow a phrase from our school song. There was a cluster of long buildings with red roofs set in a thick forest of dark deodars. Lower down on the same spur of the mountain was another set of buildings where some of the teachers and the office help lived. In between were two levels of playgrounds. Looking west from Tara Devi in the far distance we could see the plains of the Punjab with the Sutlej winding its way through them. Subconsciously, I was humming our school song, and when

I reached the line that made most sense at the moment, I broke softly into words.

"To Tara's gap through which the plains
Stretch out beyond our sight."

"You loved your school, didn't you?" she said.

"Yes, and No. It was so much of my life, how could I not love it. But I could have had more. We learned fair play, and tradition; we learned to fight the hard fight; we learned that it was the effort that mattered, and if you lost, why then you could always come back to fight another day. We learned to respect ideals, the loftier the better. We became survivors."

"So what is wrong with that? Why did you say 'yes' and 'no'?", she asked, surprised that with my eyes moist with nostalgia, I could still think of a negative.

"It's not easy to explain, Preeti. It is like your arranged marriage. With the way you loved all the principals at fault, you had not the heart to utter the truth which was screaming to come out. The same way I loved my school, and it hurts to think that it was not perfect."

"You don't have to tell me if you don't want to."

"No," I said, "like you, I too have to unburden myself. Look at us, Preeti. What do you think we need most of all?"

"Love," she said.

"Precisely," I said, "and what do little boys need?"

"Love too," she said, seeing my point.

"We were like in a military academy, one vast fraternity where we would do anything for each other. But we needed to be hugged just like you and I do now. Remember the time you put your hand across the table and held Harbaksh's hand, comforting him with your warmth. He needed it, and so did I and my other schoolmates. But boys don't hold hands or touch each other; it is not manly. While our minds soared to the trumpet call of ideals, they withered from lack of human warmth, from the love that comes from just a hug and the pressure of a hand.

I feel it's not manly to admit it; BC'S's manly ideals are so ingrained in my mind that I'm afraid, but the truth still remains: what I missed most of all was the human touch of warmth, love. I felt betrayed, most of all by my parents, because they did not try to make it up to me when 1 was home. Perhaps lifelong conformity to the avoidance of any show of physical affection that is drummed into our society had taken its toll on them already. They had lost the automatic reactions of warmth, as much victims as I was. They could, to their good fortune, blame an amorphous conglomerate such as society. I had no such luck. I knew exactly who to blame, and I don't feel good about it."

VIII

Shimla looked just the same as when I left school. We drove down Cart Road along the lower western edge of town, past St. Edward's School in Milsington, and another three-quarters of a mile till we came to a narrow, stony, dirt driveway going down on the right. Thirty yards down it, we came to the house. It was small, perhaps a two bedroom, nestled away in thick deodars. To my biased eye, it was beautiful for it even had a sloping red roof.

"It is perfect, Preeti. I like this place."

"The credit goes to my father. As you might know, he used to be in the army, a lieutenant-colonel at the time that he died. This place was intended for his retirement. He loved the mountains, and when I was little, he used to take me hiking with him. One day we went down the khud (steep valley) and then up that mountain on the other side all the way to Tara Devi. It was autumn, and pine needles covered the ground. They are quite slippery so that the hike was more an exercise in slipping and sliding than in walking. From there, we took the train back to Shimla, and then walked the remaining couple of miles from the station to here. All told, we must have done over eleven miles of walking that day. I loved his company. Everybody, particularly Harbaksh, tells me I take after him. I still miss him, even after all these years. If there was anyone who knew what I really wanted deep in my heart, it was he."

She stopped, and I could see little changes of expression cross her face, hinting at fond memories crossing back and forth across the spaces of time. Then she blinked decisively, smiled, and said: "Oh well, let us go in now; I can reminisce another time."

The house had a musty smell, not having been used for several weeks. We opened the windows to let the air in, and soon the deodar and pine aroma spread into the rooms. Ten minutes later, there was a knock at the door. It was the Gurkha chowkidaar (watchman) who had stopped by to see what all the activity was about. He lived in a hut nearby; hearing the car coming down, he had thought it best to check for strangers around the house. He greeted Preeti when he saw her. She remembered that his pay was overdue, so she gave him last month's salary, thanked him for his vigilance, and sent him on his way.

"Would you like some tea?" she asked when he was gone.

"Thank you, can I help?" I said.

"Yes, why don't you light the stove for me; and take off your shoes; make yourself comfortable."

The oil stove was similar to one I had seen my naaniji use at Dagshai, so I knew how to manage. Another ten minutes, and we were sitting next to each other on the drawing room sofa, drinking tea. Preeti's cheeks were rosy from the warm afternoon sun. All was quiet. There were no sounds other than the chirping of the crickets in the forest outside. I put my left arm around her, and with the other hand, lifted up her chin and kissed her softly. She rolled her head with pleasure and kissed me back, long and slow.

"Preeti," I said, "you are beautiful."

She purred with pleasure, put away the teacups, and lay down with her head resting in my lap.

"Sweetheart," she said softly, snuggling in closer, gently kneading my tummy with the side of her head, "I want you to make love to me, but slowly, very slowly. I wish to savor every little moment."

"There is absolutely nothing to stop us?"

"Nothing" she said, smiling dreamily.

"Where do you want me to touch you?" I asked.

"All the places where you have never touched a woman before," she answered.

"I have never touched a woman anywhere," I said.

"Then you are going to have a ball. I'm all there beneath these clothes; you won't need much imagination." So saying, she gazed seductively up at me and then closed her eyes.

Even with the clothes, I needed little imagination. They were not far removed from her breasts, the gentle rise of her tummy, or the roundness of her thighs. There she lay: supine, defenseless against the touch of my hands, deliberately stretched out so that I could explore her to advantage. My crotch was getting much warmer and I was sure she could feel a part of me rising and could sense its heat. I was not surprised then when she turned her head and pressed it down with her cheek. I placed both my hands on her body, slowly moving them on it like I would on a marble sculpture. No matter where I roamed on her body, there was not a dull moment. She was rounded and full with the tension of youth. Her thighs were full and strong, and her tummy was like low rolling country gradually rising to the higher ground of her bosom. I let my hands move instinctively, taking my cues from her responses. It was as if she was a finely tuned musical instrument, and I was playing on it. Brave music went through my being, rising slowly to a thunderous pitch. I was beginning to feel faint. Then, with one hand on her forehead, I pressed it down gently as I squeezed down on her thighs with the other, stretching her taut like a bow. She responded by extending herself as much as she could. As she lay taut, I let one hand slip between her legs and moved it up the inside of her thighs. Her breathing quickened and became irregular in anticipation. Finally, as I pressed the softness of her crotch;, she gasped and squeezed her thighs over it. Then her bosom pushed up against my other hand which was now cupping one of her breasts, and she pulled up her legs.

"Oh, Amrik," she cried, "I love you."

I could feel her heat as my hand lay between her legs, unable to move for it was caught as in a vise. She finally rolled towards me and grabbed me with her arms. Then she rolled over completely and began pressing my manhood down with her face; now with her nose, now with her lips, now with her eyes, as if she was trying to find comfort from a yearning beyond her control. But it was too much for me. I was beside myself with anguish and pleasure, feeling both tenderness and the urge to be rough with her.

"Preeti," I said, "you must get up; I need to hold you in my arms."

"My love," she whispered, as she rolled off and sat there kneeling on the carpet, "come kneel in front of me."

I did as she asked, gradually moving closer, wrapping my arms around her and pulling her in. I cupped her behind and squeezed it towards me.

"Darling, put your hands inside," she said; and as I slid them in beneath her panties, she un-zippered her slacks. She was naked below the waist as she slowly got up with me still kneeling. My face was in her pubes as she pressed it in; and my arms wrapped around her thighs, while my hands moved up her back, around her waist and on to the front where they kept moving up under her shirt, up and to her breasts.

"Preeti," I said, "take off your brassiere."

"1 will," she sighed, "just keep holding me close. And while I held her with the side of my face pressed into her tummy, squeezing her buttocks and whatever else I could lay my hands on, she removed her shirt and her brassiere, then slid her legs out of her panties and stood there stark naked in her beauty. Her bosom blossomed out, celebrating relief from the confining cups that civilization had invented. Her nipples stood erect and her breasts sagged just enough so that holding them in the palms of my hands while she pressed forward against them sent shivers of pleasure through my body. Then she pulled me up, and slowly, deliberately, took off my clothes one by one, not ever letting our bodies stay apart. We were both nude, and I had the wild feeling that I had never been so free in my life. She moved back a little, holding me at arm's length, watching my manhood straining towards her.

"I want you," she said.

So saying, she pulled me down to the carpet, and lay down on her back with me on top. Then she opened her legs and slowly guided me in. She was so wet that I slipped in easily, effortlessly, like it was the most natural thing in the world. It was now my turn to gasp.

"Heavens, Preeti, what a relief," I sighed.

"I wish to God this could go on for ever," she cried.

"It cannot, darling," I moaned, "it is unbearable."

And as I spoke, unconsciously, without my trying, my hips were moving, and I was thrusting into her harder and harder. I wanted to go right through her, being as rough as I could be, but she kept wanting it more and more, wrapping her legs around my hips, pulling and squeezing me in, as if she would not let me move back up, but only down and in. My manhood was getting bigger as if ready to burst. And then, as I thrashed around in unbearable ecstasy, it was now beyond my control, pulsating and squirting, my whole body rigid and pressing itself into her as if we would merge into each other.

Then it was over, all over. I lay there, breathing deeply, drenched in sweat, soaking her with my wetness, tired and enraptured beyond belief. Masturbation could not hold a candle to this, I heard my mind say, and then I must have gone to sleep, a deep dreamless sleep. When I awoke, I was still lying on top of her, satisfied, with not a care in the world. I stirred, and she awoke; sleepily, she pulled my head down on to her breast.

"Lie still," she said, "I want the feel of you on top of me."

"But I'm heavy," I protested gently.

"Not to me," she said, "just lie there a little while longer."

I lay there with my head resting sideways on her right shoulder, and my hand playing with her left breast.

"Preeti, I love you," I said.

"I know," she replied, "you are repeating the obvious."

"I know," I said, "but I still want to say it."

"Go ahead, love, say it as often as you like; say it all my life. I will never tire of hearing it. I love you too, more than I'll ever love anyone else."

"How do you know," I said softly, "you haven't met everyone else."

"Sshh," she replied, equally softly, "you *are* everyone else."

"Likewise," I said, "why are you so pretty?"

"So a man like you would make love to me."

"You have no shame or modesty, do you?"

"No, none whatsoever."

"I'm glad you are so shameless. I don't know what I would have done if you had been shy. I love every part of you, and I love it even more because you are so obviously proud of yourself. I could touch you anywhere I want, no matter how private, and I would feel no wrong."

"Likewise," she said.

At this, I could not resist a little snicker.

"You know, with all these likewises, we are behaving like two little children," I said.

"We are two little children," she corrected, "you're barely eighteen, and I'm just twenty."

"Oh, how wonderful it is to be a child again."

At this she began to laugh, so that I came out of her.

"What is so funny?" I asked.

"I was about to say one of those 'likewises' again, but the thought of it made me laugh, and I could not say it after all."

"I'm out, you know," I said.

"Yes, I know, the big strong man is all out of strength, sapped of it by a frail little woman," she teased.

"If you don't control yourself," I said, "I will have to do it again."

"Heaven forbid," she replied, "I'd love it, but we have to be back by three to be married."

"What was all that hurry about the magistrate when you knew we would make love here today anyway. Isn't that what you planned?"

"I was just trying to make doubly certain I could last out the day. Who could be sure what would happen? Remember, there's much a slip between the cup and the lip. Anyway, I had to do it for form's sake. You don't think Harbaksh and Mohini were dumb enough to believe we were coming here for the paints and brushes alone, do you?"

"Yes, I figure they knew. Let's see if they let on when we get back."

"Oh God, you are the limit, Amrik. Come, let's get up and wash ourselves. We have work to do."

"And what was all that we've been doing."

"If this is what you think of work, wait till you start collecting my paints and brushes, and paper, and easel and all the other things that I'm going to make you carry."

"Oh, 1 love you so much when you pretend to be angry. You should do it more often."

We both sat up, and agreed that there was nothing better than the silly nonsense lovers bandied about, and our nonsense was no exception.

"I wonder how many couples in India talk like us," she said.

"Very few, I'm afraid," I replied, genuinely convinced that such silliness was the private preserve of lovers only.

It was not long before we had all her painting, and sketching, and other paraphernalia stashed away in the back seat and trunk of the little Vauxhall. Then we opened Mohini's lunch, and sat out on the porch bench to eat it. The paraunthas were delicious, and I was really famished.

"Sex does whip up an appetite," I said, "I'm as hungry as a horse."

"You continue to amaze me; and here I thought you had satisfied all your hunger."

"And what about you? You seem hungry enough."

"Women are different," she informed me, "we can take it on and on for a very long time. Men need to recharge every now and then."

"Sounds like a very sexist way of thinking," I objected.

"It is; sex is just what we are talking about," she replied, grinning at her smart-ass comment.

"When do you think we could do it again?" I asked.

"I don't know. When do you think you'll be recharged?"

"Probably by the time we reach Scandal Point," I replied.

"Well, there you have your answer. We may be liberated, but not so liberated. Even the French would consider a public square off limits for thoughts such as ours. And the car on the way down to Solan is out of the question. The local villagers would probably kill you and I would have to become a Suttee on your funeral pyre. Remember, ours is a love marriage."

"So what you are trying to tell me is that I have to wait till the night," I finally said, summing up our discussion.

"Not I, we!" she corrected.

"Okay, have it your way," I conceded, pretending to sulk.

Scandal Point was all it was hyped up to be. On one side was the broad expanse of asphalted surface known as the Ridge. Running parallel to the Ridge and just below one edge of it was the Mall Road, Shimla's posh shopping center. Where the Ridge intersected the Mall was a fountain with a statue. We walked up on to the Ridge and gazed across at the mountains to the north. To the east and southeast, two cinemas, the Regal and the Ritz, were there on two corners of the roughly triangular expanse of the Ridge, and in the middle between them was Shimla's large church. This last was a structure obviously much used on Sundays in the past, but now relatively neglected. I was not even sure they rang the church bells any more. Down below us to the north was the track leading down to the Rivoli cinema, and just below that was the outdoor ice-skating rink, now devoid of ice. Far to the east of us, past that corner of the Ridge, was Lakkar Bazaar (lumber market). We used to come running down that way on our marathon practice, rain or shine, twice a week every summer. I remember once the denizens of the city complained to our school principal that, on rainy days, we were splashing water on to their trousers and the ladies' salwaar-kameezes (a Punjabi shirt-pant combination quite unlike western-style shirt and slacks) as we ran past. It seemed we more than made up for the lack of motorized traffic on that road (no such vehicles were permitted there, an admirable prohibition carried over from British times).

"Amrik," Preeti said, "before we go back, you had better get a few packets of condoms. You know, sex won't always be safe."

"I know," I replied, "I have peeked through some of my mother's obstetric texts, so I'm not a total ignoramus. What is wrong with having babies?"

"If I get pregnant, how am I going to make it through college, and who is going to look after the baby and pay the bills? Do you want us to go live in Karole Bagh, and ask for pocket money every time we go out to a movie?"

"No, I'm just curious what you would look like, with your tummy all stretched out."

"I will look great, if and when that happens, and I bet I could still keep your roving eyes away from other women. Now be a good boy, and get me those condoms. Consider it a marriage present for me."

So I went and bought a whole box-full; twelve dozen condoms, enough to last till kingdom come. She did not go into the shop with me, but waited outside.

"That is a big package," she said as I came out, "you sure it is just condoms?"

"No, I have diapers too," I teased. "I have to think of the future; one of us has to." Then a thought came to me that had completely escaped both our minds. "Are we not going to exchange rings?" I asked.

"People normally do, but I won't be satisfied with anything less than a diamond. And as for getting a gold band for you, your ring finger has to be measured; besides, gold bands take a few days to make. If anybody asks, just tell them we forgot them at home in the bathroom.

Preeti sure knew how to simplify matters. Very soon we were on our way back. Harbaksh and Mohini were waiting for us, but there was something wrong. Harbaksh had decided to postpone our meeting with the magistrate. The reason was in his hands, a letter for Preeti from her mother. He too had received a similar letter from her and, judging from his expression, it had made him uncomfortable enough to cancel our tryst with the magistrate.

Preeti opened her letter and, at the very first glance, her expression changed to ominous. Mummy had apparently found a match for her, and he was coming with his parents to see her in Shimla the next afternoon. Preeti showed me the letter; clearly, she had a decision to make. The letter said that Mummy had found a most wonderful prospect for her, one who would set her for life. She would no longer have to worry about her future. The boy was tall and handsome, and from a very respectable Jat Sikh family settled in Delhi. An engineer working for Escorts, he was apparently, according to her sources, highly regarded in the company. What was even more exciting, Mummy continued, was that he was completely captivated by Preeti's photograph. Who wouldn't be, I thought ruefully? His family was also quite wealthy. I looked at Preeti to see what she planned to do next.

She handed me the prospect's photograph, which had been enclosed with the letter. The man was certainly good-looking, but a bit stiff for my liking. The picture had been taken in a studio by a professional photographer using all the lighting effects he could to eliminate blemishes. There was not the slightest hint of a scar on his face, no signs that he had anything that we at BCS would accept as a sign of character. His life must be much too soft and sheltered, I inferred. Though bigger than me, I could have taken him on any time in the boxing ring, and easily improved his appearance by placing a mark or two of distinction on his baby-smooth face. But what mattered now was not whether I was tougher, but what Preeti thought of him. So I turned to her for some hint of what she felt.

"This doesn't change anything," she said. "I will take care of this matter."

'Atta-girl, Preeti,' I cheered her on silently, 'we'll show him what he's up against.'

Then, turning to Harbaksh and Mohini, Preeti continued: "It is good you postponed our wedding. Mummy is the only real relative I have, so I guess I'll have to meet this man if I wish to remain on speaking terms with her. He certainly seems to have won her heart."

'But what about your heart?' I wondered silently.

Harbaksh nodded in agreement and informed us that Mummy was expected along with her brother about four that afternoon. We had just under two hours to spare, so Preeti and I went to my room to think about what she was going to do.

IX

L ieutenant-Colonel Juswant Singh Brar ('wan' is pronounced as 'won') was the commanding officer of Harbaksh's regiment; and Harbaksh was his aide at the battle for the Zoji La. Trained in the Burma war, intelligent and compassionate, he was a sophisticated man with an excellent command both of English and Punjabi. He had married early, his wife being the daughter of Brigadier Mukand Singh Saanga. Gurmeet—that was her name—was a large woman, in the sense that she had a heavy bone structure. It was obvious that Preeti, her only child, had inherited both her frame and her looks from her father. Though the colonel was quite happy with his daughter—in fact she was a source of much joy to him—his wife had never quite surmounted the fact, depressing as it was to her, that she had borne no son. This deficiency made her feet only half a woman. Envy, marinated with liberal doses of resentment, had governed her attitude towards those of her sex who had the double misfortune of bearing sons and being acquainted with her.

She was not totally unsophisticated, though. There were times she could be charming, even to son-blessed women. Her parties, for instance, were consistently successful, but for those who had to live with her constantly, it was seldom easy. She believed in inherited virtues and family trees, and derived great pleasure tracing her descent all the way from one of the Surdaars who fought as an officer in Maharaja Runjeet Singh's army in the early days of the nineteenth century. She talked incessantly of her great ancestor's exploits—mostly imagined, her husband felt—but persistent nonetheless. So it was no surprise that the arranging of marriages, for which the knowledge of family trees was an essential handmaiden, was her constant obsession. It gave her the feeling that she controlled destiny; mating hither and thither; shuffling; reshuffling; making and breaking; playing with the fortune-strings of young men and women like a puppeteer with her puppets. It was the ultimate game of chess, played out on the Punjab plains of the busiest marriage exchange in the world: India.

Her husband's death at the Zoji La in 1948 hit her hard, very hard. A colonel's widow is not quite the same as a colonel's wife. She does not give lavish parties for the younger officers of the regiment; she does not pretend to be their mother. There were genuine offers of help from the colonel's many friends, but she needed prestige, not help. Also shattered forever were her hopes of bearing a son. Though she was only thirty-five at the time, the thought of remarrying never entered her mind. In any case, given India, that was a feat few had accomplished, even those who had been more favored by nature.

Her father and mother had both died several years earlier, and her family was essentially the two brothers she had, one five years older, and the other two years younger. She always remembered with pride the fact that her father had asked her advice in arranging the marriage of the younger one, a marriage that seemed to be quite successful, as far as one could tell.

Monetarily, she did not want. Her husband had agricultural property, which her brother-in-law was now managing for her. He had also left her the house in Shimla, and then, of course, there was his pension, coupled with the substantial monetary award that went with his posthumous Maha Vir Chakra, a decoration for gallantry that he received for his role in his last battle, the battle for Zoji La. For a woman like her, one would have thought, the award would be the ultimate vindication of her hereditary credentials, but it never was.

She knew that her husband's heart had never been hers. It was one of those things, she realized, that could not be arranged.

He loved ideals and the challenge of achievement; perhaps he loved other women too, but she never knew. While she enveloped herself in past glory and the nobility of her ancestors, he lived in the present. His life was his regiment, and the officers and jawaans knew that when their troubles grew to be larger than life, he could always be counted on to help. For him, it was simply a matter of humanity; but Gurmeet saw it differently, as something perplexing. How, she wondered, could he have the desire to befriend people much beneath him in rank?

It was early in the year 1942; the place: Burma. The Japanese armies, fresh from heady victories in Malaya, were advancing up into the Salween valley. First-Lieutenant Juswant Singh Brar and his company of troops were among those rushed from Rangoon to stem the tide of the invaders. It was mountainous territory, and the Japanese had the advantage; they had promised the Burmese independence as soon as they had gained a foothold in the country, and the latter were now cooperating. Over the years, the British had brought in a large number of Indians into Burma to build the railroads and the roads, and to exploit the natural resources of this jungle land. There was petroleum, tin, silver, lead, rubies, and three-quarters of the world's supply of teak. The locals were a leisure-loving people, so Indians were needed if the British were to successfully exploit these riches. These very Indians were now well established, having become rich along with the British. They were clearly in a much stronger economic position than the Burmese. The more successful shopkeepers, owners of taxis, and for that matter, of most of the remaining cars in the capital city of Rangoon, they hod come to be envied and hated by the locals. In fact, the Indians had come so much to consider Burma their own land that they had created a branch of their political party, the Indian National Congress, over there and made the fight for independence a fight for the combined country of India and Burma. The British then decided it would serve them better to divide and rule; so, in 1935, Burma was demarcated from India as a separate country, but still under British rule.

This mollified the Burmese somewhat, but the British had no intention of granting independence; in fact, they tried unsuccessfully, in 1939, to incarcerate the leaders of the Burmese own independence movement.

Now these very same Burmese were cooperating with the Japanese, showing the little yellow people, the children of the Sun-God from the north, the many small mountain paths by the use of which they could bypass the winding British roads on one of which the three trucks of Lieutenant Brar and his soldiers were slowly making their way up to the front. Suddenly out of the night a shot rang out, killing the driver of the lead truck; machineguns opened up from all directions; there was chaos and two of the trucks overturned as they tried desperately to find a way out of the trap. There were dead, but many more wounded; and their cries for help echoed through the inhospitable jungle.

The lieutenant had scrambled out of his truck, and jumped down over the edge of the road into the dense cover of some bushes. He was unhurt except for scratches. The firing continued for several hours; then there was silence, soon followed by the strange chatter of Japanese voices as they searched among the trucks, bayoneting any hapless survivors that were still trapped in there. Juswant sat crouched in his hideout, terrified but also full of guilt because he had been unable to help his soldiers as the Japanese killed them off one by one.

As he pondered gloomily over what would become of him if and when the enemy caught him, he felt a hand placed on his shoulder. It was followed by the burly arm of Havildaar I (Junior Sergeant) Chaanan Singh. Lying there in the warm comfort of this giant's invincible arm, Juswant felt safe. The Havildaar pointed to his bren gun.

"Sir," he said softly, "in the village, as long as I have my laathhi (stout staff), no enemy can touch me. With this here, no one will come within eight hundred yards of us. Don't worry, I will get you out. We will wait till it is just before dawn; then, even the Japanese will be asleep, and we will quietly slip out of here."

There was no fear in his voice; it was strong with the confidence of experience gained through years of fighting the Afridi tribesmen in the Northwest Frontier Province. Next morning, just as the Havildaar had planned, the two slipped out of the ambush past the sleeping Japanese.

It was now almost two years later. The former lieutenant was now a captain; and he and the Havildaar were slowly making their way up a mountain just inside Burma, on the road from Kohima where the Japanese tide had been stemmed some months back. One and a half Indian armies had stopped three Japanese armies. The Japanese had finally learned that they were not fighting against reluctant Englishmen, but against the Sikhs. These, they realized, were fighters with perseverance. Equipped with the worst weapons of the Allied forces, they had brought the Japanese to a halt, and the only way the Japanese could slow their counter-offensive was by fighting to the last man.

The Havildaar explained: "Sir, these little fellows are not afraid of death. There are probably only fifteen of them on this mountain. But they are sitting in holes with machine-guns, and we have to kill every one of them before we can advance. They will not surrender, even when surrounded. My soldiers say they are fighting for their God, the one they call the Emperor."

By the end of the day, using flame-throwers, and taking heavy casualties, the mountain had been captured, and fifteen Japanese had been killed. Mud-covered, the two of them, the captain and his Havildaar, sat in the dusk. For Juswant, it was like a father-son relationship; the Havildaar the protective father, and he the son.

"Chaanan," he asked, "why do you fight with such determination."

"Sir," he said, "I am a soldier."

"But I am a soldier too."

"No sir, you are an officer. You have to plan and give the orders. We are here to make sure they are carried out."

"What if my orders are wrong?"

"1 know you, sir, your orders will not be wrong. You and I are not very different. You have been to college, I have only learned to read and write; but you are a Sikh like me, one of Guru Gobind Singh's Sikhs; no little yellow men are going to chase us out."

"What if you were killed?"

"Well, there is my pension."

"How much?"

"Fourteen rupees a month."

"Do you have any children?"

"No, sir, just my wife; but she looks after my brother's three children too. He was killed a year ago."

Fourteen rupees! A life was worth fourteen rupees? These British scoundrels! They had gotten the world's greatest soldiers, and for what? Just fourteen rupees a man! How would his widow manage? It was impossible; and yet the man did not think himself cheated. What manner of men were these, his soldiers? What were they fighting for? It certainly was not money. It must be because they were Gobind Singh's Khaalsa (the pure); and their cause was just. A barely literate man was fighting for a cause, an intellectual cause. How incredible?

Months later, Juswant was standing by watching a. British captain having his fun with a new Indian officer, fresh from training. There was this little trough of water near the Englishman.

"Kundan Lal," said the captain to the new lieutenant, "I want you to put your head in this water."

"Why?" asked the innocent baania (shopkeeper community of Hindus).

"Because I say so."

The lieutenant hesitated, not knowing what to do, so the captain pulled out his revolver; cocking it, and pointing it at the lieutenant's head, he said: "You brown bastard, will you do it or do I have to blow your head off!"

Kundan Lal got the message. Trembling with fear, he put his head in the trough; but when he tried to raise it up a moment later, the captain pushed it down again. Juswant was standing about fifty feet away.

"You better stop that, captain," he said, "you've had your fun."

"Oh yea! And who's going to stop me?"

So saying, the captain turned around and pointed the gun at Juswant. Calm and cool, though anger seethed within him, Captain Brar pulled out his own revolver and pointed it at the Englishman.

"Captain," he said, "I am not one of your lackeys. If you wish to find out who is the better shot, I am willing to cooperate."

The captain was fuming: "I'll have you court-martialed! How dare you point a gun at an English officer."

"You swine," said Juswant to the captain, "you will be dead, shot through that filthy little whining mouth of yours, before anyone can do anything to me. Now, do you want to shoot it out?" The captain lowered his gun, turned around, and left.

By the end of the war, Juswant was a major. He had promised himself that no soldier of his was ever going to want for money; nobody would have to fight for fourteen rupees a month. His soldiers would be his family; fathers and brothers and cousins; and they would have as much right to his good fortune as his own daughter. So it was that Juswant lived for and loved his regiment. Even years after his death, Preeti was amazed to see soldiers turning up unexpectedly at their doorstep, sometimes to pay back loans for which there never had been any records, sometimes just to pay their respects to his family when they happened to be in town. Non-commissioned officers, a Havildaar today, a Soobedaar (full sergeant) tomorrow, would be standing there in front of her explaining how the colonel had sent them money when they needed it, and now that their need was over, they had come to return it. Preeti knew that they always came to her, never to her mother. She did not ask why, but in their eyes she could tell they saw her as the colonel's daughter, the daughter in whom they could sense the spirit of her father.

Preeti never accepted the moneys, assuming that her father had really intended them as gifts, but knowing the Sikhs and their pride, had pretended that they were loans. She told them what was in fact a lie, but truth in essence, that he had let it be known to his family that the soldiers of his regiment were as sons to him, and what he may have given them was what he would have given to his sons anyway. One does not keep accounts with one's sons.

After her husband's death, Mrs. Brar had moved to her elder brother's large house in New Delhi, placing Preeti in boarding school in Shimla. During the summer, she, and sometimes her brother and his family, would move to her house in Shimla. Then Preeti would get to come home and be with her family, but like me she was mostly growing up on her own in the sheltered, but at the same time independent, challenging environment of boarding school, learning to live by herself. By the time she entered college, she had become a very attractive young woman indeed, not well versed in the ways of Indian life, but educated and charming. Her English was better than her Punjabi, as was mine, but in educated circles here that is a plus, not a minus.

In many ways, though, she was quite unfit to enter Indian society. Our elders expect us to respect and even acclaim its customs, while at the same time they are providing us an education which does exactly the opposite. You don't imbue a young woman with ideals and then turn around and ask her to accept the submissive role that Indian tradition and custom expect of her. Preeti, like me, was a misfit.

When her mother brought up the idea of marriage, Preeti was appalled. She told her that she would have nothing to do with it; she wanted to pursue college and her painting, and she was not interested in a husband. But for Gurmeet, this was to be expected. No modest young lady is expected to say outright that she wants her mother to find a match for her. Preeti, of course, had done more than just say 'no', but she was only a child; you could not take her statements too seriously.

Then one day, when Preeti returned home from college, Harbaksh was sitting there having tea with her mother. He was so handsome and debonair, she felt instantly attracted to him. Without even trying, she found herself entertaining their guest. She even got around to the subject of painting, and showed him several of those she had done. The feeling of attraction was mutual, but Preeti did not know that he was married, and that too, happily. When he left, she had her first heartache. She was forever day-dreaming of him; and she just could not get him out of her mind. Her mother explained to her that Harbaksh had been her father's aide at the time of his death. In fact, Harbaksh had transferred into the regiment because of some problems with his previous commanding officer. It was his marriage, but that Gurmeet did not tell her daughter, as she was uneasy and not too enthused by it herself. The transfer had been mutually agreeable, and her father had talked glowingly of his new officer. Preeti could see why: Harbaksh was the first person in a long time who had reminded her of her father. His relaxed manner, his pride, the way he gave you the feeling that here was something warm and genuine, something that could be taken at face value. And then the way he responded to her paintings. He was in no rush to give praise like all the others, but looked at them awhile, obviously enjoying what he saw. His first comment on looking at a portrait of a local hill-woman had been: "It is lovely. I particularly like the glow in her cheeks, almost as if her skin were transparent. How did you do it?"

Then Preeti explained to him with pride how it was a matter of both skill and love; how one must feel with the subject, just as a writer must, to bring out that elusive essence that made or broke the success of a painting. Never once did he say, "How beautiful!" and let it go at that. His pleasure showed in his eyes, not just in words. Her mother had seen that painting a thousand times, but had never noticed any such thing. Preeti's interests, for her, were just a silly amusement. The real goal in any woman's life was marriage and raising a family of her own. Painting was simply one of those skills that men found attractive in a prospective bride, something that helped find a husband, but beyond that was of no real value.

When her mother told Preeti that Harbaksh had come with a proposal of marriage, Preeti was delighted. She could not let her excitement be seen, so she said, sort of noncommittally: "I'll have to think about it."

Coming from Preeti, that was the closest to 'yes' her mother could expect. She was delighted. When some days later, Preeti asked her if Harbaksh was planning to pay them another visit, she replied: "As a matter of fact, yes. And this time he will be bringing Inder with him."

"Who is Inder?" Preeti asked.

"Why, his younger brother, of course! The one for whom he was asking your hand in marriage. I thought you knew that. He will also be bringing his wife Mohini with him."

"Oh," said Preeti, "excuse me. I forgot something in the bedroom. I'll be back in a little while."

Back in the bedroom, she cried her heart out. She had never felt so crushed, so utterly miserable. Her first love, and he could never be her own. She wished her father was here; he would find a way to comfort her. What was she going to do? They would be here this coming Sunday, what would she say? Oh, how cruel! How could her mother do this to her?

As the days passed, the hurt became less and less acute. She was young, and time softened the pain. It was now Sunday, and they were here. Her mother did not permit her to wear the shirt and slacks she was so used to from her schooldays. In fact, Preeti had never been able to understand why she always objected to the clothes she liked most. Today, she had made her wear a lovely salwaar-kameez, the typical Punjabi dress for a woman. It was very attractive, but Preeti did not feel at home in it; it was not as comfortable, or as casual, as her slacks. It made her feel as if she was on display, which she was. But the long shirt (kameez) hugged her tight and accentuated her beautiful figure; and her look of resigned sadness added a tragic touch that made one's heart go out to her. For once, her mother reflected with relief, her daughter wore the submissive good looks that Indian tradition demanded of its women.

When she saw Mohini, Preeti knew she never had a chance. Harbaksh obviously loved his wife; you could see that every time he glanced at her, and the way the two of them looked when he stood beside her. They belonged together. Then she saw Inder. He was handsome like his brother, but not as self-assured. He was shorter, about five nine, but smart. He had a good figure, but was more ill at ease even than her. He was obviously excited, but his smile was more ingratiating than warm. It seemed as if he felt that his brother was doing everything for him, and all that he had to do was to do whatever he was supposed to do, and all would be well.

The talk was of everything but marriage. After a while, Preeti's mother turned to Inder and said: "I'm sure you want to talk with Preeti. We must be boring the two of you with our conversation. Why don't you two go out on the porch while we catch up on old times."

So it was that Preeti found herself alone with Inder, her proxy for a lover. He talked of his regiment, and the sorts of things he and his friends did for fun. There was horseplay, parties, drinking parties, sometimes social dancing in the mess. He never talked of books, or what he thought of life; of what he wanted out of marriage; or what she might mean to him. Finally, he said: "Harbaksh tells me you are a painter."

"Yes," she replied, trying to sound enthusiastic, "I like to sketch and paint. Do you like that kind of thing?"

"Naw," he said expansively, "the only thing these hands are good for are motorbikes and guns. No, I'm a soldier. Soldiers have no time for drawing and painting."

"How about books, do you like to read?"

"1 have read a few. I remember once I borrowed a detective novel from one of my friends. It was good, but I don't really enjoy that kind of thing. I like the outdoor life. I like my motorbike and the cinema. I like to have a good time."

Preeti was discouraged by what she heard, but she did not know much about men. The last several years she had spent in a girls' boarding school, and she knew very little of what men were really like. Harbaksh was probably an exception, like the characters in the novels she was so fond of reading. Perhaps Englishmen were like that, but not Indians. She was truly depressed, and wallowing in self-pity.

After they left, all she could say to her mother was that the boy was 'nice'. When her mother asked if she should fix the marriage, she did not say 'no', nor did she say 'yes'. Her silence was taken as agreement. The marriage was arranged, and the rest is history. Now Mummy was coming back into her life. But this time, things were different. Preeti had much to fight for. She had love, she had her man, she had her life, and she loved them all. Her spunkiness was back. She was painting again, and there was nothing her mother could do to change all that. She would not let her.

Preeti now lay in bed in my arms. She had just finished telling me what I have just told you, and now she was hiding her face in my armpit.

"My love," I said, "we have everything we need, which is not much. We have earned it all. No one can take it away. Your mother had to know one day. My father will have to know too, and soon. I am not worried about my mother. I know she will love you. Once he has seen you, even my father may come around. He is not really a bad man. When he realizes I am no longer a child, he will concede our right to make a life the way we wish. He is a non-conformist anyway, for even though he may be religious, he does not go to the gurdwara (Sikh temple). In his way of thinking, God is in your heart, not in any particular building. And he does not believe in prayer. He says that God always knows what is in your heart; you do not have to speak out loud for him to hear, not even pray in your heart; just do whatever is right. He knows what you are thinking anyway, so where is the sense in prayer. My father is a disciplinarian, unfortunately without much imagination. But discipline is for children, those he is responsible for. I am no longer a child, nor his charge, so the need for discipline no longer applies. And as for your mother, you are no longer a baby, you have outgrown the need for mothering. She will have to realize that you cannot any longer be a pawn on her chessboard. She can be your friend, and act more like a loving mother if she wishes, but she cannot determine your destiny."

"But I don't want to hurt her," said Preeti.

"Truth never hurt an honest man or woman," I said, "the only person who can hurt your mother is she herself. If she forces you to chose between her and me . . ."

Preeti cut me off. "That choice no longer exists. I have made my choice, but I still don't want to hurt her."

"Come, darling, let us not dwell on this any more. Once we go out into the sunshine, your mood will change. Life is like your paintings. A change in the palette can change somber moods to gay. In the sun, depressing browns and dark grays will give way to happier pastel blues and greens; and yellows and oranges. The solemn tones of the great masters will yield to the light-celebrating happiness of the Impressionists, as darkness yields to daylight."

Preeti lifted her head and smiled. Raising herself on one elbow, she traced her finger over my face, across my lips and nose and eyes, every now and then violating the outlines that nature had placed there. "Amrik," she said thoughtfully, "are you upset that I love Harbaksh?"

"No," I replied softly, "I would have been surprised if you did not. I love him too, in a hero-worshipping kind of way. He is an unusual man; one cannot help but love him."

"I wonder if he knows what I feel for him."

"He knows," I said, "and if you asked him, he will tell you so, even though he knows it will cause you pain. But don't ever do it. There are some things better left unspoken. And don't ever feel guilty for loving someone; hating perhaps, but loving, never!"

X

It was a touch warmer than usual. Preeti and I went out to greet her mother and uncle as the car drove up to the house. Preeti introduced me as a guest of the Virks, hugged her Mummy, and asked me to bring in the luggage. Harbaksh and Mohini watched from the porch.

Mummy was bulkier than Preeti's description had suggested, so that her kameez clung to her body as it desperately tried to enclose the excessive layers of fat which had been permitted to accumulate. Here was a woman who was clearly no longer concerned with being attractive for, as Preeti had explained, she was a businesswoman; or more correctly a busybody, one who managed people problems.

"Preeti," she announced excitedly, "I have some wonderful news for you."

"I too, Mummy," Preeti responded, "but it can wait."

"Yes, it is so hot today. I need to freshen up and wash the grime off my face," Mummy continued, while fanning herself with a magazine. But it was actually pleasant, even though warm. Living in an unsheddable layer of insulation was certainly no piece of cake, I mused; yet who could one blame? All evidence suggested it must have been voluntarily accumulated.

Harbaksh and Mohini greeted Mummy with the traditional *Sat Sri Akaal*, while I took the luggage to Preeti's room as per Mohini's instructions. When I came back, all, including Preeti's mamaji (maternal uncle) were settled comfortably in chairs, drinking *shakanjami* with ice. I poured myself a glass too, and joined in the conversation.

The talk was of events in Delhi, mostly about mamaji's wife and their two sons. The wedding of the elder one had been fixed for November. Harbaksh and Mohini, of course, were expected to attend. The bride, Mummy announced with some pride, was educated in the Jesus and Mary convent, one of the 'English' schools in Delhi. She was pretty and *so* pleasant, just the perfect match for the boy. He, for his part, was well settled, working as a contractor building houses in the city, and doing very well financially.

While the girl's grades in school had not been great, you could not expect everything. However, unlike Preeti—and here Mummy spoke with emphasis—the girl was skilled at knitting, and even knew how to sew.

"Can you imagine," Mummy exclaimed with wonder, "she can make her own salwaar-kameez."

Mummy could not get over this fact because, as she explained, you do not normally expect a girl with a convent school education to be so good at household skills. Wonder of wonders, she was also a good cook. Of course, she had the good fortune of having lived with her parents during her schooling, unlike Preeti.

"Preeti," said her mother, turning to her with a tone of apology, "we had to send you to boarding school because your father passed away. Otherwise, who knows you may have been just as good a homemaker as this girl."

"Mummy," Preeti objected, "I am a good cook."

"Yes," Mohini hastened to add in her defense, "she is just as good as I. Of course, she does not cook every day. We do have a servant, but he does need instructions and supervision, and Preeti is an expert at those. She does the actual cooking only when we have something special to make that requires more skill than one can expect from a servant."

"I'm proud of you, bayti (daughter)," said Mrs. Brar to Preeti, more in a tone of conceding than acclaiming, "someday you may even learn to knit and sew."

"When I need to, Mummy, I will," Preeti replied, trying hard to keep the edge out of her voice. "There are better things in life than knitting and sewing."

"Very few, I'm afraid," countered Mummy, sighing. "A woman has to know something more useful than just drawing and painting."

Preeti held her peace, though I could sense her seething under that quiet exterior, thinking for the nth time: 'so this is what Mummy thinks of my painting, just some idle amusement. Well, it is not the first time, but now I know that there are others who feel like me.' Here she looked at Harbaksh and Mohini, and then at me. I smiled. She understood: she was doing fine.

"Mohini," Mummy said after a while, "I think my brother and I would like to wash off the grime of the journey. Do you think you could arrange for some hot water for us?"

"I'm sure the servant has it all ready," Mohini hastened to reply, getting up and going into the house, with Mrs. Brar and her brother following her. Harbaksh and I went off to Solan in the jeep to get groceries and meat. By the time we returned, Mummy and her brother had bathed and changed into fresh clothes. Mummy's, in particular, were attractive, though of little consequence given her figure. But a change of manner had come over her, for she was excited and feeling rather pleased with herself. Her walk was quite amusing—despite her weight, she still barreled ahead; huffing and puffing a little, but with impressive, well-nigh unstoppable, momentum.

She was now bustling around looking for Preeti.

"There is something very important I have to tell her," she explained to Mohini.

"Preeti's hanging out the wash." Mohini indicated, "She'll be back soon."

When Preeti returned, Mummy got up and led her to her own room. Apparently, whatever information she had was of a personal nature. I was not a witness to what transpired, but this is more or less what it was, secondhand, as told by Preeti:

"Guess what I have for you, bayti: it is the best present you could think of."

Preeti was not interested in guessing. She had a fair idea what her mother was referring to, but even if it was something else, it was unlikely that Mummy would know what she really liked; and, even if she did, she would not approve of it, and so would have to bring something else.

"I don't know, Mummy, what is it?" answered Preeti.

"I have found the most wonderful boy for you."

Preeti remained calm.

"I saw the photograph that you sent me with the letter. Don't you think you should have asked me before you started looking for a match?" Preeti complained.

Mummy ignored her objection.

"So the letter did reach you. What do you think? Isn't he handsome?"

"Mummy, this time I want to marry someone of my own choosing," Preeti replied.

"Of course, I understand. Educated girls today want to make their own decisions. I'm not saying you have to marry Amarjeet—that, incidentally, is the boy's name—but at least agree to meet him. So, what do you think of him?"

"I don't know him, Mummy; how can I give you an opinion?" Preeti complained.

"Bayti, you know I would accept only the finest match for you. Because you are my daughter, nothing but the best will do. You will see how wonderful he is when you meet him. Your mamaji and I are going to Shimla in an hour's time. Why don't you pack up some nice clothes and get ready to come with us. The boy and his parents will be coming to see you around four tomorrow afternoon. We have lots to do before they arrive."

Preeti had no desire to go with them, but she did not want to create a scene by refusing to see the boy at all, so she said;

"You two go on without me. I'll come in my own car and I'll be there in time tomorrow."

Mummy was afraid, knowing her daughter's way of thinking and her insistence on independence, that if she pressed her any further, she might get an outright refusal to cooperate. So she agreed to Preeti's plan.

"Now, bayti, remember to be well on time. I want you to look your best. This is a once-in-a-lifetime opportunity. If all goes well, I can guarantee you'll be set for life. You'll have nothing to worry about, for the boy is wonderful, but we must do our best, for not only is your future at stake, but our family's reputation is at stake too. Now what was the good news you were going to tell me?"

Preeti decided that the time was not ripe to tell her about our plans to marry, so she replied: "It can wait; I'll tell you after this is over."

Mummy was pleased because she had not expected Preeti, judging from past experience, to be so understanding. She and her brother left after dinner. When they were gone, Preeti informed Harbaksh and Mohini about her decision to go along with her mother's plans:

"This does not mean any change in our plan. If all goes as I expect, Amrik and I will still need the magistrate day after tomorrow."

She did not elaborate any further except to tell me that she wanted me to come with her to Shimla. "You could show me your school," she said, "and stay in town till we're ready to return here. I'd prefer that you didn't stay with Mummy and me, so do you think you can find another place for yourself?"

"Don't worry, sweetheart," I assured her, quite conscious of the many decisions she had to make, including plans for them to succeed. "I'll stay in school as a guest of Mr. Whyte."

Preeti and I left for Shimla late the next morning. When we reached the town, we drove down the Cart Road beyond her house to BCS, where we parked the car just outside the iron gates, walked in past the Lefroy housemaster's residence, behind the chapel, past the tennis courts and the building where art classes were held, all the way to the first flat.

BCS was abuzz with activity, for it was the day of the School Fête, the fair held once every year in summer. Preeti had on a pale. yellow cotton shirt, black slacks, and a yellow scarf with black Polka dots round her neck to offset the other two. Her hair was tied in a low bun at the back. All in all, she looked stunning, enough to freeze activity as all heads turned to look in our direction.

A couple of senior students recognized me and came over to say hello. I was thrown into a quandary right away. I could introduce Preeti as Miss Preeti Virk, which was probably the safe thing to do, or I could be bolder and introduce her as my fiancée. I decided to go with the latter option because, whatever Preeti may have decided to do about this Amarjeet fellow, something we had not discussed on our journey that morning, she was mine, and I meant to keep her that way.

I looked around to see if any of the teachers were there, and sure enough, I caught sight of Mr. Whyte. He had seen us walk in and came over from his wife's White Elephant stall to greet us.

"Randy," he said, "welcome back to school; and who is your charming companion?"

I made the introductions: "This is Preeti Virk, my fiancée. Preeti, this is Mr. Whyte, our senior master."

Mr. Whyte shook our hands and walked us over to where his wife was standing. She was the most beautiful of our teachers' wives, but this time, meeting her was special because now I was an Old Cottonian and, as she reminded me, a man ready to start life on his own.

"Amrik," she said, breaking with the BCS tradition of addressing everyone by his last name, "this is indeed a pleasure. You have come to see us on our most festive day, and you have had the presence of mind to grace the occasion with a lovely companion." She held out her hand to Preeti and introduced herself as Florence Whyte, the wife of the Headmaster.

"I didn't know that, sir," I said to Mr. Whyte, "the last time I saw you, you were still Senior Master. Congratulations on a well-deserved promotion."

"Mr. Manning, the Headmaster, decided that it was time for him to retire." Mr. Whyte explained. "He left last month for New Zealand, and the Board of Governors picked me to succeed him. Now that you're here, surely you will stay a few days with us. Flo and I would be delighted to have you as our guests."

"As a matter of fact, sir, I meant to ask you if I could stay overnight with you, but I'm afraid Miss Virk has a pressing engagement this evening, so she cannot be with us."

Mr. Whyte was much too smart not to notice my tentative manner of speaking, so, without preamble, he decided in his own characteristic way to get to the root of the problem right away.

"Miss Virk," he said, "please allow Flo and the students to show you around the place. I have much to talk about with this lad here, things that you might find of too little interest.

The two senior students, who were still standing with us, were more than delighted with the company of two of the most beautiful women BCS had seen in a long time. As they went off, Mr. Whyte took me aside.

"Randy," he said, "do I see a cloud lurking on your horizon? Is all well between you and the young lady?"

We had walked over to the Pavilion that overlooked the second flat, and were now seated on one of its benches. I explained to him Preeti's dilemma with her mother, and the suitor who she was scheduled to see that evening.

"But you said she was your fiancée," he objected.

"Yes, that she is, informally, but her mother doesn't know that," I explained, a bit embarrassed.

"Does the lady love you?" he enquired.

"Yes, sir, of that I am certain."

"Then why don't you simply tell her mother that you wish to be married, and that she need look no further for a match for her daughter?"

I tried to explain the nature of the predicament as best I could: "Sir, before we could tell her, she had already found a suitor for Preeti. Now Preeti feels she has to meet this man, otherwise her mother will be embarrassed and their relationship permanently damaged, something she is loath to do."

"What about Preeti's father, does he have anything to say about this?"

I explained to Mr. Whyte how Preeti had lost her father in the battle of Zoji La, and how he was a decorated hero. Her mother, I told him, is a very traditional lady, quite unlike the father, who was a man of vision, and with whom Preeti was very close.

"The mother very much believes that the purpose of educating young ladies is to ensure that a suitable groom can be found for them," I explained. "Preeti loves me, and I love her, but I want her to have the freedom to choose between this suitor and me. Perhaps he is the better man."

"Nonsense," Mr. Whyte exclaimed, "how could a man who lets his mother find a bride for him be better than another who has won the bride's heart on his own? What we need now is to strengthen the lady's resolve to marry for love. I, as the Headmaster, will do my part, but you will have to do yours. Here's what I want you to do. At one o'clock, we have a soccer match between the staff and the school eleven. I want you to play for the staff—we do permit Old Cottonians to play on our side."

"But soccer is not my forté," I objected.

"So much the better because whatever you achieve will be beyond expectations. Just make sure you give it your best—you know what the stakes are. This is your chance. Leave the rest to me."

We then walked back to where Mrs. Whyte and Preeti were having an animated discussion about, of all things, pretty clothes. Preeti had on a wide-brimmed straw hat which she explained to me she had won at the White Elephant stall. Mr. Whyte complimented her on how becoming the hat was on her, which it was, and then went on to inform her that I had volunteered to help the staff team by playing for them in the soccer match due to start any time now.

"But Amrik, I hope you remember where I have to go this afternoon?" Preeti said anxiously, quite unaware that the Headmaster knew all about it.

"We'll be finished by two," I assured her, "which will give you plenty of time to spare.

There was little time to lose. Mr. Whyte summoned Bhasin, the school captain, who was a friend of mine, and explained to him that I needed a soccer jersey and shorts, and a pair of soccer boots. While Bhasin and I went off to get these items, Mr. Whyte, his wife and Preeti greeted the chief guest, General Rai, who had just arrived. After settling them in their seats in the Pavilion, Mr. Whyte went to change into his Cambridge blues. He was the staff team's captain.

I was placed in the center-forward position, the place I occupied in hockey when I played for the School XI. Bhasin was the center half for the school team and Mr. Whyte was our center half. The school team won the toss and decided to press right away. They were good, having learned their tough style of play from their coach, who was none other than Mr. Whyte himself. I found myself fighting to keep the schoolboys from scoring, playing more like a half-back than a forward. A couple of times I took some hard balls to my tummy, but I was okay. However, I wondered what Preeti felt, seeing that we seemed to be unable to get the ball out of our half of the field.

The sky, in resonance with the mood of the game as far as our side was concerned, became overcast and soon it began to rain. The game became a contest between two teams who could barely be distinguished as they became more and more covered with mud. Just before the half, the school scored. Things were not going as Mr. Whyte had planned. But when the game started again, we were cheered, for what were we hearing now? Two female voices above the noise of the schoolboys: "Come on, Thomas; come on, Amrik."

We took the cheer rather personally, for right away the Cambridge jersey was all over the playground, and we were beginning to gain an edge. We even got a few shots on goal, but Nanavati, the school's goal-keeper, was good and blocked everything. Then Mr. Whyte headed a ball towards the net, but it was not to be. It was deflected by Nanavati, hit the cross-bar, then one of our players, and went out of bounds.

The score was still 0-1 against us. Mr. Whyte looked towards me as we positioned ourselves to receive the kickoff by the other side's full back. I got the ball and kicked it sideways towards Mr. Whyte. Bhasin got to it first, but Mr. Whyte was not to be denied. With a tremendous effort, he stole the ball from the school captain and headed towards their D. I ran along with him, the two of us making short passes between us. Just at the mouth of the D, he made a quick short pass to me. There was, however, no way I could score because the ball went out beyond my reach towards a defender. Yet, as luck would have it, it bounced off this boy's hip and slowly went over my head. This was my chance. I spun around, and with my hands down on the ground, I arched my back till I was bent like a bow, as I raised my hip and right leg. The boot made contact with the ball, propelling it over my prone body and sending it sailing into the net. Nanavati didn't stand a chance as it all happened so fast. A cheer went up for a most spectacular goal. I turned to look at the pavilion, and there I saw Preeti and Florence standing and shouting, pushing their little fists up in the air in a sign of victory. Mr. Whyte came over and gave me a pat on the back. "Good show, old boy; the lady is yours."

There was no more scoring, so the game ended in a draw. I was picked by the unanimous vote of both teams to receive the "most plucky player award." General Rai was to present it to me. The rain had stopped, as if on cue, and the sun came out. Preeti and the general walked down the stairs to the field. Then the general began to speak.

"As you all know, I am an Old Cottonian and I feel honored to witness how another Old Cottonian has managed to shine in a game which I am told was not one of his strengths. I have also discovered that the young lady here with me is the daughter of a war hero, Lt. Col. Brar, who fought and died defending our country at the Battle of Zoji La against what seemed at the time insuperable odds. I had the honor of awarding him the Maha Vir Chakra. The young lady here, Miss Preetam Virk, is, by the most amazing stroke of good fortune, engaged to be married to the young gentleman who is to be the recipient of "the most plucky player award." Given the circumstances, I believe it is more appropriate for Miss Virk to present the award to Mr. Amrik Randhawa than for me. I now give you Miss Virk."

Preeti picked up the microphone and said: "Thank you, General Rai, for giving me this opportunity to honor my future husband." Then she turned to me. "Mr. Randhawa," she said, "it is indeed an honor and a privilege to present this award on behalf of both the teams and the entire school for a job well done."

I accepted the award, then took the microphone from her.

"Preeti," I said, "I love you, and I couldn't have done it without your cheers."

So saying, I put my arms around her and gave her a long and deep kiss on her lips. Why not; this was BCS, part of the modern world, not an Indian movie. Her clothes, of course, were no longer as pretty, but she was proud of the few mud marks I had left on them. I had won the battle, perhaps even the war.

XI

Preeti went straight to her room, showered and proceeded to get herself ready for the visitors. She picked a gold-brocaded yellow chiffon sari and a sleeveless, low-cut, black blouse; filigreed gold pendants for her ears; and a fine gold chain with an orange-yellow garnet pendant for her neck. Her hair was pulled back and tied in a complex, elegant bun high at the back. Her eyes were shadowed, and she wore light orange lipstick. Viewing herself in the mirror, she exclaimed: 'Why not, I might as well indulge myself.' So she dabbed herself liberally behind the ears and on her bosom with the strongest perfume she could find. Mummy would certainty be pleased.

Amarjeet, Mummy's choice as a prospective son-in-law, and his father and mother, arrived by car about four that afternoon. Preeti's uncle met them on the porch and ushered them into the drawing room. Once they were comfortably ensconced on the sofas, cold drinks were served all around. Mummy was beside herself with excitement. The boy was tall and handsome, and smartly dressed in a dark, pin-striped suit, with his beard rolled up in the manner of Harbaksh; and he had on a maroon turban neatly peaked at the front. Pakoras, samosas, luddoos, gulaab jaamans covered with the finest gold leaf, and burfee similarly coated but with gossamer silver graced the low table before the guests, along with almonds, cashews, and other assorted snacks. But they all paled by comparison as Preeti walked into the room, preceded by perfume, and escorted by her mother. A seat was cleared for her next to Amarjeet.

He turned to her and smiled. She looked back at him, the faintest hint of a response gracing her lips, but her eyes were untouched by emotion. A few awkward moments later, Amarjeet's mother inquired of Preeti how she spent her time these days, whereupon Preeti informed her that at present time lay heavy on her hands.

When asked if she liked to cook, she responded: "not particularly."

"How about embroidery and stitching? Maybe you like knitting?"

"No," said Preeti, "I have little experience of such things."

Amarjeet turned towards her, and said softly: "I'm sorry mother is badgering you with such embarrassing questions."

"Not at all," Preeti replied, equally hushed; "someone has to make these inquiries."

"I mean these are not important," explained Amarjeet, trying to endear himself to her.

"I wouldn't go that far," Preeti rejoined, "a wife has to be good at something."

"Yes, but not at these homely things."

'So he wishes to portray himself as a modern, enlightened man, does he?' thought Preeti. "Since this appears to be question-answer time," she proclaimed, "what is it you do or not do?"

Amarjeet laughed a little nervous laugh, but not disagreeable. "I don't cook, sew or knit," he replied.

"That doesn't say much for the two of us then, does it?"

"No, but I do other things."

"Such as?

"I work, as an engineer, with Escorts."

"Well, I work too, but not for pay. I do the laundry, darn socks, make beds, occasionally help with the cooking, pay the chowkidaar, and generally try to keep my mother's spirits up. But I'm sure she's told you all this. Tell me, since you've obviously talked with her, what do you think; do you like her?"

"Of course I like her. She's your mother; besides, she must be wise, having raised someone like you."

Preeti acknowledged the compliment by smiling, then countered it with the remark: "Actually, I was raised mostly by nuns."

"I don't understand. Would you explain what you meant by that?" he asked, visibly taken aback by her revelation.

"What I meant is that I spent the better part of the last seven years in boardings. First I was in the Jesus and Mary school here, then in St. Bede's college. I visited with my mother only during the winter vacations, and a few weeks every summer. She usually spent most of the year with my uncle because she felt there was no social life here in Shimla."

"Oh," he said, much relieved despite Preeti's veiled bad-mouthing of her mother; "for a moment there I misunderstood you."

"Whatever could I have said?" she wondered aloud, "I thought I was perfectly clear."

"I thought you meant that you'd been brought up as a Christian."

"That may not be far from the truth," she asserted, "I know far more about Christianity than I do about Sikhism."

"Not to worry," he assured her, "you'll learn about us in time."

"I'm not so sure; and I'm not sure I want to."

"That's a strange thing to say. Sikh women are the backbone of our community. As they say, 'behind every Sikh man stands a woman.'"

"Strange I never heard that before."

"I just made it up," he confessed, reddening a touch.

"I'll make one up too, then. 'Behind every Sikh woman stands a man.'"

"I don't see the difference."

"Well, it doesn't matter, I was thinking of another relationship. But maybe I went too far in my generalization; I'm actually not sure of *every* Sikh woman."

"Then who were you talking of?"

"Someone I know very well."

"One of your friends?"

"You could say that—one of my inseparable friends," she sighed.

Amarjeet was confused by these veiled revelations, so he decided to steer the conversation elsewhere.

"May be I could take you out tomorrow," he conjectured, floating a trial balloon.

"I can suggest one better. Why don't you take me out to dinner tonight?" she proposed with obvious enthusiasm; "there's something I want to discuss with you . . . alone."

"I'm not sure what everybody's plans are," he hedged, trying to avoid making a commitment.

"What do their plans matter to us? Are you telling me you've got to ask your mother before you can take me out?"

Amarjeet flushed with embarrassment. "Of course not," he replied, "I was just wondering whether they had something else planned for us."

"So it's settled. What shall we talk about now?"

"I don't know. Whatever you wish."

At this time, Preeti arose and proposed that they go out to the porch, out of earshot of the others. She knew from past experience that Mummy wouldn't disapprove; in fact, would be delighted. When they were alone, she said, as if thinking aloud: "Hmm! What shall we talk about? I know! How about my former husband?"

"I know all about him," Amarjeet responded, hoping Preeti would restrain herself. "Your mother told me everything."

"What did she say?"

"That he was a very nice man, a lieutenant in the army; and then she told me of his tragic death."

"Yes. That's what she thinks."

Amarjeet's consternation at the way that the conversation was going rose another notch. This girl was not at all what he'd expected. She was beautiful, even more so than her photographs suggested, and she had a lovely voice, but why such heavy perfume? And why was she talking this way about her mother? Heaven knows what she's going to reveal about her late husband.

"Why don't we postpone that for later?" he suggested.

"What?" she asked.

"What you were going to tell me about your husband."

"Oh yes, Inder! He was quite a character."

"I'm sure he was, but let's talk of something else."

"I'm surprised at you. You should take a cue from your mother, and my mother too. I'm sure Mummy asked everything about you that there was to know."

"Yes, I suppose so, but I think some things should be left buried; like the memories of past tragedies."

"All right,' said Preeti, "I'll assume you don't wish to know everything about me, but I cannot permit myself the same neglect. I'll make amends by trying to find out all about you. Of course, my Mummy has told me everything your mother told her about you. Why don't you tell me something your mother doesn't know, so my Mummy doesn't know; about you, I mean."

"What do you want to know?"

"Well, what can I say? I'm not privy to your secrets."

"I don't keep any secrets from my mother. Do you?"

"Oh yes; many. You learn that kind of thing in boarding school. You never went to boarding school, did you?"

"No, I studied in Delhi."

"Still, you must have kept something from your mother?"

"Why must you insist that I keep secrets from my mother?" he responded with barely disguised irritation.

"Oh, I'm sorry if I gave that impression; it was unpardonably rude of me. I don't at all insist that you are secretive. In fact, my mother insists that you're a very honest person, and I've no reason to doubt her, but I was thinking of something else. A tall, good-looking person like you, I thought perhaps you had relationships which it wasn't prudent to let your mother know about?"

Amarjeet was offended by Preeti's forwardness. "Well, if I did, it doesn't matter; they're in the past."

"Just like my marriage?"

"Yes, like that. What's past is past. We have to think about tomorrow."

"I don't know if I agree with you there. My late marriage haunts me; I can't get it out of my mind."

Amarjeet was becoming a bit apprehensive. Maybe, he figured, he should let her tell him about this Inder fellow. "Okay;" he said, "tell me about it."

"Inder," she said, without waiting an instant, "was a very handsome man. You should see his elder brother, he's even handsomer, and perhaps the most attractive man I've ever seen. Well, not quite. In all truth, I should say he is among the two handsomest men I know."

Amarjeet wasn't sure of the other person she referred to, but he thought it safe to assume she meant him; after all, she had said he was good-looking and tall. So his spirits regained a notch at the comment, and he eagerly waited to hear what more she had to say.

"Well," she continued, "this very handsome brother came to my Mummy one day with a proposal of marriage for me. I assumed it was on his own behalf; and he was so charming, I instantly fell in love with him. It was only some weeks later that I realized he was only asking my hand in marriage for his younger brother. He himself, in fact, was already married, so you can see how disappointed I was, and how foolish I felt. But what was I to do? I didn't know because I was only nineteen, so I made the mistake of marrying the wrong brother.

"When the younger brother, Inder, that is my husband, discovered that I didn't love him, he was sorely disappointed. He realized that he and I had nothing in common, so being a decent man, he left me alone and took himself another wife."

Preeti paused here. Amarjeet was shocked. Mummy had not told his mother anything about this.

"I didn't know he married another woman. How could you stand it?"

"Quite so," said Preeti, "it was disgusting. He would spend all day drinking, or else he would be out with his friends."

"I thought you said he took himself another wife?'"

"Oh, I'm sorry, it was merely a figure of speech. I meant the daughter of the vine. Unfortunately, he had the bad habit of mixing fun with pleasure."

"You mean work with pleasure," he corrected.

"No; officers in the army don't work, except when there's a war, and at that time there was no war. So he mixed the fun of driving a motorbike with the pleasure of drinking. And that's how he died. Did Mummy tell your mother that?"

"No."

"Well, I thought it only fair that you should know. You can never trust people who hide their secrets. At a very dear friend's last birthday, I made the resolution I would never misrepresent myself, and I'm so glad I've been able to live by it."

Amarjeet was quite unnerved. He didn't know quite what to make of her. She seemed to know a lot more about life than him, and she wasn't afraid to reveal anything. It was obvious she would demand much freedom in the marriage. There was also little doubt that she was not discreet. He was genuinely scared. All he could think of now was how to get out of the dinner commitment she had forced upon him. He had never said yes, but she'd made it seem as if he'd agreed.

"Preeti," he said, "my parents and I have some other plans for the evening. Could we postpone the dinner till tomorrow?"

"A pity," she bemoaned; "I was quite looking forward to it. I was picturing myself with a glass of red wine; and afterwards how we would dance. They have some wonderful bands in this town, you know."

"I'm sure they do," he said, "but I don't dance."

"That's no problem. I'll teach you. I remember a very dear friend of mine, the one with the birthday, who I taught dancing recently. It was no trouble at all. One afternoon's coaching, and he was dancing like a pro."

"Perhaps you're a very good teacher, but I'm not sure I want to learn how to dance."

"Okay, we don't have to dance, we could just talk. I could tell you some more of my secrets; perhaps then you'd be encouraged enough to tell me some of yours. We're both adults, you know; we shouldn't be plunging headlong into an important relationship without knowing everything about each other. It doesn't make good business sense. Isn't that the way you operate in your business?"

"Pardon me, Preeti, but there's a big difference between business and personal matters. One mustn't be too inquisitive in the latter. After all, if you're going to live together, you must be willing to leave a lot of things to trust."

"Like I did with Inder?"

"No; I mean that was unfortunate. You shouldn't generalize from one instance."

"My impression was that trust was something that developed after you knew a person very well, like in a love affair. Are you trying to tell me, with your emphasis on trust, that you'd prefer a love marriage kind of relationship to this arranged union we're planning?"

"No, not at all. I think arranged marriages are preferable. They're more suited to our culture."

"I don't know. I'd love to have an affair before getting married. This way I could trust you more. My previous marriage has made me a little gun-shy; you know . . . once bitten, twice shy."

"I'm afraid my family wouldn't approve of it."

"There you go again. One would almost think your family was getting married, not you."

He flushed with embarrassment again, but this time the emotion was mixed with annoyance, for he had come to the conclusion that she was a very clever and devious woman, and quite capable of making his meanings appear totally other than what he intended.

"That's not what I meant," he explained, "by nature I prefer a harmonious relationship with my family. This way everyone is happy, and I have peace of mind."

"Oh," said Preeti, "I'm not very close to my family. My father passed away several years ago, and after that I've lived mostly with the nuns, as I explained before. I like my independence, and you'll agree that isn't easy when you have to worry about pleasing every member of your family. Fortunately for me, there's only my mother, and she has other interests, so I've been happily left mostly to myself. Don't worry. I'll teach you how to be independent of your family."

She stopped, as if counting in her head. "Oh my," she continued, sounding as if burdened with chores, "the things I have to teach . . . I mean dancing and independence, and how to have fun. It's not going to be easy; you're much too restrained. You should let yourself go some more. Okay, okay . . . don't frown, I'll teach you how to do that too."

Preeti was feeling very pleased with herself, but Amarjeet was totally flummoxed. He commented that it was getting chilly, so it might be better to go inside and sit with the others. So they returned to their original seats. Thereafter, Preeti let the conversation and events evolve as they would; her work was done.

Next morning, a hand-delivered message arrived for Preeti's uncle. There appeared to be trouble ahead. The other party wanted an urgent meeting with him; so, by ten o'clock, he was at the Grand hotel, where Amarjeet and his parents were staying. He was told by the father that the boy was not agreeable to the marriage. Asked what had gone wrong, it was explained that there appeared to be an irreconcilable difference of temperament between the two parties, and the boy was disappointed by this discovery. No further explanation was forthcoming. Back at the house, Mr. Saanga relayed the bad news to his sister so that when I arrived, promptly at noon, I found the two sitting together on the living room sofa in stupefied, funereal silence.

Preeti had answered the doorbell. I had barely obtained a glimpse of the other two before she led me back out to the porch and announced triumphantly: "The coast is clear. It's smooth sailing from now on."

"You told them you wouldn't marry that jerk?"

"No. He turned me down."

"1 don't believe it! The man must be an idiot! How could anyone in his right mind turn you down?"

"Believe it or not, he did!"

"You must have told him about us."

"No; I'd never do that. Our love is sacred. There's no way I'd let it be touched by anything as infamous as an attempted arranged marriage."

I kept shaking my head in disbelief. I was thrilled, but still couldn't believe it was true. I knew Preeti had finagled it somehow, and I was eager to learn how. She promised to explain everything later, but for the present there were still some things to settle. As we went in, Preeti informed her mother that I was here to see her.

"This is no time for socializing," her mother reprimanded her.

"But why not?" Preeti asked.

"Don't you realize what has happened, bayti?"

"The marriage is off, right?"

"That's all it means to you?" her mother asked, appalled by the flippant attitude of her daughter to so serious a matter.

"Mummy, you saw everything yesterday. I was dressed in my best. I was very friendly; even you couldn't have failed to notice that. What else could I have done to make him like me?"

"1 don't know, but you must have said something terrible that he so quickly changed his mind. What did you two talk about?"

"I told him whatever he wanted to know. I didn't lie or exaggerate. I'm as mystified by his ingratitude as you. You saw how nice I was to him?"

"Yes, I thought you were very friendly, not at all the way you behaved with Inder." Then she reflected some more and announced: "His change of heart must be because you're a widow."

"Come now, Mummy; what has that to do with it?"

"Bayti, you should not take such things lightly. People believe a widow is bad luck."

"Why? Who did I ever bring bad luck to?"

"Your husband for one. He died, didn't he?"

"Mummy, I didn't give him the drinks, and I didn't force him on to his motorbike. It was all his own doing."

"I know that, but still, you couldn't have kept him too happy; why else would he have been drinking so often. You couldn't have been very nice to him."

Preeti shrugged her shoulders. "Is there any other misfortune you wish to blame on an unfortunate widow, Mummy?"

"I'm not trying to blame you, bayti, but people believe anyone who's a widow has had her eyes opened, and is therefore not to be trusted. I'm sure you understand what I mean. I tried my best to reassure them that you're perfectly virtuous, that widowhood has left no taint on you; but superstitions die hard. Maybe there's some truth to it, else why would so many people believe it. Nobody wants to marry a widow."

"That's not true!" Preeti was genuinely furious.

"Show me who'd marry you? Anybody from a good family would think twice about it, bayti; they were doing us a favor considering the match at all.

"I'll show you who'd marry me. Amrik, tell me, would you marry me?"

"I'd consider it an honor." I replied.

"He's just a boy,' Mummy objected,

"No, he's not. Amrik, propose to me if you really mean what you just said."

"Preeti," I said dutifully, but with emotion, "will you be my wife?"

"Yes, I will, gladly; but first tell me, why do you want to marry me?"

"Because I love you."

"And I love you," she rejoined, with emphasis and in her warmest tone.

Mummy was furious. "You hussy," she screamed, "is this what you've been rehearsing behind my back? How could you be so cruel? You must put a stop to this!"

"Why? Because I love him and he loves me?"

"Stop it, Preeti! I don't want any of this infantile nonsense!"

"Mummy. This is no infantile nonsense. Amrik and I love each other. I'm going to marry him, whatever you say. That Amarjeet of yours couldn't hold a candle to him."

"How dare you speak to your Mummy like that!"

"I'm giving you your chance, Mummy. You can have a son-in-law today, if you wish. Isn't that true, Amrik?"

"I'll marry you this very instant; just say the word."

"See, Mummy. You can have a son-in-law right now, but on my terms. I'll marry for love, and only for love. So they think I'm used, do they? Those utter fools! Come, Amrik, let's go; there's no room for us in this house."

Preeti plumped the wide-rimmed straw hat from the White Elephant stall on her head, and I picked up her already packed suitcase from her room and took it to the car, while Mummy and her brother glared at me. I'd never liked this uncle of Preeti's, anyway. A short fat man with furtive, beady eyes and an overfed, ruddy complexion, he looked just the type who would belch after every meal. Now he was glaring at me like the cornered rat that he was, but he spoke not a word. It was evident Mummy was the moving force in the family. I appropriately ignored him, and opened the door of the car for Preeti.

"Mummy!" Preeti cried out one last time, but to no avail. Her mother was beyond herself with impotent rage, and sorely disappointed besides. "So be it, Mummy; if you have anything nice to say to me, I'll be at Harbaksh's" . . . 'and married', she mused with pleasant anticipation.

XII

The nearest magistrate was in Kundaghaat, so we had to go back up the road towards Shimla. Preeti had bathed and changed into a sari, and she insisted that I wear a suit, and since I did not have one with me, she loaned me one from her ex-husband's wardrobe. It fit the mold perfectly, and I looked like a man fit to be married.

By five o'clock, we were at the magistrate's house. He was awaiting us, even though it was Sunday. With Harbaksh on our side, clearly anything was possible. Preeti and I repeated whatever the magistrate asked us to say, filled and signed the proper forms, and by five-thirty we were officially husband and wife. I thought of kissing the bride *a la* Hollywood, but Harbaksh counseled restraint, cautioning me that the magistrate might disapprove of an Indian man and woman kissing in public, whatever the occasion. So I desisted, but the moment we disembarked at Suproon, I picked up Preeti with my arms around her waist and kissed her even as we spun around in a waltzing turn. This was my marriage, and I was going to do what I damn well pleased.

Then the champagne cork was popped, and there was an impromptu celebration with drinks all around. Later, the four of us sat on the porch, with Harbaksh and Mohini reminiscing about how they had eloped, much to the dismay of Harbaksh's commanding officer and her parents, who were friends of the C.O. But the deed had been done, and like most Indians, her parents and the C.O. eventually accepted the fait accompli. All, thanks to God (Harbaksh's opinion, not mine) were now very good friends.

The wedding dinner saw more champagne, but to the accompaniment of classical Indian music, which I loved but still had much to learn about as I could not tell what 'raag' it was. Next came the typical 'shehnai' music that is traditional at weddings. This instrument has a wailing sound, which is both poignant and sad. We listened silently for a while, but I just had to ask: "Harbaksh," I said: "Why is marriage music always so sorrowful?"

"It isn't so everywhere in the world," he replied, "but it is with us. Indians are only partly hypocritical. Actual customs expose the truth, even when not intended. Marriage, as practiced here, is not usually the culmination of a tale of love; it is, more often, an attempt at a beginning. Many boys today insist on seeing the girl, by which I mean literally 'seeing', before they will agree to marry. They wish to observe with their own eyes that she is attractive, and sound of limb and body. If she has a visible defect, her chances of finding a groom are slim. Defects that are not visible are usually kept secret and jealously guarded from the entire world. The only thing a groom can be assured of is that there will be a meeting of the bodies, but whether there will also be a meeting of the minds he cannot know. And therein lies the rub. You and Preeti, Mohini and I, had a meeting of the minds. The meeting of the bodies was essentially to celebrate it."

He paused and looked at us, seeking a hint that his assumption was right. Preeti and I looked at each other, exchanged a knowing glance, smiled ever so slightly, and slowly nodded our heads to indicate that things were as he assumed.

"So, you see," he continued, unable to suppress a sly smile of approval, "we have no need for sorrow."

"But," I said, playing the devil's advocate, "the reason parents cry at their daughter's wedding is that she will be leaving her home. Now she will no longer belong to their family, but to someone else's. It is a parting greater than simply her traveling to another home."

"Yes," said Harbaksh, "parents all over the world cry when their daughters are married, but that crying is of the essence of parting, perhaps greater than what your mother felt when she saw you off to BCS each year, but there is no element of fear in it. Here, at the time of marriage, the parents are delivering their hapless daughter to the mercy of her husband and in-laws. They have tried their best to determine that these are good people, law-abiding and honest, and that they have a good reputation; also that the groom is well-educated and intelligent, as judged by his scholastic record, and is gainfully employed and making a good living; or at least has enough wealth that their daughter is assured reasonable comfort. Most importantly, that the groom and his family will not misuse their rights over the bride. But nobody, least of all the bride, knows what is in the groom's mind, or in his heart. A meeting of the minds might happen after marriage but, as to the odds, your guess is as good as mine. One thing, however, is certain, you cannot quit if it fails to materialize."

We all sat there at the dinner table, my right hand softly enclosing Preeti's left hand as it rested on the tablecloth, quietly listening to the haunting notes of the shehnai. We felt sadness, not for ourselves, but for the countless young men and women scattered across the land, many of whom would commit marriage, but never love, nor happiness. We could feel ourselves aging despite ourselves. The music stopped, and Preeti leaned towards me, resting her head on my shoulder and gazing up at me with those wonderful brown eyes.

"Yes, Preeti," I said, "I love you, and we are in a house that is an island of happiness in a land of sorrow. No one is crying over us. I like the odds, and we are twice blest, once by our love and again by the love of our friends, Mohini and Harbaksh. What more could we ask for in this world?"

"Yes, there is something," Mohini spoke up, jarring all of us out of my moving reflection.

"Mohini," I said, making an effort to recapture the moment, "what more could we wish for?"

"You have all the love that you need, but there are a few other things that you ought to have."

Preeti lifted her head up. "Presents?" she asked, her eyes all a-glow.

"Yes, presents," said Mohini. "Every married couple deserves some."

There were two small boxes and one bigger one. I asked Preeti to open the smaller boxes. One had a gold band for my finger. She looked at Mohini with tears of happiness in her eyes, then took my left hand and placed the band on my ring finger. I looked at the others around the table, beaming with gratitude.

"The goldsmith obliged," explained Harbaksh.

Preeti handed me the other small box to open. I had guessed its content, but the excitement was still there, even for one such as me who had never received a present before. It was as I suspected, a diamond ring. Tears were pouring down Preeti's eyes, and I was making a valiant effort to hold back mine. I asked her to extend her hand out and then slid the ring slowly on to her finger. "Now," I proclaimed, "we don't just feel married, we even look married. Will you kiss me?"

And she kissed me, with one hand softly cupping my cheek.

We turned towards Harbaksh. "Where and when did you two get these?" I asked.

"From Shimla. Apparently, you were not the only ones to visit that town today."

"It is a small world," I observed, and we all laughed. The spell of the shehnai had been broken. "Preeti, do you have any regrets," I asked.

"Yes," she said, "no one has cried over me. Even the shehnai has stopped wailing."

Preeti's mock sorrow over, Harbaksh picked up the larger package. It appeared to be heavy. "I think you had better come into the drawing room for this," he said.

We all followed. Preeti opened it and said to me: "You can start working tomorrow. There is no time to stand on ceremony."

It was a Smith-Corona portable typewriter.

"Why not today?" I asked. "There is so much to tell."

She placed a finger on my lips and said spousingly, conspiratorially: "There is much to do, remember?"

"Oh," I said to Harbaksh and Mohini, "I'm afraid you will have to excuse us. We will be seeing you in the morning."

There was no crying, regretfully for Preeti, just smiles as she and I left for my (our) room.

XIII

I awoke to the fragrance of roses Mohini had so thoughtfully placed in our room. Preeti lay peacefully asleep on her back, no doubt dreaming of me, I assumed with smug satisfaction, one leg bent and lying crosswise over mine, my left hand resting warmly on the inside of her thigh. I had never felt so liberated. Lying stark naked in bed was something I had always fancied. It had that flavor of the carefree which many of us yearn for, yet seldom achieve; but with a naked woman? That was beyond even my wildest dreams. I was tempted to make love again, but she seemed so contented, a modern-day sleeping beauty, that I desisted, and slowly eased myself out of bed.

Putting on my pajama suit, I wondered why such an item was at all necessary. It certainly had no function in bed. I had often thought of sleeping nude, but not ever having had a room to myself, the idea was moot. Only since I turned fourteen had I begun even to lock the bathroom door behind me. Prior to that, my father's injunction that it should be left unlocked had kept me from doing so. He claimed that you could accidentally slip on the wet floor, and knock yourself out. If the door was locked, how could anyone come to your aid? It was a philosophy of strange and unlikely emergencies. Whatever the original motivation, he justified his beliefs with appeals to this smotheringly protective and somewhat embarrassing logic of safety. It was besides the point that no one could recall hearing of anyone accidentally knocking himself out this way, but the possibility could not be denied. The women of the family ignored him and locked the bathroom anyway, but for us male children, who he assumed were made in his own image, his feeling of responsibility was endless.

Puberty came late, not till my fourteenth year. Then hormones began to focus my mind on the body. Various forbidden parts became subjects of intense interest and experimentation, at once a blessing and a bane. I could have pleasures of unimaginable intensity as and when I desired; and given the incredible lure of the discovery, I would never tire of them. But there was also a need for secrecy, hence the locking of the bathroom door in the face of paternal objection.

The word 'masturbation' was discovered in school long after the act had been perfected, but a connotation of guilt, even shame, attached itself to it early on. The problem was 'semen-al,' to coin a word. I remember one morning in school having a wet dream just prior to the six-fifteen rouser bell. It was a first, but the timing could not have been worse. My pajamas were soaked, and there was not enough time for drying. The problem now was how to make it to the washroom to brush my teeth and wash my face, knowing full well that there is nobody as callous and cruel as a schoolboy who discovers something embarrassing on another. Necessity helped invent—I wrapped my towel around the waist to hide the 'sin'. But I could not very well lift it to wipe my face in the bathroom, so I just walked back to my dorm with my face wet, let my pajamas slip to the floor prior to putting on my shorts, and then dried the face.

The transient nakedness while I lifted the towel to the face was no problem in BCS, only the soiling of pajamas with strange, pleasurable secretions in the midst of 'dirty' dreams; and since no one ever talked of it, it must be something shameful, akin to being caught masturbating, except this time without actually masturbating. I had to wear the same pajamas on the subsequent two nights, unfortunately, because laundry day was that far away. The starched, dried area of caked semen had the odor of mother's milk spilt on babies faces, and I can recall how terrified I was that some other boy might notice the smell.

I therefore made doubly sure that I never got too close to anybody. The precaution was unnecessary, as I learned later, for night emissions were commonplace among us all, and so was the odor; besides, its mustiness was conducive to pubertal dreams, something high on the list of every schoolboy's desires.

I came to terms with my rogue body about the time that Mr. Whyte began his general knowledge classes. He was short for an Englishman, but wirily muscular and the schoolboy's epitome of toughness. Any thoughts or actions coming from him were, by their very nature, imbued with manliness, so when he told us how he and his beautiful young wife, who we were all in love with, and their six-year-old daughter bathed in the tub together, we listened very attentively. His daughter, it seemed, was learning her lessons in anatomy firsthand, noting with some curiosity the uniqueness of his mid-anatomy in comparison to the relatively featureless one of herself and her mother. Her interest, however, was evanescent but, he assured us, it was merely dormant and would reawaken as her body blossomed out with the onset of puberty. This lesson in sex education, and the seductively rounded term 'blossom,' remained ingrained indelibly in my mind, and helped foster a growing interest in the female anatomy.

During the month before our senior school certificate examination, Mr. Whyte, then the Senior Master, a position next to that of the Headmaster, would discuss essay topics with us at a quarter-of-seven every morning. He would talk on anything we wanted. It was there and in the general knowledge classes that we slowly matured out of pubertal confusion into men as he lifted the veil of mystery shrouding activities that were neither studies nor games, neither necessary for sustenance nor for rejuvenating the tired mind, but of consuming interest nonetheless; and whose only value then seemed to be that of self-indulgent pleasure.

One of the more memorable topics he discussed was 'clothes'. I came away with the distinct impression that clothes in general were of about the same value as pajama suits; they were equally a superstition, one that would wither away in the face of rational inspection. Little function remained beyond that of warmth. Moreover, it was difficult to conceive, in the face of hormonal persuasion, how anything could enhance the stunning attractiveness of the naked body. Though he did conduct chapel services when the reverend was away or sick, none of us could imagine him talking of the expulsion from Eden of Adam and Eve, and the sudden feeling of shame at the sight of their mutual nakedness, another biblical fairy tale that helped spur my conversion to atheism. In fact, his sermons dealt with secular ethics and never mentioned the word 'sin', which is a religious stricture quite distinct from evil. I even suspected that he was really an atheist, and his chapel performance was simply part of his duties as senior master. He convinced me that the human body was a temple of perfection, and I derived the logical corollary that anything physiologic that followed must of necessity be equally desirable and healthy.

As time passed, I developed a delightful capacity to enjoy the sight of nudity, and my brother's Popular Photography copies were pursued with great pleasure. It was small wonder now that I found myself unable to leave the room. There she was, Preeti, lying asleep, one lovely breast uncovered, her face relaxed and utterly attractive. I had to kneel by the bed and, atheist though I was, thank Nature or whatever that had conspired to bring such loveliness into being. But my worshipping was as far removed from the religious variant as an abstract God was from Preeti. She was my goddess; not some mystical nonentity to be feared, but an ideal of perfection to be protected, nurtured and enjoyed as the esthetic food my mind hungered for. Imagine a notion as nefarious as having a sexual, even gastronomic, appetite for God. You would be instantly flung, without the slightest recourse to an explanation, into the deepest dungeons of darkness, even into blazing hellfire. But Preeti was my kind of goddess, so I lowered my head till my cheek covered her naked breast; and I tenderly caressed her face. She smiled and opened her eyes, slowly pulling my head down even further. There followed some cuddling, kissing, much cooing and sighing, and then, alas, it was time to begin the day.

Harbaksh was among the dahlias, daataning as usual and, on seeing me, he pulled out a spare stick from his pocket for me. He gazed at me a bit longer than usual, I felt, and perhaps a little more incisively. Even though he was now at least thirty years old, he seemed unable to resist the temptation of knowing what the night may have brought my way. I responded by devoting all my attention to the task at hand, which was the piece of wood I was masticating.

"It's good to be alive," I finally offered. That seemed to please him.

"It's nice to know that all is well," he added.

"Yes," I agreed, "married life is all it is made out to be."

"Uh-huh," he replied, "I ought to know."

"How could you have waited two months?" I asked.

"With much pain and frustration," he replied.

"As one married man to another," I said, "I can empathize with your feelings."

"So I see," he said, not quite able to suppress a smile.

Finally, we looked at each other, and chuckled. "There is no question," we agreed in unison, "women are God's (Nature's, I amended) greatest gift to man."

"I'll drink to that," he said, "and you?"

"At this time of the morning," I replied, "it will have to be milk, or at most tea. I may never graduate to *kaura paani* (bitter water, a Punjabi slang term for liquor)."

Daatan over, and mouths fresh from the astringent cooling of kikkar juices, we settled down to tea. By now Mohini and Preeti had joined us on the porch. Everybody looked unusually contented, though Harbaksh and I were still smiling from our private joke. As the smiles slowly ebbed, he became more philosophical.

"Amrik," he asked, with what sounded like genuine curiosity, "do you have an aversion to liquor, or is it simply a prejudice?"

"Neither," I told him. "Actually, it has much to do with a village wedding my father attended while he was still in college. As members of the bridegroom's party, he and a few other young male companions were celebrating on the wedding eve with some locally distilled liquor—*suntra* (tangerine) is what it was called—a most potent brew, hearing him tell it. As was to be expected, they all got roaring drunk. It must have been some celebration, though, seeing how my father is, it is not easy to imagine him in it. They drank through half the night. Over the next three days, my future father was so sick that he was confined to bed.

"When he finally regained his senses and his feet, he swore never to touch the bottle again. Not content at stopping there, he foolishly went beyond what was called for and promised, in a spell of misguided generosity I'm sure, that any future wife or children who came his way would be foresworn from it as well. He had been 'born again', and religion, which was as yet nascent in him, became an overt preoccupation. The bottle was banished from our home, as also were such things as playing cards which, in the hands of an idle mind, might become instruments of sins such as gambling, or so he believed. I never did touch liquor, but seeing that my maternal grandfather was an avid enthusiast and owned several very expensive decks of cards, I did learn to play a mean game of bridge."

"So you are then essentially a virgin when it comes to drink?" commented Harbaksh, rhetorically.

"You may say that," I conceded, "though I would phrase it more subtly. My father is often wrong, but this is one time I have no quarrel with him. Having a natural sweet tooth, my taste in liquor is unlikely ever to extend beyond wine and champagne."

"Expensive, huh? For our land of India, you are certainly cultivating sophisticated tastes," he observed in mock admiration.

"Consider it," I explained, "a perfect incentive to work hard and earn the enormous amount of wealth that will permit me and my lovely wife to live well, now and into the foreseeable future."

I smiled at my presence of mind and at Preeti, my beautiful wife.

The idea of doing some productive writing had been growing in my mind ever since Preeti agreed to marry me. I now desperately needed to accumulate material, so I finally asked Harbaksh: "May I pick your mind a little to answer some elementary questions about Sikhism that have been bothering me?"

"Sure," he said.

"Okay, here's what I want to know: we all know that Sikhs are forbidden the use of tobacco. But I am told Guru Gobind Singh also forbade the use of liquor, at least so my father says. Is that true?"

He smiled. "You certainly have a penchant for asking embarrassing questions. However, I'm afraid your father is correct. Religious sanctions have a way of interfering with the nicest things in life. Don't ask me why Sikhs almost universally observe the ban on tobacco, but many drink as if there were no tomorrow. Perhaps the daughter of the vine is too precious to cast aside, even at the behest of a guru. But we could also look at religious strictures a trifle more philosophically. One could then observe to the letter those that are the least onerous, and allow memory to lapse on the others."

"But," I objected to this pragmatic approach to religious strictures, "why not view them in a more enlightened manner? The guru did actually have a choice: he could have presented the proposals as suggestions rather than obligatory and binding. Christianity and Judaism have much the same problem. In the Bible, God presents to the Jews, through his prophet Moses, the ten commandments. Why not ten suggestions? It seems as if he lacked confidence in the ability of his followers to grasp their value, or that one or more of them were not justifiable?"

"You two are just perfect." That was Preeti. I had been unaware that she had been even listening to our discussion, let alone understanding it.

"Thank you," "Thanks, Preeti," we both acknowledged her compliment.

"You misunderstand," she explained, "I was referring to my sketch."

But, of course; there she was with the sketchbook in her lap, what else could she be doing? I got up to look. Harbaksh looked just like he was, wise and unflappable, but I looked strange. Preeti's sketch was a harbinger of things to come, because an artist's husband is her model. I was destined to be sketched every which way, front, sideways; clothed, unclothed; happy, sad; couth, uncouth, you name it. Such modeling inevitably led to the discovery of many strange things about myself. For instance, have you ever noticed how difficult it is to recognize yourself in profile? Well, I had the same problem, only more acute, because I had never even been photographed. In fact, as with liquor, I was virgin material for snapshots and sketches; but with Preeti's help, I might come around to the view that I would soon get to know this stranger who was me, even sideways. The mirror revealed a familiar perspective, my artist-wife another, as yet unfamiliar.

"Is that really me, Preeti?" I asked, trying to make certain it was a good likeness.

"The spitting image," she replied; "you don't know how attractive you look when animated by an exciting discussion. An artist cannot get most people to pose for her; their expressions simply fall apart. All of a sudden, they discover so many components to their faces, along with the virtual impossibility of keeping them all in their proper place when they try to. Things that come together naturally, as in a smile, fall totally apart when people try to pose. So, if the artist wants intensity and character, the essence of a person, she is better off not asking her model to pose; better just sneak up on him unawares."

I hugged my wife of many talents, and kissed her adoringly on the cheek.

"Sweetheart," I predicted, "we'll make it. With your talent and my hard work, survival should be a breeze."

"Are you trying to tell us that you will produce manuscripts of inestimable value merely through hard work, or are you allowing for a modicum of talent as well?" chimed in Harbaksh.

"Who am I to deny such talent?" I replied.

"Yes, yes, I know," he conceded, smiling, "silly questions deserve silly answers."

On my part, I was thinking: 'there is much to be said for a night of loving: the aftermath is so agreeable.'

Breakfast done, I settled down with my new typewriter. It was time to start working for a living. I started by typing: *'Arranging a Marriage,'* which I had decided was to be the title of my maiden manuscript.

As I saw it, there were only two ways to arrange a marriage: either by yourself, or through someone else. Most Indians could not see why anyone would make a fuss over your relatives arranging your marriage. Everybody believed that you married to satisfy your desires, more specifically the carnal ones. Beyond that, it helped to perpetuate your genes, those newly discovered worm-like strings of inheritance material which coded and passed on your characteristics to your progeny. In a society where, at least among the Hindus, you were born into a certain class, the maintenance of the high quality of your flesh was an imperative beyond all others, so you married within your caste. Relatives could be of enormous help in this regard: they knew many families belonging to the right class and caste, and had your 'best' interests at heart. The class system also indicated to you the fact that, as a member of a certain high caste, you were inherently superior to all those of a lower caste. Your beauty and the quality of your mind, skin, hair, nails, blood, and anything else you could imagine, were naturally superior to that of persons beneath you in the class pyramid.

Personally, I much preferred the rare, self-arranged union. Only an advanced state of despondency would have caused me to accept the other alternative. Whereas there was always the odd chance that I might find love at first sight in an arranged marriage, even there a prior assurance of such an outcome was preferable. But any such effort at assurance meant entering the uncertain territory wherein what is and is not 'arranged' is defined. For instance, since I was introduced to Preeti by Harbaksh, one could argue that he had arranged for us to meet and, since everything followed that, ours was an arranged marriage. But there is no such intention in the Indian concept of an arranged marriage. Harbaksh's method is unacceptable because it allows for the possibility that the two may agree to have an affair, of whatever depth, and then decide not to get married. That would be a calamity. Every Indian woman is like Caesar's wife; she must be above suspicion, above even the semblance of impropriety. It is taken as implicitly true that if a boy and girl were alone together and had the opportunity, they must have availed of it.

As far as the girl is concerned, the principle of ritual pollution here applies with far greater intensity than for such things as food and shadows. If she has been touched by a man in anything more than a very cursory fashion, she is considered defiled, not fit to be a wife in any 'good' family. In the Raamayan, the story of the legendary God-king Raam and his beautiful wife, Seeta, the daughter of the Earth, much fuss is made of the fact that Seeta, who had been abducted by the evil demon (*raakshus*) Raavan (though even in his evil he was so civilized that he refused to touch her unless she consented), was suspected by Raam's rescuing and victorious army of having slept, albeit involuntarily, with her kidnapper. To make a long story short, she was asked by her husband, he protesting all the while that he believed in her innocence, to undergo an ordeal by fire as a test of her purity. If she was pure, not innocent, mark you, because a victim of kidnapping and rape could hardly be considered culpable, the fire would leave her unscathed as she passed through it.

She passed the test, but was later banished from the kingdom by her "loving" husband because his subjects, who had not personally witnessed the fire test, still suspected her of ritual pollution. Raam claimed that he had given his word that the wishes of his subjects would take precedence over anything else, even over his own convictions and desires. He failed to admit that they would also take precedence over justice and morality. It was a victory of innuendo over proven innocence, of something as absurd as suspected ritual pollution over love. But that is the way of our land. Raam is portrayed as the ideal of virtue; he was, after all, the incarnation of Vishnu, the Almighty himself. Paradoxically, Seeta, who was truly virtuous, is portrayed as a touch blemished, at least in the eyes of men.

In this land, paradoxes and contradictions abound, with incompatibles often viewed as compatible. Existence is, after all, a magic shadow-show, an illusion, a play by Fate, a cosmic vindication of the principle of Determinism, one in which Free Will has no real role except to be mocked by illusion. Imagine what the application of such notions would do to my once-widowed Preeti.

The term 'arranged', then, is acceptable only when it ranges on the one hand from those marriages in which the bride and groom see each other for the first time at the wedding (this is becoming rare among the educated), all the way to the other end where the two are permitted to meet each other in a chaperoned setting, with the understanding that any physical or serious emotional probing is absolutely out of the question, because it is Western, un-Indian, defiling.

It had been my impression that almost all Indian boys felt as I did. It seemed quite reasonable; after all, I was not an intellectual or moral freak. Why then was the system of arranged marriages so powerful and so universally accepted by us? I had thought of this often, not merely since the time I had met and fallen in love with Preeti. My thoughts were now coming together, and the warp in the culture was becoming clearer. Actions speak louder than words. Whatever our elders and our religious books said, one thing was clear: their actions showed that Indians held women in low esteem.

Many of the families of the Hindu friends I knew, and some of the Sikh ones too, were convinced that it was a misfortune to have daughters. There seldom was a celebration when a daughter was born, for the goal of marriage was to produce male heirs. In this connection, I remember something my father told me some years ago. When he was still young, he recalled that there used to be a certain old woman living in our village. Oh, I forgot, I never explained to you the significance of a village. Let me do it now.

The Punjab, like the rest of India, is essentially an agricultural community, with well over eighty percent of the population living in villages. Each village can be conceived of as originally founded by some one man. It grew as his descendants and their descendants grew. In a matter of a few generations, there may be fifty to a hundred people living in a village, all related to each other. Brides were brought in from other villages, and so the community of the interrelated grew, in the manner of an extended family. Everybody was either an uncle or an aunt; a brother, sister or a cousin. Only in a few professions, such as those of scavengers, those who dealt with the skins of dead animals, those who disposed of human waste, and those who were weavers and cobblers, would there be outsiders, people of lower caste; and sometimes Muslims. There would also be the moneylender, or 'baania,' as he was known in Punjabi, who belonged to a certain class of Hindu shopkeepers. All the rest would be your relatives. What then happened in any village was essentially a family matter.

The job of this woman who my father recalled was to help eliminate unwanted female Infants. Given the Indian system, all female infants were unwanted, at least in villages like ours. Whenever such an infant was born, this woman was called in. She would strangle, smother or drown the helpless baby and dispose of it. I shudder at the thought of the story, but there also were redeeming acts. The fact that there existed female cousins of mine testified to the truth that some fathers and even mothers-in-law would not permit the practice in their household. It was clear that love and integrity never quite died.

But the dark source of the problem still remains, the dowry system. For the majority of Indians, to have female children is a curse. Among the Hindus, it is almost universal, though changing among the better-educated families, particularly in the Punjab, for the bridegroom's family to demand a dowry at the time of marriage from the parents of the bride. It is common for the parents of female children to have to spend their entire life's savings in the weddings of their daughters, and sometimes even to go into debt; and that in a land where people are fiscally conservative to the point that they prefer to buy and sell things like houses outright rather than with borrowed money.

At this point in my thoughts, Harbaksh walked in, and found me still staring at an essentially blank sheet of paper, unable to find an acceptable first sentence.

"So how is the budding writer doing?" he asked.

"Not so good," I said, "you know a lot more about the dowry system than me. Tell me, what are the feelings of the givers and takers of a dowry?"

"Not very healthy, I'd say."

"I've tried to look at it in a detached manner," I said, "but I always come up against the problem of conscience. I don't believe anybody is really devoid of one, so how then do our elders live with the knowledge that they have demanded payment, or acquiesced in giving it, in order for a marriage to take place?"

"Well, fortunately," said Harbaksh, "it is not common among Sikhs, though not rare by any means, and certainly on the increase. As far as Hindus are concerned, various mitigating arguments have been given. The dowry, it is claimed for instance, is not a payment for a son-in-law; rather it is your effort at providing a comfortable life for your daughter— consider it as a wedding present to her. In many instances this is true; after all, it is often used to buy household goods and other amenities for the newly married couple. In fact, the jewelry and the bride's clothes that are part of the dowry are accepted as belonging to the bride. But other things, such as cash, which is generally the biggest component, gold other than jewelry, and the various items of clothing such as suits and the like that are provided to the groom and his family, are under their control. Sometimes, the bride's parents may even be asked to provide property, such as a house, for the groom's family. In some instances, further payments have been demanded after the marriage, maybe even years later, accompanied by veiled and not-so-veiled threats concerning the welfare of the bride."

"What you are trying to say then is that the groom's family essentially lives off the bride's family. Obviously, if they have more than one son and no daughter, they would really have it made."

"Quite so," said Harbaksh. "It is assumed, since in most instances the husband is the only earner, that he deserves to be paid by her family for looking after her. Transactions are of many kinds, but here it seems that society has decided that the only value of any significance is monetary or other tangible wealth. Marriage has been transformed into a commercial transaction. Sex and the emotional value of the woman, and her inspiring love, are downplayed. She is instead viewed as a sexual receptacle, a breeder of children, someone to do the housework and look to the comforts of the man. It may also be that these attributes of a wife are considered detracting from the lofty goals of our philosophy, in the sense that they are somehow unworthy of a virtuous human being; even dangerous, for they are 'maya'—illusion—things that charm the mind, tempt it to stray from the straight and narrow path to salvation, a trap one must try to steer clear of. Ironically, by the same token, tangible wealth is also maya, and thus equally to be avoided, but hypocrisy ensures that it is not.

"Whichever way you look at it, in the final analysis it seems that though individual couples may view sex all the way from enchantingly elevating down to animal, philosophy seems to have relegated it mainly to the realm of lust, at best a foolish temptation that leads astray, something not becoming of an ideal human being. By having love marriages, you and I have made a tradeoff. We have sacrificed much wealth, and gained enormous love and happiness. I know we are winners, though I daresay most of our countrymen would mock at us as idealist fools who, in their ignorance, besides having shown poor business judgment, have foolishly dared to defy the collective wisdom of the ages, which is tradition. Our karm (morally significant acts) would ensure that in the next lifetime we would suffer Nature's retribution by being reborn into the misery of a low caste, or the mindlessness of an animal."

It was difficult to keep from smiling at this ridiculous Indian vision of brimstone and hellfire, but I had to get him back on track.

"I think there is more to the dowry problem than you have suggested," I interjected. "Do you believe it is possible for a woman to truly fall in love with a man knowing that he and his family have demanded and received what, in essence, amounts to blood money from her parents? She would have to suppress this knowledge from her mind to do so. Even then, there would remain a subconscious fear, namely, how far could she trust a person who has stooped so low once, not just surreptitiously, but brazenly and openly? If he professes love for her, can she really believe him? A man like that could be capable of lust, but not possibly of love! He cannot help knowing what he has done and what he is in essence, a blackmailer, no matter how well he attempts to hide his actions under the guise of custom and tradition. But what troubles me is this: if the system is so degraded and sick, why have people not rebelled against it?"

"Perhaps you are being a bit harsh," replied Harbaksh. "There are many happy arranged marriages, and certainly many in which the couple love each other, but as a general rule, they do start from a position of disadvantage, particularly where an onerous dowry has been paid. Your ability to live with it probably depends on your level of intellectual sophistication. Those who do not think deeply or independently, and are willing to ascribe the events of their lives essentially to Fate, not to human action, may have few problems. But such people are limited in the level of happiness that they can achieve, for the very reason that they are protected from the moral outrage that a dowry should arouse. Happiness, in their minds, is a low level state of satisfaction and contentment, primarily because, having neglected the intellect, they have chosen to live, in effect, at a semi-human level. Real, all-consuming happiness demands a keen awareness of one's metaphysical reality, of the fact that man's distinguishing feature is the intellect and his potential essentially intellectual. You neglect it at your own peril, not so much to your physical self as to your emotional and spiritual self. A mind that is dull to moral outrage is equally insensitive to the experience of happiness because, if you want the latter, you must be keenly aware of the former. You cannot have one without the other.

"As to why people have not rebelled against the system, I don't think I can answer the question to your satisfaction. Not yet, at least. I have thought over it long and hard, but have never quite been able to nail down a fully satisfying explanation. I am evidently overlooking something of fundamental importance, but I don't know what it is. Look at it this way: the system has endured for several thousand years; there must be something which all Indians accept that permits them to tolerate it, and even to boast of its success. Look, for example, at the smug satisfaction with which they point to the high rate of divorce in western cultures. The arranged marriages in India, they point out, almost never end in divorce. How then could you claim that love marriages are better when so many of them end up on the rocks?"

"I have a trite defense for that claim," I answered; "it is better to have loved for a while than never to have loved at all. But, seriously, I can see how a love marriage is a high-stakes game. Your goals are loftier, and your demands keener. You love someone for a reason, not simply because of the difference in sex. Love, being what it is, needs to be continually nourished. It withers if the reasons for its existence cease to exist. It has exacting standards, and will not tolerate hypocrisy. If the husband or the wife no longer is what he or she was once perceived to be, or if the initial perception was flawed, misguided, wishful, to begin with, then love dies a sure death. One could then continue to live at a lower level as in many an arranged marriage, pretending as if love never existed or mattered. But the love bug is a child of enlightenment, of aspirations beyond those of mere satisfaction, of a will that dares to rise to the lofty. It cannot tolerate its own death, because it would be sacrilege. There is only one answer to that: divorce.

"A love marriage, by its very nature, is more demanding; it is also less forgiving because in it the moral is magnified, both in its positives and its negatives. When you aspire to an enlightened existence, the price of failure is high. It is not for the faint of heart, or the casual. You can see why divorce would be common where love marriages preponderate, and rare where arranged marriages are the rule."

"I believe you have it, kid," agreed Harbaksh, "but even what you have termed trite is not that, kid. There is something profound in it, having to do with how you view yourself. Are you a person in your own right, an independent entity, or are you just one of many millions? Is happiness a valid goal and something that you control, or is your existence of so little consequence that such an issue is of no significance? Remember, the best arguments that have been given against the need for happiness are those that belittle your existence as an individual. When someone starts talking to you of the billions and billions of stars, and the billions and billions of galaxies, and then points out how you are just a speck of dust in an ocean of eternity, he is trying to destroy the 'I' in you, your feeling of individuality, of self-worth; he is trying to destroy that in you which soars to the clarion call of ideals and dreams impossible dreams; that feels existence with an intensity that will not be denied; prides in the heroic, and wishes to cheer at the sight of achievement. Yes, he is trying to destroy your self, the admiration that you feel for the miracle of life that is you. He is trying to make you feel how inconsequential life and, by extension, you are by dwarfing these with allusions to the vastness of the universe and the infiniteness of time. In the face of such a perspective, it seems irrelevant whether you are honest, or lie and steal; whether you have love, or simply rape and plunder. Whatever you do, you will still be but a speck of dust that exists for a very brief and inconsequential moment in time, and then be merged again and lost in the eternity of existence, making not an iota of difference. The moral imperative is rendered meaningless, ridiculous; in effect, destroyed.

"Once he has convinced you of life's evanescence in the context of the eternity of the universe, he will then further undercut your feelings of reality by revealing that the universe too is but an illusion. It is all in your mind. Your mind, by then, will be in such a tangle that it will not know what to believe and what not to. It will not even trust its own existence. How then could it think of right and wrong, and things such as happiness? They would mean absolutely nothing."

"But why would anyone want to do such a thing?" I asked, unwilling to concede the existence of such evil.

"I don't know, kid, but there are many such people. The small fry are simply losers. I believe they derive satisfaction by dragging down everyone else into the same state of misery as theirs. Perhaps, there is vicarious pleasure in it for those who have given up on everything else. Who knows, maybe the driving force is the guilt so easily acquired by acquiescing in the blackmail we call dowry, something that owes much to the institution of arranged marriage. One thing I know: there is no way a true love marriage could ever degenerate into such a commercial venture.

"But what about the big guns, the philosophers, the ones who preach that mystic drivel which attacks the self? I'm not so sure of their motives. Read philosophy, read the scriptures, kid. Maybe one day you will find the fatal flaw. When you do, let me know."

For a while, we sat there in silence. I was still unwilling to accept that humanity could be so callous and hypocritical. Deep inside, I knew that everything had a rational explanation, and that there must be one for what moves these mystics. I had to put my finger on it, and Heaven help me, one day I would. Lost in daydreams, I sat there, listening to the brave music of a distant drum, fantasizing a rescue of my troubled land, this land of so much sorrow.

XIV

I awoke next morning with the nagging, pervasive feeling of unfinished business. My parents had to be informed of my marriage and the change of career plans. So it was back to the typewriter. I started with the usual greeting that I had used for the past five years:

"My dear Beeji,"

Boys at BCS had used a variety of greetings, depending upon family custom and circumstances. Some wrote "Dearest Mom", others "Dearest Mummy", some even "My dear Ummaji". There were as many ways as there were provinces and cultures in India, but none, as far as I knew, used my manner of address. That was a surprise, since Beeji is a common term for mother in Punjab. Most, however, were anglicized, reflecting the strata of society the writers came from. The endings too varied from "Your loving son" to "With love" or "Love and Kisses," but I simply wrote "Yours affectionately". I had a mental block using the word 'love'. Despite fondness for my mother, it seemed incongruous using 'love', and 'love and kisses' was totally out of the question. I was hugged when my mother saw me off to school, but never kissed.

I remember two blond-haired brothers with a Sikh father and an Austrian mother. The mother used to see them off at the Delhi Railway Station. She used to cover their faces with so many kisses that I would feel embarrassed just watching. She even cried as she waved when the train pulled away. My mother occasionally had water in her eyes, but it would make me so uncomfortable that I avoided looking at her face. So it was even now when I was all grown up, married and in love, that I could not bring myself to change my greeting to 'Dearest Beeji' or 'My loving Beeji.' I could not use the words 'mother' or 'mom' or 'mummy' because they lacked the ring of authenticity. There was no possibility of addressing her thus in real life, and since a letter was simply talk put down on paper, it did not call for a change. One concession I did make to Western culture was in the use of the word 'dear.' I never used that word, in English, or its Punjabi equivalent, when talking to my mother, but not using it in a letter appeared too formal and cold, so it found its way in. Perhaps it was my subconscious initiating a gradual change in our relationship. Once I had even written a letter to my father, to which he asked my mother to reply. I addressed him as "My dear Papaji," but did not mean it in the same sense as when addressing my mother. So this is what I wrote now:

> "My dear Beeji,
>
> "I am having a wonderful time here, but the purpose of this letter is more than simply telling you how nice a place Solan is, and how wonderful Harbaksh and Mohini are. Solan is charming and they are wonderful, but I do have a lot of other news, and it is all good. In fact, it is the best news I have ever penned—pardon my error, typed—in a letter. It is better than telling you that I stood first in my grade, or that I made the BCS hockey team. It is so good that I think you had better brace yourself for it.
>
> "Your son is, as you may well suspect, all grown up; and, as you know, he is now eighteen, and so no longer just a boy. In fact, he has become a man and, like all men, has begun to think of making a life for himself. As Fate would have it, he met someone very wonderful here. She is Harbaksh's sister-in-law, Preeti. It was love at first sight. I know this is not the kind of news you expected to hear from your son, but I am very much in

love. There is more: she loves me too, equally as much, so we did what we just had to do. We got married. You have a daughter-in-law, someone you will be as proud of as I am of her.

"Before you start getting worried—after all, things done in haste, almost on the spur of the moment, and without the advice and experience of elders may well be a mistake—I want you to know that she is very lovely. I find her more attractive than anyone I can think of, and so does everyone else. She has an education similar to mine, and we think very much alike. She even sketches and paints, just like me, except that she is much better.

"I don't want you to feel that I wasn't thinking of you when I got married; it was just that we could not wait. Harbaksh and Mohini were with us when we went to the magistrate, and they completely approve of what we did. Harbaksh has indicated that he will be writing to you, but I felt that it was better not to wait, so hence this letter.

"There is just one more thing. I have decided not to become a doctor. I know Papaji will be quite upset, but it was always his idea, never mine. I never wanted to go that route in the first place. Instead, I am planning to study arts with the aim of becoming a writer. I know I am good at writing, and am strongly motivated for it, so please don't send the fee to Hindu college. The reason is that I will be registering in St. Stephens as soon as I come back to Delhi, which will be in a couple of weeks.

"I'm sorry that I did not give you the opportunity for a big wedding with all our relatives present, but you know how I feel about such things: for me, marriage is a very private affair, and our Indian weddings are too public for my liking. Besides, Papaji would have insisted on making it a simple religious ceremony, and I did not want any of that. Beeji, I don't want you to worry. This is the best thing that could have happened to me, and you will love Preeti when you see her. One more thing: I am going to change the way I have always ended my letters, so brace yourself for it. I am going to express my feelings for you more openly; so here it comes:

With love and kisses.

Amrik.

P.S. This letter is typed on the typewriter Harbaksh gave me as a wedding present. Preeti will also be going to college in Delhi to study fine arts. She, my wife, sends you her love."

The crack about typing versus penning detracted from the overall serious tone of the letter, but I have always felt that humor has a place in anything we do. It prevents us from slipping into pomposity; allows for that little uncertainty that is, of necessity, always part of everything. View it not as a debasing humility, but an acceptance of reality as it is. The truth is always known in hindsight—it may be guessed at prospectively, sometimes quite accurately, but not known—so it does not hurt to make allowance for that little surprise waiting around the corner. People call that the wisdom of experience; lessons learned in the school of hard knocks; but I don't like this implicit equating of life with difficulty and suffering. My objection is simple: when you start viewing life through blue glasses, it tends to look blue; you also can no longer see the warm reds and oranges. So I much prefer to simply call it good commonsense. Humor is our cushion par excellence against shocks; it makes the unforeseen palatable. It also is the spice of life, the most eminently human attribute in us all. Think of it, have you ever seen a man with a good sense of humor end up in a mental hospital? I haven't.

I showed the letter to Preeti. She liked the way I had eased myself into the bombshell, but she could not let pass an opportunity to tease. "You have said a lot of nice things about me, but I don't see any mention of a widow, and about marrying an older woman," she pointed out. "Are you embarrassed to admit that your wife is your elder and a widow?"

"Preeti, I married experience. No! I did not mean it that way; I was not referring to the school of hard knocks. I simply meant that I married someone who could appreciate what it means to be loved and to love; someone who knows how it is without them. The thought that you are older and a widow never crossed my mind. I simply see you as a very lovely woman, one I love to share my desires with. But, repartee aside, neither my father nor my mother would be the least bit upset with a widow or a wife older than their son. My father may be very conservative in most things, but he is a radical when it comes to customs. He scoffs at the notion that a widow should not remarry, and as far as age and beauty are concerned, he would be satisfied if my wife was good and obedient, and completely devoted to me. Beauty is irrelevant to him, for it smacks of Maya; and he very much believes in that concept, a concept that explains much of his ascetic approach to makeup, jewelry, fancy weddings, and life in general."

"He's a mixed-up male chauvinist, if you ask me. 'Good and obedient, and completely devoted!' My foot!" retorted Preeti.

"No more than Harbaksh was when he talked of the Guru and his Sikhs professing great respect for women, yet indulging in polygamy,' I countered.

"Perhaps I will have to straighten him out the same as I did Harbaksh. Somebody has to do it, why not me?"

I had qualms about anybody trying to change my father's ideas, but Preeti saying that to him could have just the sort of shock value that might actually make it work. Anyway, the problem was not in the here and now, but in the future. I would cross my bridges when I came to them.

It was a pleasant morning, so Preeti and I walked the mile odd distance to Solan to mail the letter. This way we could be alone away from her mother who had just arrived from Shimla an hour earlier, and the still uneasy relationship between her and me. Mrs. Brar was now resigned to me as her son-in-law, but she did express the desire that I call her 'Mummy,' just like Preeti. The word had a strange taste in my mouth, but what the heck, if the old woman—she behaved old, did she not?—wanted it, it was no big deal for me. So I agreed. Now I have a 'Mummy' and a 'Beeji,' but notice an odd incongruity. My Beeji has a traditional name, but a liberal bent of mind, whereas Mummy has a modern name, at least for us Indians, yet a wholly conservative mindset. Ironical, is it not?

Mailing that letter lifted a big load off my mind. Besides placing the ball in the other court, it brought me back in tune with my philosophy of life: what has to be faced and done, ought to be done, and without procrastinating through fear. May be not if you wish to avoid hurting someone, when there is a chance another way out could be found, but when you are deliberately trying to keep someone in the dark who ought to know, then the sooner you shed light, the better. And now that it had been done, I could get back to my own business, which was the business of writing.

So the typewriter was opened again, and I was back on my blank sheet, with "Arranging a Marriage" typed at the top.

I typed on: "India is divided into two approximately equal camps. The two live in constant tension and distrust of each other, yet must make love or the nation will perish. How they behave is the essence of our culture. Whereas once we resorted to the barber and one's relatives to make 'perfect' matches between the sexes, we are now in a technical age and are increasingly making use of the newspaper. Its matrimonial columns are a boon to travel-weary fathers, mothers, uncles and aunts, and they open up increasingly wider markets for prospective brides and grooms. But there is a problem. Observe an ideal entree:

> Handsome Jat Sikh boy, 5'8", seeks
> beautiful, convent-educated, Jat
> Sikh girl, tall, slim, charming,
> fair-complexioned, loving, homely, enterprising,
> good cook, knits and sews, excellent lover,
> virgin, willing and able to bear children,
> has similar tastes and talents, paints, sings like a nightingale,
> loves to read, has good sense of humor,
> has modesty but lacks it when necessary,
> has courage, integrity, belongs to
> honorable family, with amiable
> parents who are rich and generous.
> Reply with photographs (front and side poses)
> and detailed resume, including marriage
> incentives, to
> A.S.Randhawa, 13/220 Khajoor Rd, Karole
> Bagh, New Delhi."

At about this time, Preeti walked in. Looking over my shoulder at the nascent manuscript, she said: "Ahem, do you think I would have replied to that?"

"Not you; Mummy."

"You cannot place an ad like that. It calls for the requirements too openly. For instance, even though her qualification as a lover is what you are really interested in, you cannot mention that. Besides, how would she know without having made love, and that as you know is a no-no. It is an insult to her modesty, and she would be ritually defiled in the process of finding out. You also cannot say anything about the ability to bear children. Only a widow or a divorcee who is barren or has children would know the answer to that, and that you have ruled out by demanding she be a virgin. In any case, it is not proper to ask questions about the womb. You have to assume it works.

"You want a convent-educated girl who also knows how to cook, sew and knit? And you want a girl who is both homely and enterprising? You must be kidding! No such girl exists. And then 'front and side poses?' What do you think she is, a convict? Nobody is going to send you photographs of their daughter. The last thing they want you to know is how she looks. Besides, how do they know you won't circulate them around to others. She could become the talk of the town. Modesty? You cannot demand that she have it and then lack it when necessary. Bedroom behavior is learned on the job. All you can have is an apprentice; the rest is up to you.

"Are you asking for a quote on the dowry? Forget it! No one will be willing to commit that on paper. Such things have to be negotiated."

"I would be happy to settle for the highest bidder," I said.

"I'm sure you would, but high bids and good-looking girls don't mix. If a girl is tall, slim, charming, beautiful, and fair-complexioned, and also has a convent education, she does not need to answer newspaper ads, nor need a dowry. On the other hand, if wishes were horses, and you could pull it off;" and here she became reflective, "we could rent ourselves a comfortable apartment in one of the nicer parts of Delhi. Sure sounds tempting! We could live well . . ."

She looked charming, her eyes wandering off into fantasyland, where it is always sunny and cool, and never rains, where every day is a picnic. When they finally refocused, she continued: "But coming back to the matter at hand, if she has a sense of humor, she will be laughing so hard at your ad, she will have no time to reply. So allow me to use my veto power over what you may or may not ask for, and then see how it looks."

So saying, she picked up a pen and started slashing out one item after another. What was left was this:

> Handsome Jat Sikh boy, 5'8", seeks
> beautiful, convent-educated, Jat
> Sikh girl, tall, slim, charming,
> fair-complexioned, loving, homely.
> Reply to: A.S.Randhava, 13/220 Khajoor Rd. Karole
> Bagh, New Delhi.

"But that omits almost all the important things I am looking for," I objected.

"How sad. But you are in no position to complain about omissions. This is a long ad, the way ads go. How much money do you have?"

"After the condoms and the money for petrol for our trip to Shimla, I have a little over a hundred rupees left."

"Forget it, you barely have enough money to place this ad in the newspaper, and at the same time have enough for petrol for our forthcoming trip to Delhi."

"May be I could get a loan from you."

"I have money, but I am not exactly a rich widow, you know."

"I love you. You are so sweet to me."

"I have no choice. You are the only husband I have, and the only lover too. You are so helpful in inspiring me to 'shed my modesty when necessary'. Ha! Ha! Ha!"

She was chuckling, and her pupils were large and dark, with loving on her mind. But I had work to do, so I negotiated a rain-check. There were more pressing needs for the moment, so I continued with my writing:

"The matrimonial ad is an interesting exercise in futility. All the things you need to know are between the lines, and no common code exists by which you can decipher that. Arranging a marriage is a high-stakes game where the truth is stretched almost to the breaking point, virtues grossly exaggerated, and blemishes omitted altogether. You cannot hire private detectives, because you are not dealing with criminals, at least not overt ones. In any case, you are not interested in the actions of the girl; you want to know what is in her head. Yes, how she is packaged too, but that a little spying on your own would accomplish just as easily and a lot more cheaply than a detective. Besides, what looks good to the detective may not look good to you.

"You also have to remember that the parents are simply trying to protect their wares as best they can, and if you find the sample a little less than attractive, it is quite likely they will add incentives, like the dowry, to change your mind."

This was depressing business, but one has to make a living, so I continued to type, pointing out the flaws in my ideal ad just as Preeti had done, and explaining that what was left was not worth the paper it was printed on. Yet the arranged marriage market was flourishing, people were getting married everywhere and none were being divorced.

Some of the men were having extramarital affairs. Since Indians love to poke their noses into everyone's business, extreme secrecy was called for in such ventures. There was not much a wife could do if the husband were found out. She might go on strike, but that could be counterproductive, heightening as it would the value of the mistress's services. A divorce was almost impossible. First, the laws were such (and this I had from Harbaksh) that it was extremely difficult to sue for it, and second, if a woman did obtain it eventually, she would have nowhere to go. Her parents would not want her back in their house, particularly after having paid a sizable dowry to get her married; and given the fact that the vast majority of Indian women have no visible means of support, such as a job; and alimony is essentially nonexistent or too meager to be of survival value, she would simply be out on the street. Yes, that is right, the street.

What is it like to be on the street? There is nobody on your side. There are no shelters for abandoned women, or for women

who have run away from their husbands. The state has no stakes
in the system, and there is no welfare agency. You could become
a prostitute, but that is the equivalent of committing suicide. So
what happens? You continue to live as the wife and help keep
the divorce rate at the negligible level it is, the level which
Indian men, and some co-opted, 'well-educated' women, boast
of. If only there were a different index, a 'Happiness index' or
a 'Demand index' or an 'Achievement index', indices that
assessed how much one asks of a marriage, how successfully,
and with how enlightened a result; indices that deal with the
bond of intellectual survival, the eminently human survival,
not simply physical survival; how would India stack up under
such circumstances against the rest of the world?

I don't know too much about conditions abroad, but even a
dimwit could see that things could not be much worse. I don't
have to go very far for examples. My parents' and Preeti's
parents' marriages were the only ones of the arranged kind I
knew enough about, and they sure were failures. In contrast,
Harbaksh's marriage was a roaring success, and mine too, so
far. Even if, through a most malign, impossible quirk of fate,
Preeti and I were to break up, what had existed and happened
between us would be enough to override any grief that would
follow. It would be an injustice then to call ours an unsuccessful
marriage; a tragedy, may be, but not an unsuccessful marriage.
We had seen the light, achieved the unbelievable, soared to
great heights; so what if it had all been eventually lost? History
had been written, and it could not be erased. But look at the
other side: there was no history to erase; it would never even
be written; it would always remain a blank sheet, as if the
couples had never existed.

Could it be this that was the secret behind those who sought
to belittle the meaning, the significance, of the individual?
Could they be wishing to protect those in the system from
collapsing under the weight of the nothingness that they had
consigned themselves to? Perhaps it was. Why else would we
be steeped in an otherworldly philosophy? A blunder of this

magnitude must rest on a philosophical blunder of equal magnitude. My father had always told me that we must not get too involved in the concerns of the world, in material well-being; that the goal of life was essentially spiritual. We are, in essence, a spirit trapped in a body, a spirit that cries for release. The more we identify with worldly concerns, with the needs of the body, the more entrapped the spirit becomes. The real reality is the spirit, everything else is 'Maya', both an illusion and a trap for the unwary. Worldly desires lead us astray, make us forget the perfection that we are, burying the spirit ever deeper and deeper.

Now turn around and look at the matrimonial columns. One glance at them and you realize that this is the most materialistic society in the world. People talk of the sublime essence of the Vaids (usually spelt Vedas, which makes little phonetic sense except to linguists), of the beauty of Indian spiritual thought. You would think they had never opened a newspaper. But they have. The same spiritual philosophy is present every now and then on the op-ed pages, berating us for our Western ways. What Western ways? A woman who wears a shirt and slacks is a slut, but a woman who sleeps with a man she does not love is a virtuous housewife? A woman who tries to look attractive, wears jewelry and lipstick, is a hussy; but one who is plain and subdued, and thinks so little of herself that she has lost her pride, and simply lives secondhand for her husband, obeying whatever he wants her to do, is an ideal? It is not Western ways these columnists are complaining about, it is the desire to live, the desire to be somebody, to be happy. What makes them so afraid of people who have something to be proud of, of those who capitalize the word 'I'?

Strange that I say that. 'I', when it stands by itself, is always capitalized. Maybe the founders of English have a message in it for all Indians. I do know a little bit about Christianity; as a matter of fact, quite a lot. The five years I spent going daily to chapel were not a total waste; I even won the Divinity Prize. But wait a minute! Christianity is as opposed to capitalizing the

'I' as the Hindu scriptures are. So then how did the English convention of capitalizing the 'I' originate? It must be their sense of life, which has survived the vicissitudes of the Christian onslaught. Maybe it is the human spirit, the true spirit, not that little fragment of the Almighty that the Vaids talk about, or the soul the Bible talks of, which has triumphed. It is the triumph of the spirit that so few know. Not the soul; not that one-billionth of the Universal Spirit that sits here trapped in the body, crying for release; it is the spirit that derives from the body, enjoys it and revels in its pleasures. It is the spirit that knows there is no other spirit; no ghosts in heaven; no angels or gods; no non-materialistic entities that violate all the laws of Nature; no soul. It is the spirit which knows that it is not in conflict with the body. It knows that when the body dies, it does too; and that is all there is; the rest is just a fairy tale.

But we don't want to believe it, do we? We go around worrying what to do with the dead; should we cremate them, or bury them? And if the latter, with embalming fluids and in a coffin that would help preserve what has already decayed beyond any resurrection, or simply in a 'kuffan,' that simple piece of cloth in which the Muslims bury their dead. And then look at the Parsees, members of that prosperous community that lives in Bombay, but whose ancestors were the inhabitants of ancient Persia long ago. They leave the bodies on their Towers of Silence, to be devoured by vultures; life into life, they say.

Why do we do all this for the dead? Because we think there may be a soul? The Christians believe it will re-inhabit the same body, the Hindus one that is new, animal or human depending upon your karm. Of course, the latter feel that the ultimate success story is that it won't inhabit any body at all, but will become one with the Universal Soul. They call it 'mukti', 'nirvaan', 'moksha' . . . salvation. But there is no soul. It is a cruel fiction. We would all be better off, particularly the living survivors, if the dead were simply disposed of in the most hygienic manner possible, and with the most consideration for the feelings of those who loved them, if they were ever loved, and let it go at that. Cremation suits me just fine; but no suttee, please, no suttee! I don't want any woman, loved or not, committing suicide ever a failed piece of flesh. The blues in life do not deserve, must never be allowed, more than temporary sway.

My article was shaping up nicely. When Harbaksh walked in, I asked his opinion. "It is excellent," he said, "and true. But you want it published, don't you?"

I nodded my head.

"I don't think any editor would want to do that. It's like offering his head as a sacrifice to society. He would be cut into tiny little pieces and then offered to the vultures, as you have so colorfully put it; and you will be forced to follow him as a 'suttee'."

"Come now, you must be exaggerating. This is a country of laws, with freedom of thought and speech, and freedom of the Press."

"Well, you can try, but don't say later that I didn't warn you. Where would you like to send it?"

"The National Express, maybe, or the Illustrated Weekly," I replied, looking at him with the expectation of advice pro and con.

"I'm not sure of the Illustrated Weekly. It is really a family type of magazine. But the Express sounds like a good idea. Finish the piece, write a covering letter, and I'll drive you over to Solan to post it."

By early afternoon, my first article was already in the mail. My fingers were crossed, and would remain so throughout the days to come. I was excited. If this manuscript was accepted, my decision to become a writer would be vindicated.

Mummy and her brother were driving back to Delhi, and were trying to figure out how to save as much of their friendship and respect in their circle of friends as they could, and then mourn their common misfortune in more conducive company than was available at Solan, by ultimately bringing the brother's family with them for a vacation to Shimla. Preeti and I were not invited, fortunately. Preeti wanted me to pretend disappointment, but I told her I was not much of an actor, and Mummy was no fool, so that scheme was quietly shelved. We simply wished her a happy journey, both of us hugged her sizable presence., and then waved her and her brother goodbye.

XV

Preeti was at the easel, eyeing with favor the low valley to our east, with the town of Solan tucked away into its right flank. Nothing more than a conglomeration of houses clustered along the road as it went coursing across the low shoulder that passed from our mountain to the one beyond, Solan was a low point on the road to Shimla.

"Amrik," Harbaksh remarked, "do you not see the invisible hand of the Creator in this vale of perfection? If you were a visitor from outer space, would you not wonder about the invisible artist who created all this?"

"Put in those terms, I would say 'yes.' But I would be careful about it vis-à-vis a Creator. A book from your collection has some interesting philosophical reflections on this very question. It points out that it is impossible to conceive of a beginning, a time when there was nothing."

"But why? Everything has a beginning, and a cause that causes the beginning. You can't dispute that, can you?"

"No, I don't. It is what the author calls the 'law of Causality.' But he points out that the law merely explains how all things are formed by a change from something else. It assumes that something exists, which by operation of the law changes to something else. But the catch is that the process is a transformation, not a creation de novo. Something can come only out of something. Out of nothing, only nothing can come, and nothing as you know is just that— nothing!"

"So?"

"So you cannot have Creation, the Universe, arising out of nothing. Existence can only be derived from something, but if something exists, then the Universe already exists."

"But what did that something that exists come out of?" he persisted, trying to make me regress to a beginning.

"It is regression ad infinitum," I said. "How far you go back does not change anything. Something only comes out of something, and just as something cannot come out of nothing, so too something cannot become nothing. The Universe thus can have neither a beginning nor an end. The Hindus have tried to get around it by saying that the Universe is merely a transformation of the Creator himself. They even talk of multiple Universes, to which I must cry foul, because it violates the definition of Universe: 'all that exists.' But they have not achieved anything different from the others. The question still remains: from what transformation did the Creator arise? Their answer is not clear. The best one can make of it is that it is an infinite cycling between the Creator and the Universe, the former never ceasing to exist; the latter merging into the former at intervals. But it is just a play on words. They have merely substituted the word 'Creator' for the word 'Universe,' even though they insist on using them separately to explain us and everything we sense. The whole scheme is vacuous though, since it is based on unbridled imagination, not evidence."

"But you do admit that a force, such as a Creator, is necessary to produce the transformations as things do not come into being all by themselves."

"As long as by 'coming into being' you mean a transformation, I have no quarrel. But why postulate a Creator? By that term you do mean a being or an entity, don't you?"

"Yes, I mean God,"

"Okay, if he is a being, then he must have recognizable properties, right?"

"Yes, of course."

"What kind of properties do you have in mind?" I asked.

"Well, the usual ones."

"Name one."

"Omnipotence," he offered.

"But," I pointed out, "that is a no-no. To be omnipotent means that he can do anything, even violate Nature's laws. But each entity, by its nature, is capable of only certain things. Man can jump, hop and so forth, but he cannot fly. An omnipotent being, like a genie, would be able to make us fly; would be able to cause any rock to float on water; would be able to instantly change water to wine, and back. In fact, he would suspend in this manner another philosophical law, the 'Law of Identity,' which states that each entity has properties unique to itself, such as: water does not flow uphill; sugar sustains; cyanide kills. But if something that you think is cyanide does not kill, then it is not cyanide. If it flies and has wings, it is not a man. All experience shows that the Laws of Nature apply without exception. If an exception were to be found, then the specific law violated would have to be changed to conform to this new finding; but we would still have a law, only slightly different. The new law would still apply without exception."

"You have me a little confused there," said Harbaksh, "what are you driving at?"

"What I'm implying is that miracles, that is, violations of the Laws of Nature, not just the laws we know, but all of them, even those of which we are presently unaware; or, stated more simply, impossible events, cannot happen. Existence is not capricious. It obeys certain rules, and since that is so, there cannot be an omnipotent entity because, for it to be truly omnipotent, it would have to violate the rules. It would require the impossible to be possible. And that, you can see, would make nonsense not only of reason, but of language too. After all, the impossible is termed that because it is impossible, meaning that it cannot happen."

"All right, let us forget about omnipotence. How about omniscience?"

"It's just as bad," I replied. "If he is omniscient, then he knows what will happen before it happens. Suppose he knows it is going to rain tomorrow. Now, if you also suppose that he is omnipotent, then he can make it so that it is sunny tomorrow. But if that were to happen, he would be wrong about it raining tomorrow, and hence he would not be omniscient. If it nonetheless rains tomorrow, then he could not be said to be omnipotent, because he could not make it sunny. It is either or, he cannot be both omnipotent and omniscient. In fact, he can be neither, because if you believe he is omniscient, you are stating that everything that is to happen in the future is already predetermined right from the beginning; just as if you roll a ball, the forces acting on the ball predetermine what will happen. What you are saying, in effect, is that whatever happens, it is out of his hands. Once the Universe was created, everything that was to happen was predetermined. The problem with that is that it eliminates the possibility of omnipotence, since nothing can be changed; and, as I have just shown a little earlier, it becomes nonsense since one cannot demonstrate a beginning, a time when the course of events was said to have been predetermined, that is, a Creation of Existence. Without that, the whole sorry scheme collapses. I do not enjoy saying it, Harbaksh, but that is the way it is."

"But I do wish to believe in a Creator, a benevolent being who looks after us all."

"And lets us die too? Come on, if you want to look at his handiwork, you have to look at everything. They say there is a sentence—I'm not sure that there really is—in the Koran, which states: "do not read the Koran, while under the influence (of alcohol, or whatever)." Now you cannot just read the first phrase: "do not read the Koran," and leave it at that. It would be dishonest. In the same way, you cannot confine yourself to benevolence; you have to take the world as it is, the good with the bad. Now do you wish to believe in a Creator who is both benevolent and malevolent?"

"Perhaps not," he conceded, "but it is sad to contemplate his demise."

"No, not demise. That would be possible only if he exists; but if an omnipotent, omniscient being actually exists, then there is no question of a demise."

"You won't let up, will you?" he said, finally conceding the argument.

"I owe you too much for that. Besides, it was your book," I replied.

Preeti had stopped her sketching, and was standing there listening to us. She had been obviously engrossed in the intricacies of our discussion, and now wished to sum up her feelings: "I love the both of you," she said, "why could there not be more of you?"

"Because it would violate the Law of Identity," I replied, chuckling, making light of a truth she had dared to state, even if so obliquely.

Harbaksh did not evade her statement. He went up and hugged her. "It is good to know someone who loves so much," he said. Then, turning towards the house, he announced: "I believe tea must be ready."

But I could not help getting one back at Preeti. Walking up to her, I asked softly: "Is it polyandry you have on your mind?"

"Hush," she said, "you would not take advantage of a woman in love, would you?"

"I would," I replied, "but this is neither the time nor the place. Later, may be."

She squeezed my hand, then furtively brushed my rump. By then, we had all walked back into the porch where Mohini had just brought tea.

The days passed wonderfully slow, as if Nature intended our honeymoon to last forever. One day, Preeti and I walked over to the meadow where she had taught me the waltz. We had a picnic as before, but this time we had brought along a bottle of red wine coaxed out from Harbaksh. It sat there on the lightly decorated sheet, which we were using to sit on, flanked by half-empty wineglasses. As if planned, there was also a crystal bowl with moist grapes lending an ambience that was most becoming—straight out of Omar Khayyam, I thought:. "A jug of wine, A loaf of bread, and Thou beside me sitting in the Wilderness; Ah! Wilderness were Paradise enow."

Preeti sat there, a winsome lass, a Paradisian houri, one among many beautiful things, and asked me to sketch her. Then she completed the scene with me in it. As the afternoon wore on, she painted in the colors. In a few hours, the basic outline of the painting was complete. The rest could be done at the house. She named it "The Picnic."

"Darling," she said when she was done painting, "I would like us to do something interesting."

"Such as?" I asked.

"Making love," she replied, quite unabashed.

I looked at the trees, then at the path we had come up, then around at the mountains. "I don't have a condom," I said.

"I do," she replied.

"Are you not afraid someone may come by?"

"Yes," she replied, "that is why I want to do it."

I was not quite sure what she meant, and it showed in my expression.

"You know," she explained, "one always talks of freedom, but never quite has it. We tend always to remain captives of society's mores and taboos. I was born naked, and so were you: and but for these clothes, and hair here and there, I am still naked. Why then does society want me to be ashamed of it? With you near me, I feel safe enough to defy it and feel how it is to be myself, just myself, without cover. Every animal is beautiful just as it is, only we try to wrap ourselves up like manikins to create an artificial beauty."

The message and desire were clear. "Do you want me to take your clothes off?" I asked.

"No, I want to do it myself."

So saying, she disrobed completely, and strolled around the meadow, through sun and shade, a naked woman in her natural element. I could see that she was still restrained, as if yet learning to walk. The feel of the breeze on her naked breasts, and her belly, and her thighs, it must have felt strange.

"Would it help if we danced?" I asked, "The body feels nicest when it expresses in movement what the mind senses in thought.

So we danced, I fully dressed, she fully naked. After a while, she let go my hand, spun out of my arms, and danced around the meadow all by herself, as if in a ballet. She was no ballerina, but the beauty of movement is in us all. How well we do it rests on the perfection with which we envision it in the mind, and then how faithfully we command our body to do what the mind has conceived. She soon came running up to me in small steps, light as a feather. Without seeing them, I could sense the shimmering of her buttocks as she closed in, and it took all my will to keep a hold of myself.

"Preeti," I implored, "why are you doing this to me?"

She laughed. "Because I have to. I have to feel one with someone, and you are the one."

She then indicated for me to disrobe as well, saying: "I know it is more difficult for a man than a woman to feel one with Nature, but I want you to try."

I was not sure I could. We men pride ourselves on our strength. We think of ourselves as rocks that can withstand any force of nature. We are there to defend; but to exult, to feel the pleasure of simply being free, without any challenge to face, that does not come easy. Women are closer to Nature, for they deal with such things as having babies. There is no dignified way to have a baby; you just have to descend to the appropriate level of Nature; nothing less will do. The fault is not in Nature; it is in what we believe to be dignified. Similarly, men assume that a naked man cannot be dignified, but a woman can be. We worry about things one cannot control. Avoiding them tenses us, and there goes the feeling of release. I determined to relax, not try to stop what might happen on its own. I would let my body do whatever it wished. Perhaps then I might experience what it means to be free.

I had never been naked out in the open. The feeling was like a tingling of my fiber, completely fresh and overwhelming. We walked hand in hand, barefoot. She stopped, opened the hair tied in a knot (joorhha) on the top of my head, and let it loose. I shook my head, letting the hair fall.

"There," she said, "you are as Nature intended you to be."

Then we danced again, the same waltz that we had danced so long ago in an age when we were merely acquaintances probing at love. This time, though, she hummed along with me, as it should be, man and woman, husband and wife, partners in pleasure. But as I looked into her eyes, something was happening to me again in nether places. I let it happen till it prod her belly.

"Preeti," I pleaded, "can we stop dancing."

"No," she replied, "today is my day, and you must do my bidding. I love you too much to let you hide yourself in me so soon. You must be more than bodily naked to me; you must be naked in your soul too. You must give yourself up, be whatever I wish you to be, at my pleasure. You must not have a care in the world; just surrender into my hands and let me play with you. You must be for me what you are to me, my most consuming obsession, my only obsession."

And she continued dancing, mercilessly. Then, when all seemed lost, she threw me down on the grass. I closed my eyes as she sat down on top and lowered herself on to me. When I opened them, there I lay, flat on my back, my knees pulled up, looking at her naked beauty. Her breasts lifted as she lifted her arms out to the wind, and with her face worshipped the sun. I thrust into her while she stretched her body up, daring me to cup her breasts. I was making sounds of pain when there was no pain, just an anguish that was the most intense of pleasures. She was too, but soon she collapsed as I came to a climax, lowering herself on to my torso, crying with deep gasps, wordless sounds of pain and pleasure, till it was over and she sank down on me and rested.

When I awoke some time later, I noticed the cool breeze on my naked limbs, and the coolness of her skin as she lay crouched on top. I was out, and lo and behold, I had on a condom. When and how she put it on I could not recall, but somehow she had kept her head when all was lost to me. My fear was over even before it began.

I don't know if you have noticed, but the period you awake some time after sex is one of profound thought. The body is satisfied and utterly relaxed, and so is the mind. Thoughts proceed undisturbed by other concerns, and so it was with me. There was no question of Preeti's delight at shedding her clothes and wandering the meadow all by her 'unaccompanied self,' as she had put it, unaccompanied by the weight of propriety and that which is paraded as proper. She was not special in any way, except that I loved her, and she was beautiful, even heavenly. Did it then not imply that all women, and men too for that matter, would have similar desires, and would revel in them the same way? They may not accept the possibility of accommodating these desires as easily, but they would have them nonetheless.

But what of those who so sternly enforce the dress codes? It was not likely Preeti would ever get to wear shorts in India. She may have in the closed environment of her boarding school, but in the real world outside, she would not stand a chance. The insults people would heap on her would bring her to tears, and make her swear never to leave her home. How about skirts? Well, in convent schools, young Indian girls did wear frocks as uniforms, and even skirts, but wearing one in public when you were beyond the age of, say, sixteen, would be much worse than wearing shorts. People would not only be rude to you, you would also be ostracized, as if you had converted to Christianity, and were deliberately insulting your culture. But why was our culture so frail, so easily wounded?

I had often wondered at why this widespread distaste of Christianity and 'western' ways. It applied only to Indians, never to foreigners. Perhaps most of the converts to that religion, at least in North India, were from the lowest castes, the untouchables. They had converted because it brought favors from the British rulers, thus allowing the otherwise impossible transition from utter despair to a life of reasonable comfort and security. This knowledge, that most converts to Christianity once belonged to the lowest caste, was not lost on the Hindus, and perhaps a few Sikhs felt it the same way, though in my experience to a lesser degree. Now that the British were gone, I wondered how these Indian Christians would fare. The few I knew kept a low profile.

The next morning it was almost four days since I had sent my article to the National Express. The editor must have it now, I thought; maybe he was even reading it. I wished I could read his thoughts, that I was omniscient; but you cannot just wish and then have.

Harbaksh and I were sitting drinking tea. This beverage brings out the thinker in me, and so too in Harbaksh. I had read a lot more philosophy, and a philosophical discussion was overdue anyway. It was not surprising then that he turned to me and asked: "In your article, you mentioned that there is no such thing as the soul. What makes you so sure? After all, it cannot be seen or sensed. How then could you know that it does not exist?"

"That's easy," I replied, "there is a philosophical rule that whenever the existence of anything is proposed, the onus of proof lies with the proposer. In this case, since you suggest that there is a 'soul,' you must furnish the evidence and proof behind your assertion. I can only be asked to refute the evidence or line of reasoning that you present, but I cannot be asked, in the absence of proffered evidence, to prove the absence of something that I believe does not exist. Now, do you have any evidence for your proposal?"

"No, not really, except to say that almost everybody believes in it. You don't really expect the two or more billion people on the face of this Earth, most of whom believe in the soul, to all be wrong?"

"If they have no evidence, then yes, I would assert that they are all wrong," I replied.

"But you do realize the implications of what you are saying?" he asked. "If there is no soul, then everything based on its existence is as naught."

"Yes," I agreed, "an edifice built on a false premise is by definition false and totally untenable. It is irrelevant how faithful to logic and reason its proponents may be after that initial premise, because a house built on a foundation of cardboard must of necessity collapse."

"But why cannot there be a soul, that little spark of perfection in us all?"

"I wish you had not said that," I replied. "It betrays a notion, perhaps only subconscious, that everything else about us, meaning everything for whose existence evidence exists, is imperfect. Why would you wish only the nonexistent to be perfect? Isn't it the saddest thought for a mind to harbor?"

"I have a healthy respect for the body," he countered, trying to defend himself, "but you can see for yourself that it is not perfect. It ages, decays, and ultimately dies, and every now and then falls ill."

"That is true," I conceded, "but that is the way it is supposed to be. It would be imperfect if it were not. Its perfection lies in its variety, in its infinite variability, in its ability to surprise us every now and then. View it as the dynamic process that it is, never the same, ever changing; and age, that remorseless engine of consumption that we all decry, why, it is but a dating of the continuing variation that is life. We dislike death, but it too has a perfection in that it is inexorable and inevitable. We marvel at the transformation of the inanimate to the animate, the inorganic to food and on to living tissue; why not at the reverse, which is death? Wedded to life as we are, our frame of reference is life. Its loss pains us, but that by itself is not enough to decry it as imperfect.

"Immortality is a yearning, not necessarily an indicator of perfection. To yearn is one thing; it does not follow *pari passu* that what we yearn for is perfect. Immortality, once achieved, may turn out to be ennui, a state of satiety, not Paradise. There could be nothing more boring than Eternity. It would be like a phonograph record stuck in a groove. Remember, perfection would mean that nothing else would change either. Trees and shrubs would be in perpetual bloom, leaves would never fall; there would be no seasons, no floods, no destructive storms, no dust, nothing that you might view as a blemish. Then a time would come when you would begin to yearn for blemishes: bleak, wintry landscapes; snow; rocky, treeless plains; a woman who is hard to win; the challenge of uncertainty; everything you now view as imperfect.

"But we are going astray. The real question before us is not whether the soul is perfect, but whether it exists at all. To answer that, we have to be clear about what we mean by it. Could you give me some definition, anything tangible that you can conceive about it?"

"For one," replied Harbaksh, "the soul is nonmaterial."

"That tells me nothing," I replied, "for I cannot think of an entity that is not material, in the sense that it is not susceptible to the senses. Both matter and energy have properties that can be sensed, or their presence indirectly inferred, but for something to be nonmaterial means that it has no properties that are detectable because, if it is detectable, then it is not nonmaterial."

"But can you not conceive of an independent spirit, something existing outside the body, or even inside in the sense that it permeates it?"

"If you are talking of the mind, of consciousness, it does exist; in fact, I would insist that it does, because if it does not, I don't know who else in us is doing this discussing."

"All right," Harbaksh agreed, "let us accept that the mind is the soul."

"But then," I countered, "all the evidence points to the fact that the mind operates only so long as the body is alive; to be more precise, the brain is alive, but ceases to show any evidence of its existence after the brain dies. I, for one, and I'm sure everybody else too who has looked dispassionately at the problem, have found no evidence of a mind existing independent of the body. Look at it this way: if you propose that the soul or, as you have agreed, the mind, exists irrespective of the existence of the body, then you have postulated something which can have no detectable properties; that because it is nonmaterial. If that is so, then it has no identity, because identity is just the sum of its identifiable properties; which means that, by definition, it does not exist. Everything in Existence has identity. That which has no identity cannot be part of Existence, meaning that it does not exist. Q. E. D., Quod Erat Demonstrandum: that which was to be proved, has been; or, Quite Easily Done, as we used to say in school."

Harbaksh smiled at me. "I'm impressed, and convinced. Where did you learn to argue so well? he asked.

"In the Debating Society in school. Mr. Whyte ensured that we all learned the rules of logic well; they were drilled into us by force of argument, argument with him. He was merciless, permitting no detours, no cheating like the kind which all those who believe in a soul do. Perhaps I have honed my skills since then, but most of it I owe to him."

"Your argument is convincing and, as I am a man of reason, I feel compelled to accept it," said Harbaksh, "but something troubles me about such an acceptance. Look at all the religions of the world. They spend an inordinate amount of effort trying to convince you to value your soul, to look after its interests, in the present within the body; and in the hereafter in Heaven; or in Hell, or Purgatory, where it is cleansed by expiatory suffering and where it will know no rest; or in unity with the Universal Soul; or in its voyage of transmigration into the same or another body. If there is no soul, they are simply making a fool of themselves and of us in the bargain."

"Mostly of us," I rejoined, "perhaps of themselves too if you grant that they are honest. But many of them are not. They are simply con artists operating on the grandest scale, almost unchallenged, and for the longest period the Earth has seen."

"Is that why you prefer to call yourself an atheist?"

"Well, I want to make sure you understand me right when I say that I am an atheist. Atheism is not some sort of religion like all the others. It is the absence of one. If there were no religions, an atheist would simply be an ordinary human being just like anyone else. He would not have to carry any special label such as 'atheist.' He would never have to discuss vacuous things such as the nonmaterial, because such ideas would be considered self-evidently absurd. But religion has messed up that perspective on the atheist. He is no longer considered just a human being, but a disagreeable one who insists on differing from most of the others. He is considered an outcaste, and this primarily because all the others believe themselves to be special, in that they are religious human beings, not just ordinary ones. Who would have ever thought that the irrational would pride themselves on their irrationality, and make pariahs of those who remain rational? This book of yours had a most interesting quote which more or less sums up the attitude of the religious, the God-believers, the believers in the nonmaterial. The ascetic Tertullian, from the early centuries of Christianity, asked why he believed in God, is reported to have said: "Credo quia absurdum," meaning "I believe because it is absurd." That, you must agree, is the ultimate arrogance of the religious."

XVI

Though not a practitioner of religion in the literal sense, Harbaksh nevertheless gave its proponents the benefit of the doubt and assumed that they were "good". He further assumed, that the teachings of religion were the basis of man's moral foundations. My doubts were now revealing cracks in these assumptions.

I often wondered about the value of theologically inspired codes of ethics. Religion per se was based on the irrational. The religious did not deny it, even taking pride in their irrationality and the acceptance of their beliefs on faith, a process they themselves defined as acceptance without rational evidence or proof. For them to question was to display a lack of faith. But why such a willingness to believe? In everyday survival, they would never trust their worldly valuables to anyone without meticulously checking his credentials, and they all hailed the laws against fraud and theft. Why then were they willing to be duped in the far more important intellectual sphere? Could it be that the mental, the spiritual, being more intangible, was the less important of the two, so why bother checking? In their teachings, they disparaged the everyday world and assigned all importance to the spiritual. But their actions belied their professed teachings: they seemed to demand proof of trustworthiness only in the worldly sphere, not in the spiritual.

Something even more fundamental concerned me. I had found no basis for the belief in a supernatural being, or any other nonmaterial entities, such as the soul; and neither to my knowledge had they. Why then propose their existence? What had they to gain? What was the need for these entities? Experience showed that no good ever came from pursuing the irrational. It solved no problems, created more, and seriously damaged one's grasp of reality, the relationship of things to one another, and one's skill in the use of reason and logic. As far as could be assessed, the nonmaterial had a very definite negative survival value. Why then would someone so fervently pursue it? Here again, as with the concept of arranged marriages and the dowry, the motives of small fry were easy to fathom. If miracles could happen, if wishes could be horses, if such could be granted by an omnipotent being, it paid to subscribe to such a belief.

For those who have neglected it all their lives, the act of thinking and reasoning is trying indeed. But if it could be replaced with begging or wheedling, then why bother with reason? All you had to do was to fervently believe in an all-powerful being who could not only grant wishes, but was also susceptible to flattery, the more absurdly outrageous the better. Witness the praises heaped on him in the act of supplication we term prayer. To reinforce the effect, we go so far as to do it on bended knees, or with forehead to the ground.

For the intellectually adept, however, this explanation makes no sense, as they are not fools. They are likely to know that irrationality begets only the irrational; that reality rolls on pitilessly and majestically, totally unmindful of piety, or wit, or tears; that the fruit of the irrational is itself irrational, and so of little value. But wait! This must imply that their codes of ethics too must be irrational. After all, they are derived from the irrational; or are they? What if they had evolved in the secular culture and then been smuggled in? The irrational would have no qualms about theft and misrepresentation. A cursory overview reveals no obvious flaw in the codes. Murder, after all, is reprehensible, as are theft, lying and cheating.

But Nature is not capricious. The Law of Causality has no exceptions, so bad causes breed bad ends. The only question is, which causes? I lacked the answer, but perhaps Harbaksh could help, so I posed the question to him.

"Look, kid," he said, "I don't have the answer, but I do have all the books you will need, written by the finest minds. Read them, understand them, and examine them, for somewhere within them is the answer to your question."

I looked at the books and realized that there was a lot to read. Besides, I was not one with infinite patience. At eighteen, you want your answers right away. I could attempt to wade through a variety of commentaries on the scriptures, but it seemed neither wise nor necessary. If their basis was flawed, did it make sense allotting so much of my precious time to the pointless musings of countless mystics? The data I needed would come from studying the rational. Who better to ask for help than Preeti? She had few preconceived notions and, as a woman, was much closer to reality. She worked daily for survival, like all women do, or at least most of them, so it was unlikely she would stray too far off the mark for what I needed to know.

When asked, her suggestion was: "Why don't you just try to see what would happen if there were no religion or religious teachings? Begin with the first thing in the morning."

"You mean like walking around the dahlia patch and drinking tea?" I asked.

"No, even earlier."

"Like in bed?" I asked.

"Yes, that is the way the day starts, is it not?"

"Okay," I said, "I awake and find myself in bed with you."

"What happens then?" she asked.

"I touch you. You are naked and warm, and we begin to make love."

"You have a one-track mind, don't you?" she commented.

"Well, what do you expect of me? I am no masochist, you know."

"Calm down, calm down, I am not complaining. I am merely stating for the record that you don't think of very much else when you are with me."

"Yes, that is true," I conceded.

"Now, if this were a religious household, would you do anything different?"

"Yes, I would be saying my morning prayers."

"To save your manly soul from me?"

Seeing my look of exasperation, she turned more serious. "So far, then, we have seen that morning prayers are not something that would come in the natural course of events. They also interfere with one's most basic needs, namely the desire to make love, if not all the time, at least in the morning."

"What are you driving at, Preeti?" I asked, not really upset, but a little unnerved at the ease with which she had taken my mind off the weightier concerns of life.

"We are just going through the day item by item. But, if you don't object, let us stay for a moment with making love first thing in the morning. Do you think the religious approve of love?"

"Are you kidding! They hate it! They have even tried to change its meaning. It is the most self-interested thing anyone ever does. There is no way they could control a person who violates their exhortations so blatantly. 'Thou shalt live for the sake of others', they preach. When you make love, if you are doing it for others, you sure are making them pay a heavy price. No, there is no way they can approve of romantic love. What they call love is a feeble, totally deluded hallucination in which you pretend to love a nonmaterial entity, and that entity in return loves you. No, not quite. That entity, they say, loves you unconditionally, all the time, whether you love him, it, whatever, or not."

"At least they could have made God a woman for you men. It would be more natural and interesting," Preeti offered.

"As a matter of fact, it once was," I replied. "The Mother Goddess. Remember the Indus Valley civilization?"

"That was in the good old days, when men were closer to Nature," she explained, "but now that men are further removed from the concerns of life, they will accept anything, even a male God."

"But, Preeti, they are not talking of romantic or sexual love. They are talking of something entirely different," I protested.

"Like the love between comrades-in-arms, who would sacrifice their life for each other if need be?" she asked.

"No. An omnipotent God does not need your sacrifice. He cannot be threatened in any way."

"So then how are you supposed to express your love for him?"

"By obeying him."

"But, husband dear, he does not talk to you. You cannot even sense him."

"His commands are in writing, in the scriptures," I explained.

"You don't seriously believe that they come from him, or her, or it, do you?" she asked.

"No, of course not, they were conceived and written by men."

"Who," she continued, "were dishonest enough to ascribe them to someone you could not argue with. Obviously, they wanted no dissent. They were pulling the wool over your eyes. They were up to something no good."

"That figures," I said, "why else would they need a phony author, one who could not even be contacted?"

"If I know men, they are either fools or a bunch of bastards, with the exception of you and Harbaksh, of course, and perhaps a few other souls."

"What do you think they were up to?" I asked, visibly impressed with her no-nonsense, earthy way of getting down to the heart of the problem. Harbaksh and I, in all this time, had achieved very little, primarily because we were too polite to call a spade a spade, to call liars liars.

"They wanted you to do something; on second thought, many things considering the sheer volume of the scriptures, that were not in your interest. If they were, there would be no need for an unquestionable authority. They could simply inform you, and the sheer logic of the argument would be enough to win your acceptance."

"Okay," I said, "I accept your thesis. We men were bamboozled by a bunch of jokers. But what about you women? How did they get you?"

"It is interesting that you ask. You may have noticed that if a woman wants to, she can use her wiles and her not inconsiderable charms to bring her man back to the straight and narrow path which is love, rather than letting him stray all over the barren desert seeking fruit where none exists. So she has to be muzzled. The Christians did it quite simply. They portrayed Eve as the temptress, the one who could, with her womanly lures, inexorably draw you away from the 'goodness' preached by the mystics. They were even afraid to suggest that her charms lay in herself, lest men realize what they were giving up; they sublimated them in the apple, and added a henchman, the Serpent, to boot."

"I don't believe it really was an apple; it was actually the fruit of the Tree of Knowledge of Good and Evil."

"They like to say the knowledge of Good and Evil, but what they really meant was the knowledge of Reality, the knowledge that makes you independent and permits you to survive on your own," she explained.

"It makes sense," I agreed, "but what about in our Indian religions?"

"I could give you a wonderfully chauvinistic quote which says it all. It is from the Atharv Vaid, and I quote: 'Enjoying love, children, fortune, wealth, by being always behind thy husband in his life's vocation, gird thyself for immortality.'"

Her sarcasm was not lost on me. "So you achieve immortality secondhand?" I asked.

"Yes, we must help our husbands attain it first. Only then can we achieve it. If he does not make it, neither do we. To put it more personally, if I try to be happy and independent, I am not only destroying my own chances for immortality, I am jeopardizing yours as well."

"But why should your happiness be an impediment to mine? If you were unhappy, my happiness would be destroyed too."

"Not according to the scriptures," she replied. "My happiness, if you can call it that, must only come from your achievements, not my own. The only ones of my own that are good for me are those which were made in your interest." She stopped for a moment, then continued, "Can you imagine how it is in a polyandrous marriage? Just think of it, a wife having to get three men through immortality all by her single self!"

Her colorful examples were amusing, but also enlightening, so I said, "I like your analysis, Preeti. It makes a lot of sense."

"Of course it does. Eveything about me makes a lot of sense, or have you forgotten?"

"No, I cannot forget. You are too good to be true."

"Darling, truth is much too good to be believed. What you see and admire is true. That is why you cannot forget." She let that sink in, then continued, "have you noticed how, among the village folk, and those of the older generation, especially where the women are illiterate and, in this way, totally dependent on their husbands for survival; how in those circumstances, they always walk several paces behind their husbands? In our society, men and women do not hum the *Blue Danube* together—the husband does it first, and the wife follows. They are not partners, but employer and employee, master and servant. A husband who concedes equal status to the wife, as you seem to, violates the spirit of the scriptures, violates the norms of our culture, threatens the rights of all men, and not just his own immortality, but the very survival of our system. He threatens to bring reason into his life, even into his bed, and banish the mystics and their God to the nonexistence they crave."

"Bravo, Preeti," I cheered, "that was beautiful. You force me to say something I never tire of saying."

"What might that be, my husband and companion?"

"I love you."

She caressed me gently on the cheek. "Stay with me. We will go a long way."

"I intend to," I said, "we'll breakfast on love and sex every morning, may be sometimes at lunch, and certainly after dinner."

We both sat silently, satisfied with our efforts, enjoying the pleasure of being together. Then she smiled slyly, as though some thought had just entered her mind.

"You know," she said, "this reminds me of the first time I was being married. There I was sitting next to Inder, and the *Bhaeeji* (Sikh priest) was lecturing us on how we should behave towards each other. You would think it was some sort of class in sex education for just the two of us, but done openly in the presence of a couple of hundred witnesses. Well, he spent most of the time on me, haranguing me never to forget how it was my duty to keep Inder happy, how I must not think of anything else in life but him. I must banish from my mind the thought of other men, for they no longer were my concern. If I was to believe his words, my world would be narrowed to the confines of the house, mostly the kitchen and the bedroom, and its other occupant, my husband. Everything else was as good as dead."

"What was his advice to Inder?" I asked.

"He was to bring home the bacon," she replied.

"That's it?" I asked, astonished at its brevity.

"More or less," she said. "Of course, there was a lot of nonsense about how he was to take care of me, and love me, and teach me the right path in life. After all, the husband is the wife's guidance through the pitfalls of human existence. In the process, while he was doing all that, I was to bear him children, and rear them, teaching them unquestionable obedience to his every whim and wish. Oh, what a lot of hot air! Here was a man giving advice, unasked for, to two well-educated, modern individuals, while at the same time anyone could see he knew not the slightest thing about love and happiness. He was, after all, the staunchest upholder of our culture. You know, a civil marriage beats a religious ceremony any day. There is absolutely no comparison."

"May be you say that because you are in love with me," I suggested.

"Not that alone," she replied, "there is an honesty and intimacy to a quiet civil marriage that is totally missing from a big religious, and very public, affair. You know why all the relatives and friends are really there? It is to bear witness, to make sure the husband does not just walk out on you later. You would think it was something you and he were being compelled to do, to get married."

"Well, you are not far off the mark there, are you?" I commented.

"Yes, may be not. You are right. In most arranged marriages, it is a kind of giving in, by one or both of the participants. They are giving up on romantic dreams, on wanting the very best for themselves. They are settling for a compromise. It is in essence a loss of integrity. What an awful way to start a new life!"

"Yes," I agreed, "we are only talking of the better arranged marriages. Look at what happens to the poor, the seventy or eighty percent of Indians who barely make ends meet. The marriages there are almost all a total exercise in compulsion, particularly where the girl is concerned. She marries whomsoever her father wishes her to, and that is that. Pitaji (daddy) is physically stronger, and he controls the meager supply of money. There is not much she can answer to an argument like that."

We were quiet again for a little while, and then I asked, "You mentioned earlier that most men are either fools or bastards. Which one was Inder?"

"Fortunately the former. He did get increasingly drunk as wisdom dawned on him and he realized what he had got himself into, but he never hit me. I truly felt sorry for him when he got himself killed. I was not demolished with grief, but I did feel sorry. I remember how so many commented on how well I was bearing my loss. Little did they know that my sorrow was not for a loved one; it was merely for the loss of a human life. He might have made a good husband for another woman, but he had married me, not that other woman. It was such a waste, and I felt bad. Our marriage was a total failure, but I was depressed, not relieved, at his dying.

I was sorry for what she had had to go through, so I waited a while before continuing with our conversation. "Would you care to sum up your thoughts?" I said finally, wondering what she would do next with that wondrous and wonderfully housed intellect of hers.

"I could say it this way," she answered. "Everything has to do with obedience. A wife must obey her husband, unconditionally, absolutely. Given that tenor of thought, the philosophic basis of the Indian method of attaining immortality is this: you be an ideal wife to God, and I will be an ideal wife to you. This way we will both achieve the ultimate."

"Which is?" I asked.

"Union with him; the utter loss of our independent identity; our dissolution, not simply a dissolving. We would cease to exist, with no way of ever being re-separated. And that, husband, is what is termed eternal bliss, not the superlative sexual orgasm that you and I have been so stupidly assuming."

She was right, and I nodded my head in agreement. It pretty much laid to rest what little respect I might have had for the scriptures.

"Well," I said, seeing that we had reached a sort of endpoint, "what do we do now?"

"We can move from the bedroom to breakfast, in the intellectual sense, or we could literally have breakfast."

"That is a stellar idea," I agreed. "Let us eat."

"Now that I have enlightened you so much," she said, "do you think you would like to practice what I preach? Would you like to learn how to make breakfast?"

"If Mohini does not object, I would love to. At least I can then see how the other half lives."

So I was given my first lesson, actually a hands-on lab session, in making eggs and toast, and oatmeal. The servant yielded to the mistress and desisted from helping me. He could not, of course, wipe the smirk off his face, and I could well imagine what he was thinking: 'Why would an educated man want to do the work of a wife, especially when she is still alive? The ways of modern men are strange indeed. They let the wife walk beside them, even let her talk to other men in their presence, and sometimes even let these others hold her and dance with her. Do they not care that she might get tempted away, that she might start thinking of other men? Why give a woman ideas when you don't have to?'

But I knew better: a woman without ideas is not a woman worth marrying.

XVII

"S **teeped in Violence."** I typed it in as the title of my next article. This was going to be easy because there was so much personal experience. I began:

"The land of Gandhi is a land of violence."

Preeti came and sat down beside me, glanced at the paper, then looked inquiringly at me.

"There is so much from my own life alone that I'm not sure where to begin," I explained.

"Perhaps you should start by telling me the story of your childhood," she suggested. "This way you can sort out your thoughts."

So I narrated the story to her:

I was born in Lahore, which is now in the Pakistan part of Punjab, at home, like almost all Indians of that time. There was another one of me, a twin, but he died soon after birth, sullying my arrival with the dark hand of death.

Life was peaceful till the age of four or five. Then war broke out all over the world. One relative died in Singapore; another on a bombing raid in Norway; others were still fighting the Japanese in Burma. But at that age, death held no terror; it was barely understood. All I can remember is how my friends and I used to invent stories of the bravery of our relatives and other Sikh soldiers of the Indian army. We literally believed in Guru Gobind Singh's symbolic claim that one Sikh could fight a legion, to back which we spent a lot of time tabulating the number of Victoria crosses that our community had won. The exploits of Sikh soldiers, often true, but more often greatly embellished by us, were always glorious. Then there was the booty of war, such as when an uncle came back with a sword belonging to a Japanese officer who had been killed in a battle with a Sikh regiment. It had a hilt decorated with inlaid ivory. The officer's death did not, at the time, bother us because death was not something awful, it was simply something that happened in war. I am not sure if we even associated physical pain with it, but death's occurrence in war was always glorious, war itself being simply conceived as a game, a test of strength if you will, like a wrestling match.

We frequently argued among ourselves about which was the most powerful nation on Earth. The consensus was Roos (Russia). It was difficult to think otherwise given the vast expanse of green representing it in my elder brother's atlas. Any country that big had to be powerful. We had no notion of an economy, or poverty, or technological achievement, or even of freedom. We were a colony of Britain, but Roos was ruled by Russians, so a free country; its people, it followed, must be proud and happy. One of my uncles was so enamored of leftist propaganda at the time that he even became a member of the Communist Party. When he later learned what communism really was in practice, he quit; but at the time, the slogan of equality, seen as it was from the perspective of a subjugated people, was irresistibly appealing. So it was not surprising that we rooted for Roos against Hitler. Besides, even the British were friends of the Roosees, so why not us?

Every summer, I vacationed at Dagshai with my uncles. Neither Beeji nor Papaji ever accompanied my brother and I on these vacations. Papaji never took a break from his work in Lahore. Beeji did take a few days off to take us to the princely city of Patiala, where my grandfather lived, but then she would go straight back to Lahore to look after her patients and my father who, unfortunately for her, really needed looking after. He did not even know how to buy cloth for a shirt. It was easy enough, because all he wore were white shirts, and all he had to know was what material to choose. But he never learned, primarily because there was no need to. The way he looked at life, he had his work and his teekas (learned commentaries on the Sikh scriptures) to keep him busy, and my mother could take care of his clothes.

Our tailor was a Mussalman, a Pathan, one of those fierce people from the Northwest Frontier Province, the arid, mountainous region between Punjab and Afghanistan. He was a big man, but really not fierce. Given their beards and size, my uncles from my father's village looked far more daunting, and considering the way of life in those areas like Faridkot and Ferozepur, there was reason to fear them. The appellation, 'The Wild West of India,' for that tract of land was not inappropriate. Murder and daring armed robberies by dacoit gangs were not at all uncommon, and then there was the code of revenge, much like that in Sicily. It was a matter of honor among Jat Sikhs (Jat means farmer) that a crime against you or even an insult must never go un-avenged. The fights were mostly over water and land, since most Sikhs are Jats. It is said that a Jat spends one third of his life farming, another one-third taking revenge, and the rest in court. But this is a gross exaggeration. My uncles were gentle people who would never pick a fight unless there was extreme provocation. They all did own guns, but these were mostly for hunting; and for protection too, of course. Only dacoits, usually ex-army men with dishonorable discharges, used guns for crime. The rest were hard-working farmers, and when you have worked hard for what you have, you protect it with your life. There was no other reason to be fierce, for the code of honor was essentially the code of property rights.

With the end of the war, things began to change in Lahore. At first, there were the victory celebrations. Being such a major part of the army, these were a matter of pride among the Sikhs. I remember my father taking me to the huge Tattoo the British had organized at the Maidaan, which was a huge, open field used for such events, and for other public functions, including the circus. There were mock battles with tanks, the noise of shelling, and low fly-overs of airplanes over the crowds. I remember one of the planes was a night bomber, painted black. It was said to have radar in its black nose-cone. Then there was the unfortunate episode of Wing-Commander Majoomdaar. This was later in the afternoon on our way back from the tattoo. This pilot was doing aerobatic maneuvers over the city and he even flew over our apartment complex. Something must have gone wrong because rumors began to circulate that he had crashed. My brother and I ran over to the Mall Road. Away in the distance, there was smoke. The plane had hit the Filetti's hotel, near the Malka Boot (Victoria's statue). By the time we reached the scene, the police had cordoned off the wreckage. Pieces of the fuselage were scattered about the grounds and on the roof of the two-storeyed hotel. A large portion of a wing lay close by and the pilot, we heard, was dead.

That was the last of the celebrations. The freedom processions began soon after that. There were big meetings, invariably followed by processions through the streets. One day after school, my brother and I went to the Mall Road to see one such march. There must have been over fifty thousand people, all shouting 'Inqilaab Zindabaad' (Urdu for 'long live the revolution'). Suddenly, out of nowhere, shots broke out, not quite as loud as rifle fire, soon followed by white smoke. It was tear gas! We ran, but it was too late. The gas overtook us, stinging our eyes, and we spent the entire evening sitting at the water taps, trying to wash the irritant out of our eyes with cold water and ice wrapped in handkerchiefs, but to no avail. It reminded me of the time in Dagshai a few years earlier when I had rubbed my sleepy eyes with chili-contaminated hands. This was my introduction to political activity and crowds.

There followed days with curfew: you could not go into the street, and the assembly of three or more people was banned. We used to wonder whether children were exempt; surely the police would not shoot at us harmless children. But we never put our belief to the test; we only watched. My father had made it crystal clear that we had to stay home, and stay out of trouble; and when father said something, disobeying was out of the question. His disciplinary fervor was exceptional, and his slaps resounding.

One day, an Englishman was stabbed to death as he and his mame-sahib (an English wife) were coming out of the Regal cinema down the block from where we lived. Soon we were beginning to hear rumors of stabbings of British officers and civilians every day. Lahore was not the land of Gandhi. Peaceful, nonviolent resistance was unnatural here, had never been the way of the Punjabis, nor would it ever be. Gandhi was paid lip service, except among Congress party members. The Punjabi heroes were revolutionaries and those who avenged grievous wrongs. One such was the young Sikh, Udham Singh, who followed Sir Michael O'Dwyer, the lieutenant-Governor of the Punjab who, I have learned to my chagrin, was also an alumnus of BCS, all the way to England, and shot him dead in 1940. The reason was his approval of the machine-gunning on Baisaakhi day, in the early 1920s, of a peaceful protest crowd, at Jallianwala Bagh in Amritsar, by General Dyer. It mattered little that Udham Singh was hanged after that, for he had kept the honor of the Punjabis.

By 1946, though, things were beginning to change. The Muslims now demanded an independent country of their own, Pakistan (the land of the pure). By pure, they meant purely Muslims; at least, that is what we felt. There may be another more enlightened interpretation, but in practice, and as far as the Hindus and Sikhs were concerned, it meant a country in which none of us would be permitted to exist. Events bore out this belief. The people being stabbed now were Hindus and Sikhs, not Englishmen.

One day in 1946, there was a headline in the Tribune: "Eighty Relatives of Justice Teja Singh Killed in Rawalpindi Area." How could anyone have eighty relatives, I wondered? Later, as I began to understand how we Sikhs all come from one village or another, and how almost everyone in a village is related to everyone else, the astounding size of the family became understandable.

Rawalpindi is situated near the Frontier Province, and was the first area where the Muslim League of Mr. Jinnah, the separatist leader of the Muslims, struck. Long lines of Pathans and Afridi tribesmen descended on the villages of the mostly shopkeeper Sikh communities around Rawalpindi, looting, burning and raping, and carrying away all the better-looking young women back as booty. I came to know of the savagery graphically from a book of photographs, 'The Rape of Rawalpindi,' which one of my brother's friends had somehow acquired. It was banned by the British, ostensibly to prevent an inflammatory reaction, though we suspected ulterior motives. A compilation of aerial photographs, it showed columns of gun-toting attackers burning villages, and dead bodies and ruins all over the place. Many among the Hindus and Sikhs wondered whether the British were beginning to take sides. What, we asked, had prevented them from sending in the army to stop these kabailis? Nothing, we concluded, except the satisfaction of seeing fratricide among the Punjabis; and no Englishmen were being killed any more.

By 1947, the religious trouble had reached Lahore. Stabbings of Hindus and Sikhs, and burning of their homes and shops were now occurring on a daily basis. We lived on Temple Road across from St. Anthony's School where I was a student. Close to us was the Muslim locality of the Mozung, a poor to lower middle class area. Long processions of salwaar-clad young Muslims, mostly factory workers and others of the blue-collar classes, began passing in front of our housing complex with increasing frequency, originating from the Mozung and headed towards the Mall Road. Salwaars, which among Sikhs and Hindus, are the pant-like lower part of ladies clothing, were the typical dress of Muslim men. Shouts of 'Pakistan Zindabaad' (long live Pakistan) and 'Allah-u-Akbar' (God is great, or something like that) were heard as they passed by. There was anger and determination in their mien and voices. Rumor had it that they all carried daggers tucked in under the upper ends of their salwaars.

It was my first real exposure to terror. Fear I had known before, with tear gas and the plane crash, but not terror. What if some of these burly men decided to break through the gate of our apartment complex? My imagination could envision them all going berserk and doing just that, making mincemeat of my family and me in no time at all, plundering our apartment, and setting fire to the buildings.

Then one hot night in April that year, about the time we were ready to fall asleep, there was a commotion in the Mozung about two hundred yards away from our house. Our beds were on the roof of the three-storey building, the ground floor of which we lived in. Besides being much cooler, there were less mosquitoes to bother us up on the roof than on the ground floor. My mother and father in those days used to sleep in their bedroom on the ground floor under a ceiling fan, not like in Delhi where they slept out in the yard with us all. They apparently still behaved like a married couple. Here up on the roof, we had an older cousin or an uncle or two with us.

From our vantage point on the roof, we could clearly see what was happening. A large crowd of salwaar-clad men was setting fire to a tonga, a horse-drawn passenger carriage which was then the mainstay of travelers wanting a ride within the city. They had taken the horse away, and then sprinkled petrol or kerosene on the tonga, and lighted it. Next they set fire to the small, narrow house of the tonga owner; he himself had obviously fled earlier. Their actions were initially puzzling. Seemingly not content with simply watching the house burn, they instead appeared to be actually trying to manage the fire. It soon became clear why.

Lahore is an ancient city, at least as old as Rome. Like Rome, it has legendary founders, Luv and Kush, the twin sons of Seeta, wife of Raam, the legendary God-King of the Hindus, and one of the incarnations of Vishnu. Rome has the Tiber, Lahore has the Ravi, but Lahore lacks hills; it is flat. In the center, there is the ancient, fortified, walled city, and then there is the part that grew around it later in the times of the British.

The Mozung, even though it is on the outside, very much resembles in the style of its buildings those of the walled city. The houses abut one on another, with intervening walls either common or very close to each other. The tonga-owner's house had side walls almost touching those of the neighboring Muslim homes, and it was this feature that had precipitated the frenetic attempts at containing the fire. Armed with long poles, the arsonists were pushing in the walls of the burning house into the flames to keep the latter from spreading. An hour later, the house had been completely gutted. Then the Fire Brigade arrived and put out what remained of the blaze. It appeared perfectly timed to save the Muslim houses, but late enough for the Hindu's house to completely burn down. The Fire Brigade, it later transpired, was mostly Muslim, or had a Muslim officer.

After this, the burning of Hindu and Sikh homes became increasingly common; indeed, a daily occurrence. The inhabitants of the apartment complex in which we lived organized a night patrol, comprised of adults armed with stout sticks, swords and one gun. My father owned that gun, but he had never learned how to use it. He was a Sikh farmer by birth and temperament, but since becoming a lawyer and moving to the city, he had transformed into an ordinary hardworking man trying to support a family. Little of the farmer's hardiness remained. I remember wondering, even at that time, what good people like him would be against the burly Muslims of the Mozung, factory workers and the like, the same men who reputedly carried knives in their salwaars and had passed by our house shouting 'Pakistan Zindabaad.' He was too citified to stand up to these ruffians. Now a peacemaker because of his impartiality and his rigid adherence to principles, he was no physical fighter, certainly no match against a mob; and, as things stood at the time, our problem was physical terror.

A respite came one night a few weeks later. We were jarringly awakened from sleep about two in the morning. The cause of this rude awakening was a series of loud explosions and flashes of light, interspersed with machine gun fire to the northwest of us, in a section of Lahore called Rajgarh. The Muslim League was apparently taking out one of its 'Pakistan Zindabaad' processions through the streets of this area, hoping to instill terror in the hearts of those sleeping in the surrounding homes. To their everlasting dismay, racing out of the darkness, heading straight towards them was a jeep carrying a group of ex-army Sikhs. The Muslims tried to scatter, but it was too late, as masses have huge inertia. While hand-grenades rained into their midst, machinegun fire raked those on the outside. It was a massacre, the dark hand of avenging death cutting a swath through them.

The silence that followed lasted almost a month. All burnings and stabbings ceased; the city was quiet. The gruesome message had done its work, but the peace was not destined to last. The violence started anew. My parents then decided, some time in May or June, to ship my brother and I off to our maternal uncle who lived in the smaller city of Bhatinda in Ferozepur district about a hundred miles to the south of Lahore. The metropolitan area was becoming unsafe, and since schools were closed most of the time anyway, what was the point of staying? My parents stayed behind to make their living and to protect our property the best they could.

Bhatinda was a peaceful railroad junction at the edge of the western desert that encroached on the Punjab. Dust storms, far darker than any in Delhi, were a daily occurrence. My uncle was the magistrate, one of the two most important people in the town, the other being the Deputy Commissioner. Because of my uncle, we were never charged for a ticket at the cinema. We also got the best seats, upstairs in the boxes reserved for the more influential and genteel people of the town. The cinema was not much of a building; the boxes had a roof over them, but the main section was open to the sky. At the front under the boxes was the box-office; behind it was the rectangular main hall, enclosed by two side walls and a back wall on which was the screen. The lack of a roof permitted only one show a day, after dark. Indian movies run a full three hours, so it was not possible to have a late night show; besides, there were not enough people in town to make it worth the trouble.

The cinema was interesting for more than just the movies. The electricity failed frequently. People would then pull out flashlights, shining them on the screen, occasionally even at the boxes where the genteel women, who were generally the better looking ones in this class-ridden society, usually sat. There would be catcalls, whistles and general pandemonium. Out of nowhere would come storm-lanterns and hawkers shouting 'paan, beeree, cigarette.' Paan is a betel leaf, which is used to wrap betelnuts, nutmegs, lime, and other condiments, and then chewed. The leaf is green, but for some reason it dissolves in the mouth, leaving a red juice from the various condiments it contains. It is quite tasty, and has a cooling, pepperminty flavor. Habitues are wont to add tobacco to the contents of the paan, and they have the dirty habit of spitting out the red juice every now and then. They also tend to favor one corner of the mouth over the other for chewing, tending over time to make their faces temporarily or permanently crooked.

Eating paan was forbidden by our father. Sikhs in general looked down on paan-chewing as a degenerate and dirty, Hindu shopkeeper habit. But the real reason for its skimpy use by us was the possibility that tobacco may be incorporated into it by those who ate pan on a regular basis; and tobacco, as everyone knows, is forbidden to the Sikhs with a severity equal to that against cutting hair. Beerees, one of the other items hawked by the vendors, are a flattened, Indian form of cigarette smoked by the poor, a dried leaf being used in place of paper to hold the tobacco.

But the interruptions of the movie were not always man-made. Every so often, we would be hit by a dust storm. This time, all activity ceased. There were no flashlights, vendors of paan and beerees, or storm-lanterns; just pitch darkness. During July and August, the monsoon rains were in full swing. The desert bloomed, but unhappily the cinema was not built for inclement weather, and it was anybody's guess whether there would be a show on any particular evening, and whether it would last out the full three hours, or be abbreviated. All things considered, the cinema was a delight. If you tired of the movie, you could always look up at the stars, except when it rained. Then the hall emptied rapidly, and you were never sure whether the movie would resume or not. The management would issue passes which functioned much as a raincheck, permitting movie patrons to try their luck another day.

On the fateful 14th of August, 1947, independence came to the subcontinent along with a partition into India and Pakistan on the basis of whether an area had a predominantly Hindu and Sikh population, or a Muslim one, respectively. Lahore went to Pakistan. Riots all over Pakistan had started long before partition, and an estimated million or more people were killed, most in the months that followed. There were several million refugees. My parents fled the fourteen miles to the border and across into India with the help of an escort of soldiers in two trucks provided by a military friend of the family. All they brought with them was what they could load into their tiny Opel Kadett car. The rest was lost to the ruffians, our neighbors from the Mozung.

As Hindu and Sikh refugees poured into the eastern and more southern part of the Punjab, tensions began to mount. People were resentful of the Muslims who still continued to live peacefully on this side, while Hindus and Sikhs like us had lost their homes and relatives to arson and slaughter on the other side. The peace on the Indian side was too good to last. Violence erupted in Bhatinda one late September or October afternoon. A train had just arrived from the Pakistani princely state of Bahawalpur to the northwest of us. Everyone except the Christian driver and guard had been slaughtered. The bodies had been pulled out and thrown into the Sutlej river at the border. All the train now contained was blood. Within minutes of the spreading of the news, people in the refugee camps were shouting "blood for blood." Gunfire erupted in the old, walled part of the city inside the citadel that stood up on a hill in the center of town. For a while, my uncle, along with the Superintendent of Police, tried valiantly to control the situation, but when the mob directly threatened their lives, and the police showed a reluctance to obey orders against people of their own religion, they gave up and left the city to the killers.

From then till dawn, there was a general slaughter of the Muslims. These were mostly very poor people, generally illiterate, who had not the foggiest idea what Pakistan was all about. The richer and more political Muslims, who were very few in this city, had left for Pakistan months earlier. Those remaining were the unwitting victims of religion-crazed, political fanatics who saw the world with tinted glasses colored with the irrationality of religious fundamentalism, and who now conspired to set the world ablaze with incendiary interpretations of the scriptures. It was the story of India repeated over and over again for hundreds, perhaps thousands, of years; except that this time it was not safely in the history books, but was being enacted live before our eyes.

On the morning following that night of killing, we were all standing on the walled roof of our house looking out at the city where sounds of gunfire were still to be heard. Our house was the very last one in town, beyond us being only sand dunes. At about this time, two boys, about eleven and thirteen years old, went running past us into the desert, chased by two tall Sikh men, one with a spear, the other with an axe. My uncle ran down into the house and fetched one of his rifles, a Savage, I still remember the name, and shot two warning shots between the children and their pursuers. Both parties stopped dead in their tracks, waiting to see what would happen next. My uncle shouted at the Sikhs to go back or he would shoot to kill. The boys took courage from my uncle's words and came running towards our house, easily scaling the seven-foot wall that enclosed our courtyard. How did they do it? It must have been fear, the kind that brings out almost superhuman abilities in us all so that we can avail of that one-in-a-million chance. Once inside, my uncle locked them in a small room, and tied our two big, vicious, black, Tibetan herd dogs (Odan dey kootay) to the door. The male dog had often escaped from the house and had a reputation for terrorizing the town, so it was unlikely anyone would challenge these animals. My uncle had kept them as protection against dacoits, but under the present circumstances, if somebody sneaked into the house, there was no way he could get past the animals. The boys were safe.

The two Sikh refugees and their friends hung around the house for several days, even threatening my uncle if he did not give up the boys, but he had the gun and that was the final argument. A month later, when peace had returned to Bhatinda, my uncle put the boys on a train to Pakistan, and he received a letter from them several months later thanking him for saving their lives. They had made it safely across the fifty odd miles to the border and into Pakistan.

Acts of humanity were not confined to people like my uncle and other Hindus and Sikhs. They happened in Pakistan too. My parents survived because the day before partition, our Pathan tailor quietly came over to them and warned them that their group of flats was targeted for an attack that night. They had been good to him all these years in Lahore, and he could not bear to see harm come to them. He had, apparently, just returned from a meeting in the Mozung, where the political leaders had told those gathered there to prepare to attack the houses on Temple Road that night. Daggers, kerosene, and other things had been distributed, and all that was left was to wait for dusk. My parents immediately drove over to their colonel friend in the cantonment, and never saw their flat or their other belongings again.

It was in December that I saw my first corpse. We were going southeast on the train to Patiala where my maternal grandfather lived. On the way, there was a place called Rampura-Phool, where the railroad crossed one of those irrigation canals with which the Punjab is criss-crossed. The train here slowed to a crawl, exposing us to a stench the like of which I had never known. A train carrying Muslims fleeing Delhi on their way to Pakistan had been stopped at the canal crossing, and everybody slaughtered. Trains were few, so they were packed with people hanging from the doors and windows, and sitting on the roof. After the killings, the bodies had been thrown into the canal. Some of them had become bloated and got stuck under the bridge, threatening to block the flow of water and the integrity of the structure.

As our train was crossing the canal, I was looking out through the window. My aunt pulled my head in, but not before I had seen several of the swollen bodies. That scene never left my mind. I did not get nightmares, but I acquired a permanent fear of crowds and mobs, and of the religious. I don't trust them, and I am afraid of political processions and politicians who stand up on street corners and give rousing speeches. I mistrust anyone who appeals to the masses.

When I finished, Preeti turned at me and, in her own inimitable way, captured it all in one simple statement: "So you never had much of a childhood, did you?

"No," I replied, "it takes a conscious effort of the mind to visualize what people mean when they refer to the innocence of childhood. My generation never knew it; the world of events took care of that, and innocence was shattered."

"Do you think anyone was converted to atheism by these massive religious atrocities?" she asked.

"I doubt it; on the contrary," I replied, "the Muslims became more fervent Muslims, the Sikhs more fervent Sikhs, and the Hindus more fervent Hindus. It was self-evident from the events of the times that security lay in the collective; and the easiest such group to envision was that based on religion. Besides, that is where all your relatives are. There is no question that violence is irrational; what better source then to act as inspiration than the largest of all its repositories, religion.

"Other movements too have promoted violence," I continued. "Look at Communism in the Soviet Union; quite as equally irrational, if you are to believe what is written in

Harbaksh's books, and quite as blood-thirsty. As individuals, we are all sane and peaceful, but as a collective, we become like a pack of wild dogs. Various philosophies denigrate the individual, fostering violence in equivalent measure. Religions, individually and as a group, are the most anti-individualistic. At par are the various forms of collectivism—communism, fascism, Nazism, and other socialist—isms. Here in India, we are told that socialism is for our good, but the more I understand it, the more collectivist it seems. I don't trust it. Pandit Nehru says that it is the political system that suits India, and that is the one he has instituted, but I have my doubts about his wisdom this time. For the present, I will give him the benefit of the doubt until I learn more about the system; but I already sense it will not pass muster. Anyway, I have my honor roll of criminals. Religion presently heads the list, with communism and fascism following close behind."

Preeti tried to play the Devil's advocate:

"But almost everyone believes that religion is the source of all good," she said. "Don't you think you are being much too harsh? Your experience of it in the birth-pangs of independence might have given you a skewed view of it."

"Perhaps, but even when I take that into account, Preeti, my verdict is still the same. In fact, viewing it at a more fundamental level has made my distaste for religion greater than it was soon after partition. But leaving religion aside, there is a more general equation for violence, viewed more broadly than in terms of overt physical violence. Terror is not committed simply against the physical victims of terrorist acts; it is also committed against those who are frightened by it."

"You mean the threat of violence?"

"Yes. If somebody holds a gun to your head and forces you to part with your money on pain of death, would you not say it was a violent crime?"

"I see your point," she replied, then added her own observation: "society's attitude to women is of the same genre. I know that from personal experience."

"Preeti, in my article, I want to put my finger on the basic, most fundamental source of violence, whether overt or merely coercion. The law recognizes both as violence. But if you extend the thought process a little further, you discover that the definition of violence really boils down to any act in which something is taken from you unjustly against your will. This would include fraud and theft. But now for the real thing."

Here I stopped for dramatic effect. Preeti understood, but could not hold back a telling smile, just to let me know that I was becoming a bit too melodramatic.

"My love," she said, "you are a philosopher, and for that reason I'm glad that I married you. There is never a dull moment. So what is this breakthrough thought for which even your lover has to wait?"

"Preeti, this is serious business; stop playing around with my feelings. Do you want my article to stay on line two forever? That is the least that will happen if you put loving on my mind."

"That sounds tempting," she responded, "but you must remember that I do love you; in fact, so much that I am willing to forego loving for the moment. Perhaps, at the back of my mind, I am also thinking of the money you will earn if you go beyond the said line two. So tell me, while I am still inclined to agree, what is this crucial discovery?"

"Well, it is not entirely my own idea. I did glean it partially from one of the books, but I have been able to see it in the perspective of life here in India. Okay then, here it is: 'the source of violence is the desire to take from another something against his will.'"

"That's it?" she said. "Come on, I don't see anything earth-shaking in that statement. Its truth seems self-evident."

"Yes, but how often have you seen people holding back on their desire to take what belongs to others?"

"I would think that most people would subscribe to the principle, and live by it."

"On the surface, yes; but when the chips are down, seldom."

She made no comment, just looked at me, awaiting an explanation. So I continued: "Take the caste system, for example. When our Aryan ancestors instituted it several thousand years ago, their intent was to subjugate those beneath them. The king and his noble henchmen placed themselves at the top of the pyramid as the Kshatriyas—the warriors. Well, not quite the top. The very top was reserved for Brahmins, the priests. The two of them, the Brahmins and the Kshatriyas, have since then functioned as a team, systematically exploiting the rest of us.

"The Kshatriyas claimed all power and property. This they demanded as the price of their protection. But from whom were they protecting us? From themselves, the good old protection racket; very old, very archaic. The farmers farmed, the artisans made tools, clothes, houses and the like; the merchants and shopkeepers spread them across the land, but the Kshatriyas and Brahmins? No ma'am, they did not work. Ah, yes, the Brahmins did teach, language and some science, but essentially only to Brahmins or Kshatriyas; and yes, the latter did fight battles, reputedly performing deeds immortalized by hired bards, frolicking as heros of the great epics, the Raamayan and the Mahabhaarat. But they did no work in any real sense. Their wars were mostly those of conquest and glory.

"Consider the Ashvamaid Yug, the horse sacrifice, the one where a consecrated horse was let loose, and followed by a chosen band of soldiers belonging to the king wherever it went. The monarch claimed hegemony over the land that the horse traversed, so all this territory was proclaimed by this band of thugs as his rightful property. Anyone who disputed that claim was dared to fight. This is naked aggression as clear as daylight, yet it is lauded as the right of great kings in the epics.

"The Kshatriyas were rich, but whence those riches? The king used them, the Kshatriyas, to collect taxes, by parceling away much of the land between them. This netted them almost half the produce of the farmers. A major portion went to the King's treasury; another big chunk was donated to the temples; much of the remainder remained with the nobility.

The Brahmins also invented a variety of rituals which involved large donations to the temples by the king. In return, they deified him so that no one would question his authority. I remember when I was small how I used to think of the Maharaja of Patiala as god-like. He was certainly handsome, and so were his sons, and the Maharani (queen) was said to be the most beautiful woman in the state. But I was disappointed when I saw him. He looked like any one of us, only more expensively dressed and accompanied by a number of courtiers amid much pomp and show. The deification, in my mind at least, was fake.

"Later, when I met the princes who frequented the dorms of BCS, I consigned this nobility stuff to the realm of nonsense, an outsized fraud. There is an Indian aphorism: 'The buffalo belongs to the one who owns the club.' Indian history bears it out.

"The lowest caste, the Untouchables, was essentially made of people of the conquered races, most likely those who inhabited India before the Aryans. Their rulers were co-opted into the ruling class of the Aryan conquerors, as such and by intermarriage, but most of the population ended up as Untouchables, essentially slaves, although paid a bare sustenance. Because they were darker than the Aryans, we can see in the hegemony that followed their conquest the origin of the extreme color consciousness in our society. You could not have failed to notice how our marriage ads always ask for a fair-complexioned partner."

Preeti nodded her head in amused agreement.

I continued: "Maintaining the caste system called for a lot more coercion. You had to forbid voluntary liaisons between individuals. Who married who had to be carefully controlled, otherwise within a few generations the system would crumble, and with it would be lost the profits of privilege. Several traditions had to be instituted to maintain the status quo. The father, in relation to his family, had to be elevated to a status equivalent to what the king's was in relation to his subjects. This required absolute obedience to the father's wishes. We see it nowadays generalized as obedience to the wishes of our elders. A son could not marry without his father's permission. For the daughters, of course, there never was any question of doing otherwise. A son who defied his father's wishes could be excommunicated from his class, which was a major calamity, deprived of almost all his privileges, and burdened with the onerous tasks of the lower classes. The king could also dissolve the son's marriage, and even banish him from the kingdom.

"The enforcement of this highly unjust system required progressively harsher measures; and a marked subjugation, a major feature of which was an intense effort to punish anyone who dared defy it. This did not always work, so the Brahmins developed an even better method of control, the scriptures, giving people a moral imperative that attacked individuality and personal ambition. The target was desire and personal happiness, the kind of inspiration that leads a man to think: 'I should live for myself, not for the collective.' Such men are dangerous because they question the existing moral code, the division into castes, the priests and the rules that this group had devised. If allowed to survive, they would topple everything, so preventive measures were called for, teaching people that pride and personal ambition were merely vanity, but humility and living in the service of others was a goal worthy of the best. Most of us today are still duped by that stroke of genius, wallowing in guilt every time we achieve something of great personal value."

"Why were women more oppressed than men?" asked Preeti.

"Being weaker, they were easier to oppress. Another point to remember is that a woman is often the inspiration behind a man. I am rebelling against the system partly for love of you. Before we met, my rebellion was sullen and half-hearted, but now I know what dreams are possible, so my revolt is total. Women, clearly, can be far more dangerous than men, so they had to be subjugated even more."

"Amrik," she summed it all up in a tone of admiration, "I think you have something worth saying, so go ahead and write your piece."

I started typing again. By the end of the day, my second article was ready.

XVIII

The letter was short and terse. Two sentences stood out among the others: "I would like to see you as soon as possible. There is something important that I wish to discuss." Mr. Gopalan, the editor of the National Express, had not said that he would publish my manuscript. Instead, he wanted to see me. Preeti was overjoyed at the news.

"Oh, Amrik," she said, "I love you." Saying that, she threw her arms around my neck and kissed me full on the mouth, out in the yard in full view of everyone else.

"We don't normally see passionate kissing in public," said Harbaksh, "What is the occasion?"

When I told him, he rushed off for a bottle of champagne, but Mohini was a bit dismayed at the prospect of our leaving. Harbaksh popped the cork, and soon we were celebrating.

"Here's to the new writer in the family," he said, "may your successes be many, and may they never end!"

I thanked him for his encouragement and guidance, drank the champagne, and then turned to Preeti. "We might have to live in Karole Bagh for a while," I said, "until we can find a place of our own, and money enough to rent it."

"I would be happy to loan you any amount you need," said Harbaksh.

I looked at Preeti. She shook her head. "No," she replied, "thanks for the offer, but we'd like the sweetness of making it on our own."

It was obvious to anyone that the four of us were more than a family. Words seldom needed to be spoken except as a pleasure; and when used, they were more for added emphasis than for mere communication.

Next morning, we were packed and ready to leave. Preeti had finished her scene of the Solan valley, and presented it to Mohini.

"This is a down-payment on my promise to redecorate your house," she said, "just keep some wall space for the others to come; maybe even build some more rooms. Who knows how many more romances like ours will be hatched here."

It was an emotional farewell, even for me. BCS had created a stoic, but now my heart was full with happiness and excitement. Harbaksh took me aside and said with uncharacteristic gravity: "Amrik, I have some advice for you, probably unnecessary given the way you think, but I'll give it anyway. Always remember it is your life you have to live. You and Preeti are among the happiest couples I've known, and if you permit me a little mysticism, I would say yours is a marriage made in Heaven. Cherish her and love her, and don't let anything come in the way."

"There'll be no compromises," I assured him.

But there was more, so I waited. Words were not coming easy to him; not like him at all, for he was always so self-assured.

"What is it, Harbaksh?" I asked, a little concerned. "Is something wrong?"

"No, nothing like that; just something I should've told you a long time ago. What I want to say is that I have known for a long time that Preeti's marriage to my brother was unhappy."

It took courage to say, and it hurt, but he seemed relieved. Then he continued, now more composed: "I had always suspected it, though neither of them said a word to me. After you came into her life, I saw the difference. She changed before my eyes. She was her old self again; once more the same vibrant girl I had known the first time I saw her. Unfortunately, it also confirmed what I had suspected about her and Inder all along."

"She told me about the marriage," I said, "it was not a happy one."

"I know, and I've felt guilty all along. Bringing you into her life has taken a load off of me, as if I had been forgiven my error. I owe you thanks."

"It wasn't your fault," I said.

"Oh, but it was," he insisted calmly. "I knew better than to arrange a marriage. Inder was quite an irresponsible person. He drank a lot. In fact, his C.O. complained to me about that and the dissolute nature of his friends. The few I met, I instantly disliked. Wealthy landowner family types, but worthless; and Inder let them take advantage of his good nature. He started gambling, and I suspect more, though I had no evidence. I thought the responsibilities that go with marriage would sober him up; but my plan failed. Until you came along, I thought I'd destroyed Preeti's life as well."

He stopped to get hold of his emotions, which were now flooding back. I had never seen him so moved before.

"You're being too hard on yourself," I said, "you did the best you could."

"No," he continued. "I played God. It was unforgivable because I let no one do it to me. Anyway, I wish to thank you for making everything right again. I want you to consider yourself my younger brotheer. I'm closer to you than I ever was to Inder. And another, I was serious about that loan. I'd give it as a gift, but knowing the two of you, I doubt you'd accept. Nonetheless, don't you and Preeti go shortchanging yourself because of some silly notions about what is and is not proper to accept from people who care about you."

"I understand; I won't forget, and I appreciate the offer."

On the way down to Kaalka, Preeti asked me what Harbaksh had said. I told her even people as strong as him needed to unburden themselves sometimes. She never asked for more, for she had guessed the rest. She put her head on my shoulder and said: "I love you. I will live anywhere with you, and go through anything for you. I am so happy, I want to cry."

I put my free left arm around her and pulled her close. "I'm supposed to be the stronger of the two," I said, "but I know in my heart that I need you more than you need me. A woman cannot feel the same way as a man. She has to have divided loyalties. She will have children and there will be times in her life when they must come before her husband."

"But fathers love their children too," she objected.

"Yes," I agreed, "but not with the same biological intensity. For a mother, her child can be her whole life. For a father, it is seldom that."

"Right now," she said, "you are my whole life. I hardly ever think of children."

"That is just the way we want it at present. When we've made something of our lives, then I will sit back and you can have children."

"It takes two to make a child, you know."

"Uh hu, but the man's part is just fun and games. You do all the work."

"You must know something about childbirth," she said, "your mother is an obstetrician. Do you ever feel that Nature has been unfair in making women do all the work of pregnancy and labor?"

"Well, my mother views it differently. She says that many women enjoy their pregnancy and, as for labor, they scream a lot at the time, but somehow forget everything afterwards. It seldom leaves a scar on their psyche. She thinks pregnancy and labor may even be the cement that binds a mother and child."

"And breast-feeding too," added Preeti. "Most of the girls I knew in college did not like the idea of suckling their babies. I feel different. For me, it is almost the equivalent of a sexual desire. I want to hold my baby to my naked body, and I want him to use me, to live off of me."

"How about her?"

"That's fine too," she smiled, "sex is not important in breast-feeding."

"Will you have any desire left over for me?" I asked.

"Perhaps," she replied. "I have to think about that. I'm a woman with a one-track mind, at least to begin with."

"My mother says I was a twin, and twins have a tendency to run in families. Our first may be twins."

She did not answer right away, for the possibility of twins had apparently never crossed her mind. Then she brightened up. "Well," she said, "at least we don't have to worry about it for the present. The way you tell it, there'll be no place for sex so long as we stay in Karole Bagh." She paused for a moment, then continued: "will you miss me?"

"What are you talking about?" I said, "you'll be with me."

"I'm talking about sleeping together, silly" she said.

"We'll find a way."

"You know," she smiled slyly, "I wouldn't mind making love to you in public."

"Neither would I, but this is not an ideal world. We are not supposed to arouse other people's desires. It might give them ideas."

"What's wrong with that?" she said. "The worst that could happen is that you would have another brother, or maybe even a sister. Wouldn't that be fun?"

"I don't know," I replied, "I'll feel almost like a father."

"Come now," she said, "just a few days ago you were only a boy, until I came along and made a man out of you."

"That you sure did," I agreed, "I've never grown up so fast before in my life."

And so we carried on, talking of everything under the sun; and it was a hot sun. By lunchtime, we were in Karole Bagh. There was only the servant at home. He came out and helped me with Preeti's bags. My own were negligible, as they had always been. Delhi was much cooler, now that the monsoon had arrived. There were scattered puffs of clouds in the sky, but to the southwest you could tell more rain was on the way.

"Will you and beebiji (young lady) like something to eat?" the servant asked, "Beeji may not be here for another two hours."

"Thank you, Govind," I replied, "lunch will be just fine."

We went in and washed our faces with the water that had been stored in the tub that morning. There is always a water scarcity here, so everyone keeps a portable metal tub in the bathroom. You leave the tap open all night; by morning, the tub is full.

As for drinking water, we did have a refrigerator which sat out in one corner of the verandah. But the electricity went out with regularity many times a day in summer, particularly on the hottest days, so we had a backup system in the form of unglazed earthenware pots—surahees—that have long, thin necks and swollen, pregnant bottoms. They sweat through their surface, the evaporation keeping the water inside nice and cool. Two surahees sat inside the bedroom, which was the coolest and darkest part of the house since it had no windows. The drawing room was not as cool. It had a skylight built into the ceiling to let in light, as this room too had no windows. There was a room at the back belonging to the third family that lived in the house. On the east of the drawing room was our bedroom, and on the west, the bedroom of the neighbors who owned one-third of the verandah, the same neighbors with the beautiful daughter named Aasha. The front wall had the door into the verandah, so there really was no place for a window.

There were two other rooms in the house: one on our end of the verandah, which my mother used as an office, but which I felt would probably become our temporary bedroom. Her desk, of course, would have to remain, and the bed which she used for her patients after she had done some procedure on them in the adjoining treatment and examination room, which was largely filled with an obstetrical and gynecological table, would have to serve as our bed. Of course, the linen would be changed, but the smell of iodine and spirit from the neighboring room, which was between the office and the bathroom, would have to be lived with.

We had lunch by ourselves in the drawing room (there was no dining room). Most Indians generally sleep after lunch, but Preeti and I decided to make a working afternoon of it. She dropped me off at the National Express building and drove off to the Civil Lines area where the Delhi Polytechnic, of which the School of Fine Arts is a part, and St. Stephen's, are located.

I was shown into the office of the Editor, Mr. Gopalan. He motioned me to a chair while he sat behind a desk. There were many books on shelves along the walls, and an air-conditioner in the window, behind and a little to one side of the desk. He was surprised at my young age but, after commenting on it, got down to business.

"I see you don't approve of our marriage system," he began. "What is wrong with us? Don't you like us?"

I had already decided to be as forthright as possible, so I knew what to say. "Yes, I don't like the system," I replied, "do you?"

"Uh, let us leave my opinions out of the discussion for the moment," he answered, "what we want to know is your opinion."

"Well, what is there for me to say. I thought my article says it all."

"I know. It says a lot. I just wanted to be sure you meant what you said. I take it you're not married; you look too young for that." He did not wait for me to answer, but continued: "I don't think you should be so hasty to pass judgment on the rest of your countrymen and their customs that date back thousands of years, before you yourself have experience of what you're writing about."

I decided not to tell him about Preeti for the present, but to argue the point on its own merits. "Mr. Gopalan," I said, "I am eighteen years old, and I have spent all those eighteen years in India. I live in a cramped house in Karole Bagh, where I am thrown into close contact with the rest of my family, my neighbors, and the numerous guests who keep visiting us for extended periods of time. I also have friends in the neighborhood, whose houses I visit. I cannot help knowing what goes on. Besides, I do read your newspaper, and I read books. As you may have noticed from the article, I also have what passes for a good, formal education."

"Where did you study?" he asked.

"Bishop Cotton School."

"That is the hill school in Shimla, is it not?"

"Yes, that's the one. We call it BCS."

"I know, I know, my son has a friend who studied there. He is about four years your senior, so perhaps you don't know him. So you had an English education." By that he meant education in a school with British teachers, and therefore somewhat Westernized.

"Yes."

"And is that where you got your ideas about our marriage system?"

"Some of them," I replied, "but I have read a lot on my own, and I feel strongly about what I've said."

"Mr. Randhawa," he said, "I like your style and your honesty. I could use a man like you. Mind you, I'm not saying that I agree with you, but you argue your points well, and you have a good grasp of the facts. Are there other things about India you disagree with?"

"I don't know whether 'disagree' is the proper word, but yes, there are other areas where much is wrong."

"Have you written anything else besides the article you sent me? By the way, the typing was very good."

"Oh!" I said in surprise, "the typewriter was a marriage present from a friend of mine."

Too late to take back; the cat was out of the bag.

"Mr. Randhawa, I am sorry. You should have told me." He was profusely apologetic. "I had wrongly assumed that you had no personal experience of marriage. This changes things completely. So what kind of a marriage did you have?"

"My wife Preeti and I had a love affair before we married."

"How did you manage that in our restrictive society?" he asked.

"Come now, Mr. Gopalan, you know as well as I do that love marriages are not all that rare in our land."

"Quite true," he agreed, "as an editor of a newspaper you get to know of everything. But they are still rare. How did your parents take it?"

"Only my mother knows as yet."

"How is that possible?" he asked. "You just said that you live in the same house with them."

"Yes, I do, but you see, my wife and I just drove down from Solan where we got married and were staying with the friend who gave me the typewriter. I came straight here before I went to see my father. My wife has gone to inquire about admission in college. She wants to be a painter."

"Are you happy?" he asked.

"Do I have to answer that?"

"Not if you don't want to," he said, "it is just that I like to know something about my employees. It makes for better relations and better decisions on my part."

"Are you offering me a job, Mr. Gopalan?" I asked.

"We will come to that in a moment. But first, do you want to answer my question?"

"Yes, I do very much. My wife and I love each other, and it is the most wonderful thing ever to happen to me. Look, Mr. Gopalan, do you think somebody who is eighteen and just out of school would be writing articles for a newspaper? Don't you think it a bit odd?"

"As a matter of fact, I think it very odd."

"Mr. Gopalan, you have to be in love to want to take your life into your own hands and make something of it. I have had these ideas, the ones in the article, in my head for a long time, but I would never have written them down but for my marriage. I now have a family, I mean my wife and I, and am determined to no longer be dependent on my parents."

"Thank you for telling me this. I appreciate it. Now would you answer my other question, have you written anything else?"

"Yes, I brought it along." So saying, I took the article, "Steeped in Violence," out of the small paper bag I was carrying and gave it to him. Then I sat back while he went through it. When he was finished, he turned to me.

"Mr. Randhawa, you have the job."

"What job?" I asked.

"I want you to write a regular column for me every month. I would prefer every two weeks, but I don't know whether you'll be up to it. We will name it whatever you wish."

"How about *My Troubled Land,"* I suggested.

"I think that's fine. I can pay you one hundred rupees per article; I mean per column. Sometimes, if we have a long article, we might wish to have it in more than one installment. In that case, I will pay you a hundred rupees for each installment. Do we have a deal, Mr. Randhawa?"

I stood up and shook his hand.

"We have a deal," I said, beaming with excitement and pleasure. "God, this is wonderful. I can't wait to tell Preeti!"

"My secretary will have the papers ready for you to sign in about half an hour. But there is one more thing. I am a little curious about your wife. I wish to see with my own eyes what kind of person could make an eighteen-year-old Indian want to begin earning a living. Do you think it is too much to ask to meet with her?"

"Not at all," I replied, "it will be my pleasure. She should be here shortly to pick me up, and I'll bring her in then. Will you still be here?"

"Oh yes, I will. A newspaper editor's work is never done. One more thing; I almost forgot. Professor Srivastava from Benares Hindu University already writes a column for this newspaper that will alternate with yours. It is called *Our Ancient Heritage.* As you can guess, its viewpoint is quite the opposite of yours, but I think it will help produce a happy balance for our newspaper, even though he is fifty and you are eighteen— the voice of wisdom against the voice of impetuosity. Remember, Mr. Randhawa, we are here to please our readers, and there are all sorts of people out there.

I did not tell him that I already knew of the Professor. Before long, I would have the Geeta squared away; then we would see who was impetuous and who wise. With Preeti by my side, I would make it. What were those words in our school song? Ah yes . . .

"Our motto, Cotton's motto,
We must never, never, never be o'ercome.
When both friends and fortunes fail,
When wild fears and doubts assail,
With our motto we'll prevail,
And overcome."

Oh, how I loved my school! I wanted to sing the rest of the song, and I wanted to do it out loud:

"And so from those who've gone before,
To those who're yet to come,
We pass the motto loud and clear,
All evil overcome.
As true as is a brother's love,
As close as ivy grows,
We'll stand foursquare throughout our lives,
To ev'ry wind that blows.

"And we'll not forget that motto, Cotton's motto . . ."

Bishop Cotton . . . a religious man. He must be—he was a bishop. How then could he have such wonderful ideas? Well . . . he was an Englishman, and brave words are an English tradition. They had tempered Christianity with their own brand of pride and tradition, and had made it into a livable, even an admirable system. Just imagine, a bishop founding a school that had turned out an atheist like me. Ah, such was life!

XIX

Delhi was much cooler now, making a walk under the Gulmohur trees in Connaught Circus a pleasure. Tall, dark and ominous clouds were gathering up in the southwest. They foretold of imminent rain and weather that turns one's mind to picnics. Imagine sitting on the bank of a canal, a basket of 'sucking' mangoes next to you in the cool water. All afternoon, you enjoy the fruit. Satiated, you undress, dive into the water, and swim with the current, washing the summer out of your soul.

None of the picnics I had been to were like that. They were family affairs, generously stocked with uncles and aunts. Never had I been with anybody the likes of Preeti. Heaven had certainly eluded me. Often it would rain, sending us scurrying for cover under the trees. We would get soaked anyway, but who cared; it was hot enough to cook. But imagine Preeti soaked in the rain. I could envision her clothes greedily clinging to her body, and I going crazy just standing there watching her.

I was not the only one who daydreamed in the rain. The month of Saawan, or Saun, as we Punjabis call it, is the month smack in the middle of the monsoon. With the first raindrops, you can see the heat fleeing the ground, and the sweet smell of parched earth wetted for the first time intoxicates the senses. The fragrance never comes again; no matter how much more it rains, for the earth is done heaving its sighs of relief. But all of a sudden, there are birds and grass, and the greening of the trees. It is a resurrection, the desiccated mother of all life being reborn, replete with all her treasures.

Saawan is also the time for love songs, but mainly in the movies. Outside the dark never-never land of the cinema, in the stark brightness of real life, love songs are rare. There are girls folk-dancing in some forgotten villages, and even village boys and girls singing, but these are far cries from affairs of the heart, since watchful parents abound, waiting to nip amorous 'evils' in the bud. In cities, the temperature falls and there is a sigh of relief, but mostly one remembers the monsoon as a time of flooded roads, with stranded buses and cars, and with the vehicles that survive passing you by and recklessly splashing muddy water on your white trousers and shirts. There are, of course, picnics and compassionate school principals who declare a holiday to commemorate the coming of the rains, but apart from a few brave couples who manage to make it to a garden unobserved, there is little romantic celebration.

While I sat there day-dreaming under the Gulmohur trees, it began to rain. I realized that time was beckoning me to get back to the Express building, for Preeti should be returning any time now. But she was nowhere to be found. My worrying was pointless though, for half an hour later she drove up, all smiles. She was delayed because she had had the foresight to go to St. Stephens as well, and bring back some admission forms for me.

I pulled out a hundred-rupee bundle from my pocket and handed it to her. "Here," I said, "our first earned income."

"The National Express?" she asked, suppressing the desire to say 'yippee' because people were watching.

"Yes, this is what I will get for every column that I write, once every two weeks. Mr. Gopalan has hired me to write a fortnightly column called "My Troubled Land." "Arranging a Marriage" is the first topic and "Steeped in Violence" will be the next.

Preeti beamed with pleasure and said mischievously: "You should see yourself now. You look like a schoolboy after his first kiss."

"No way," I replied, thinking back on my first kiss. "Nothing could beat my first kiss; neither money, nor a job, nor even recognition.

She smiled, her eyes warming up at my sentiments, then she asked, wondering if I knew what I was doing: "Do you know that you handed me the money? Indian husbands are not expected to behave this way."

"I am not any Indian husband, love; I am your husband. I never learned to spend money, so it is better off with you. Give me some whenever I need it. In the meantime, let me cherish the feeling that I am looking after you, even if only a hundred rupees worth."

I reflected momentarily on the significance of the cash. It was the same old paper, ruined as a commodity by the printing on it, that man had invented a millennium ago to capture thoughts and events in the unique symbols we call language. But now it was a promise, an acknowledgment that something had been received and something could be demanded in return. I was satisfied.

"I will keep the money if it means so much to you," she said, "but now that the celebration is over, we better be heading home. The music has to be faced sooner or later."

"Not yet," I said, "Mr. Gopalan bought us a reprieve. He wishes to see you."

"Why?" she asked, genuinely surprised. "I am no writer!"

"But he wishes to behold the inspiration behind the writer, the modern-day Helen of Troy who could launch an eighteen-year-old into a career of writing and give him the courage to take on a whole nation."

She squeezed my hand with pride and, with anticipatory relish, announced: "Let us not keep our editor waiting. I am beginning to like him already."

I made the introductions, then Mr. Gopalan addressed Preeti: "Mrs. Randhawa, would it be too forward of me to say that your husband has done well trusting his own heart and his eyes? He never told me you were so beautiful."

Preeti blushed, and then looked at me. "Honest, Preeti," I pleaded, "I said nothing one way or the other."

"Mr. Randhawa," explained Mr. Gopalan, "you have much to learn. The words were in your eyes; they did not need to be spoken. I could imagine her as beautiful even before I laid eyes on her, but I mistakenly half ascribed the glow in your expression to your youth; that is why I am now surprised. Well, what can I say except that I am delighted to meet you, Mrs. Randhawa? Your husband is a talented man (here he smiled as if to suggest that he should have said 'boy'), and he is most fortunate to have you as his wife."

Preeti had now regained her composure. "There is more to us than meets the eye, Mr. Gopalan," she said, "but for the present let me say that I am proud of my husband, and that I love him. I know it is not customary for Indian women to state such things in public, but I have to say them anyway because I believe sentiments like that, when truly felt, are worth expressing, tradition notwithstanding."

"And what else is worth saying, Mrs. Randhawa?" he asked, intrigued by her boldness.

"I will leave that for my husband to say in his writings, for you, for your newspapers, and for your readers. I am not a deep thinker, but we think as a team. I don't take credit for his thoughts, but I do keep them fresh and exciting. Sometimes I cannot tell whether the words I utter are my own, or I am merely mouthing what he has persuaded me to accept, but I will say this, I never cared much for ideas before, but now they are a matter of life and death, as if life were one continuous dream of ideas and their absence a dreary oblivion."

"Bravo! I am certain your husband is proud of what you have just expressed. But perhaps, Mrs. Randhawa, it is you I should be offering the column to, not him."

Preeti smiled at me and then said: "No, Mr. Gopalan, he is the thinker. I am there to make sure he never gives up."

"That is as it should be," he observed. "Tell me, Mrs. Randhawa, I notice that you are wearing a shirt and slacks.

These are not the clothes I would expect a newly married Indian woman to be wearing; rather I would have thought a beautiful saree, one of those brocaded types that look so lovely on our ladies, and I am sure would look even lovelier on you."

"I would, Mr. Gopalan, at a party, but I am a working woman planning to join the School of Fine Arts so that I can learn to paint for a living. I will have time to be decorative for my husband, yes, but not often. He will have to be satisfied with my mere presence and, once I have them, my paintings, though he will not want for love."

"I admire your frankness, Mrs. Randhawa, and I can see that I am bound to hear, and hopefully see, a lot more of you," said Mr. Gopalan, "but before the two of you leave, may I ask you one more question. This one is for Mr. Randhawa. Seeing how your wife is dressed, what are your views on the kind of clothes our Indian women should be wearing?"

"I agree with my wife's point of view," I replied. "In fact, clothes will be one of the subjects I plan to write about for *My Troubled Land.* But there is something more you should know. I am convinced that I am one of those lucky few who are in complete agreement with their wives on almost anything they can think of."

"How long have you been married?" he asked.

"A little over two weeks? Why do you ask?"

"Well" . . . here he hesitated, then seemed to make a decision, and continued: "I was about to say something that is generally ascribed to the wisdom that comes with experience, but in the presence of the two of you, I think you might very well be right. I am glad for you."

So saying, he stood up, shook my hand, congratulated us, and said 'namaste' (an Indian greeting with folded hands) to Preeti. We were almost at the door when he called for us to wait. "Just one more question, if I may be permitted, Mrs. Randhawa. What is your attitude to our Indian form of greeting, the namaste, I mean? Do you think men should shake the hands of women just as they do of men, or do you think it is not proper?"

Preeti smiled, held out her hand and shook his. "Mr. Gopalan," she said, "you can feel that my hand is warm. It means that I have friendly feelings towards you. But merely because I touched you and am willing to convey those feelings, it does not follow that I have compromised myself in any way. I remain as I was before I touched you. The handshake was just a way of expressing a common feeling of humanity. It is as it should be."

"Yes," he replied, "it is as it should be; and I am honored."

Once outside, Preeti said to me: "I don't know what kind of a man he is, but I like him."

"Me too," I said. "That was quite an experience. But what did you mean by 'there is more to us than meets the eye?'"

"I was thinking of how I am a widow and you are younger than me. We not only broke the tradition of arranged marriage, but more or less violated every other rule as well. We made love before the marriage, even though in our eyes it was like what you said: 'The occasion for solemnity is when you fall in love, not when you marry.' We were already in love, so it was all right."

"You don't believe in free love, do you?" I asked.

"No, and neither do you. You have sex because you are in love, not because you must have sex. You wouldn't want to devalue sex, now would you?"

"You're right. I am about as conservative on this as you."

"Isn't that a silly way to classify things?" she observed. "By using the word 'conservative', we are implying in some sense that the idea is old-fashioned and, *ipso facto,* of value only because it is traditional. Whatever happened to right and wrong? I don't like labels, you know. People should take the trouble of asking you your exact opinion on everything, and then listening to your answer without preconceived notions in their mind. Labels are like many other short-cuts, packages of preconceived notions which may have general application to a group, but are often quite unfair and inaccurate when applied to an individual. I think they are a sign of intellectual laziness."

"Mr. Gopalan was right, Preeti. You are a fountainhead of ideas. Now I have so much to write about— 'clothes,' 'free love,' false generalizations,' 'false notions of a woman's sanctity,' and even 'expressions of feelings in public.' I am now set for the next several months, all thanks to you. I owe you much . . . and I love you; what more can I say?"

Preeti did not answer; she merely squeezed my hand as it sat on the wheel. That squeeze carried more meaning than words could express. I thought back on her handshake with the Editor. If it had anything like the warmth I felt now, Mr. Gopalan was not likely to forget it for a long time. Thinking back on it, though, it was amusing. Preeti pretty much knocked the daylights out of him. Oh God, I was so proud of her.

XX

It was pouring rain when we got home. Beeji was waiting for us in the verandah, but Papaji was on his afternoon siesta. That would normally be followed by a walk in the evening, in Ajmal Khan Park, the little green oasis about two hundred yards down the road.

Preeti said 'Sut Sri Akaal', meaning God is Truth, (I use this greeting too, but have never paid attention to its meaning) to my mother, and then stepped forward and hugged her. The way Beeji hugged her back, I knew she liked Preeti; there was even water in her eyes. I waited to see what she would call her. Surprise, surprise, she called her 'Preeti' instead of the more common 'bayti'. It made no difference really, but I had fallen in love with the name, and it was heartening to hear Beeji say it.

Beeji beckoned me to come, and hugged us both together. My mother is a small woman, barely five feet tall, but she has class. She has the genuine warmth common among women who successfully work for a living and simultaneously manage a home. It is actually more, for it requires genuine intelligence, which Beeji had aplenty. Yes, intelligent and warm, that is it. She also is the first woman doctor from Patiala State, and her patients are very attached to her. She obviously has a lot going for her.

Beeji took Preeti into the drawing room, but asked me to wait in the verandah. I have no idea what transpired, but both their eyes were moist when they came out, and Preeti looked happy. I never asked her what happened. If there were something for me to know, she would tell me in her own time. One thing I did learn. Papaji had been told of the marriage. He was not angry, only disappointed that I had not seen fit to tell him. I was happily surprised, and felt a little guilty because I had been unfair to him.

We all had tea in the verandah that afternoon. As evening set in, word spread of my marriage, and many of the neighbors came to bless us, twirling moneyed hands in a circular motion over our heads and then, not at all unpleasantly for us, dropping the lucre in Preeti's lap. I did not like this custom, knowing that money, even in small amounts, went a long way for these folks, but there was little I could do. Any attempt at refusal would give offense, so I just sat there and confined my thoughts to its pleasanter aspects. By the time the last person on the street had finished 'seeing' the bride, it was close to nine o'clock. These visitors were known to my parents, but mostly strangers to me, though perhaps there had been times when we exchanged greetings on the street. Yet, even though I sensed an obligatory element in this custom, it also nurtured a common feeling of humanity and, above all, it served to satisfy their curiosity about the bride.

Preeti was a little embarrassed sitting there in a shirt and slacks because it felt un-Indian. I told her not to dwell on it—there would be ample opportunity to wear pretty sarees. She already had many from her previous marriage, and my mother would certainly add to those. In any case, it was enough that she was allowing these strangers to gape at her, even though she wasn't decked out like a doll. If she could take it, this little concession to custom would win us at least the grudging respect of the neighborhood. Besides, with her looks, I could imagine every man here envying me, and every girl wondering how I won her.

The neighbors' daughter Aasha also came, later, when most had gone. She congratulated the two of us, and was about to leave when Preeti stopped her and asked her to sit down beside her so they could talk. Embarrassment showed on me and Preeti certainly noticed. Vinode, Aasha's brother, who was a year older than her and two years younger than me, was having difficulty comprehending that I was married. He did not consider us significantly different in age, so he kept expressing his surprise at my being married. Finally, when we were out of earshot of the others, he came out with it. "Amrik," he said, "she is beautiful! You've got to find me someone like her."

"Of course I will," I assured him, "what are friends for?" Just let me know who you have an eye on, and we'll find a way. Marriage has some advantages when it comes to arranging meetings."

He knew my views on love and marriage well. Call it a holy mission, or what you will, it was my intention to subvert the system if that is what it took to get a girl and boy together. Once we had a dwelling of our own, bachelor friends would have a place to meet the girl of their dreams. If necessary, I would cover for them so that they stayed out of trouble. In effect, Preeti and I would be another Mohini and Harbaksh.

Preeti sensed right away that I had had a crush on Aasha, so I figured they were talking about me, gingerly, of course. Aasha was a warm person, whose hand I had held in the darkness of a cinema once while she sat between her brother and I, but we had never gone out again. She always seemed to be tied up in chores or with homework. Try as I would, it was seldom possible to be alone with her. Now I was hoping that she did not care for me with the kind of intensity I had felt for her, because it would pain me if she felt hurt.

That night the rain was heavy, and accompanied by lightning and thunder. Preeti and I, as expected, were housed in Beeji's office, but for the night only. Come next morning, it had to be relinquished to her patients by nine. Preeti accommodated by keeping her make-up things on my mother's dressing table and her clothes in my parents' bedroom. The house was small, and this bedroom was the only thoroughfare to the bathroom, so that we would be running across someone all the time, no matter where we went in the house. Real privacy was only available at night in the cramped office.

Then there was the problem of the bed. It was not built for two. I would have much preferred to remove the bed and sleep on a stuffed cotton mattress on the floor. There was one other problem, a less expected one. When we finally turned in, Preeti was quiet; too quiet, in fact.

"Preeti, is something wrong?" I asked apprehensively.

"Why didn't you tell me?" she complained.

"There is no way to change the bedroom arrangements today. I'll try for something better tomorrow," I explained.

"No," she replied, "about Aasha."

"Preeti," I assured her, "it never went beyond holding her hand in a cinema once, as I told you before."

"But she is beautiful."

"Yes, I'm afraid she is."

"Do you still care for her?" she asked.

"She has not changed, darling. If I stopped caring, I would be blind to beauty and unfair to her. I love you, and Heaven knows I cannot love anyone more. Why must I then pretend that others mean nothing to me? It would be inhuman. She was nice to me, but as far as I could tell, she did not love me, not the way I love you and you me, and . . . she is not a woman to inspire me to take on the world like you.

"Amrik, it hurts," she complained, huddling close to me. "It hurts to know you have warm feelings for another woman."

"I could lie, my love, but I can't, not even if the truth affects what you think of me. When I proposed to you, I resolved to be as visible as possible, never to protect myself behind a lie or a half-truth, or even a deliberate omission, for the simple reason that any such would imply a fear that you may not understand me. Darling, everyone says that marriages go sour sooner or later. Mr. Gopalan more or less implied it when he asked me how long I'd been married. But our marriage is never going to sour, not because of me, and knowing you, not because of you. My mind will never be a mystery to you; nothing will ever be hidden, and I am not hiding anything now."

She was mollified, but she had one more doubt. "When you held her hand," she asked," did you feel like you feel with me?"

"I was sexually excited, if that is what you mean, but she was reluctant, even with her hand. I was disappointed, and it never reached the stage of elation that I felt simply dancing with you the first time in the meadow. There were really more clouds than sunshine. She does not think like you or me. She would never break with tradition. I was excited, I admit, but not inspired, nor did I dream of saying foolish nothings to her. Perhaps I was never in love; it was just simply a healthy attraction, and nothing more. I'm not sure."

Preeti rolled over towards me and traced her finger over my cheek and the side of my neck. "I'm in a strange house," she said, "and I feel insecure. I wanted to be friends with her, but I've never been in this position before."

I hugged her close and tried to will my confidence into her. "You won't ever lose me," I promised. "Do you know that Aasha's brother, Vinode, couldn't keep his eyes off you? He has a crush on you, and he kept asking me to find someone as pretty for him. Darling, it is not you who has to worry, it is other women. Look at Mr. Gopalan, you certainly bowled him over. But I don't feel jealous; rather, I feel proud that so many people want you. In fact, I must have done something right that you are actually jealous of another pretty girl."

"I am jealous, love, but I shouldn't be, because I know that you are crazy about me. But you are strong and true of purpose. I worry that I may not be able to live up to what you expect of me."

It was obviously more than a problem of jealousy. I thought about it awhile, then it struck me. It was so obvious that I felt foolish not having thought of it earlier. "Preeti," I said, trying to explain the problem, "when a woman gets married, she expects to make a home. You don't have one, except in an abstract sense with me. Right now you are living in someone else's home. It is not your husband's, but his parents' home. It can never really be ours. But tomorrow we'll begin looking for one, and we'll also begin to look for other sources of income, such as tutoring children who need help with their studies. I could teach English and Math, and you could teach fine art. Darling, we'll win out in the end, because I want us to have our own home just as much as you do. Please don't embarrass me by making me feel that all I can offer you at present is this little room, and that too only for the nights."

This last sentence finally broke the ice. It brought out the mother in her. Men are physically stronger than women, but whoever said that they are emotionally or psychologically stronger too, particularly as compared to a woman in love? She sensed this, because in no time at all, we were kissing and making up, saying sweet nothings and making promises that we never needed to make. They were foolish and redundant; even the very idea of having to promise seemed insulting. Was it even imaginable that our feelings for each other could ever change? Impossible!

I told Preeti what I thought of promises, and she smiled. "Darling, you're right," she agreed. "I made a mistake allowing myself to think that I could lose you. It was foolish because you would be lost without me. I have to trust my senses. My eyes, my ears, my lips, my fingers, they don't lie to me. I feel spent, as if I had been fighting myself, foolishly and needlessly, imagining possibilities that could not possibly be, knowing what I know. But before I go to sleep, tell me one thing: what do you feel for her?"

"I feel sorry for her, for if she cares for me at all, she must feel a void which I cannot fill. It makes me feel almost cruel; and guilty. I hope she finds another man, and soon."

"I'm sure she will. She is pretty enough, and she must be a good person for you to have cared for her."

"That she is," I agreed, "but her mind is not as fertile as yours. Yet she is pure of heart and has the strength of a woman, even though she is only fifteen."

"Amrik, hold me close. I need you."

And so I held her, and pressed the softness of her body into mine. We made love, in that tiny bed, in the warm room with the ceiling fan, and with dried sweat on our bodies. Soon all was forgotten as we lay in the bliss of each other's arms. Lying side by side, satisfied, we knew that nothing could come between us, and on that note we drifted into slumber.

XXI

The succeeding days were busy. Beeji's offer of their own bedroom for us had been politely, but firmly, refused. Instead, she was persuaded to replace the office bed at night with a mattress on the floor. Preeti and I now had ample room to sleep. For me, it, floor or bed, made little difference, but there was some concern that Preeti may not be too enthused with the arrangement. But she did not seem to mind at all; in fact, she enjoyed it.

"Positive thinking?" I asked.

"No," she replied, "look at it this way: sleeping on the ground has the flavor of camping; and we all love camping. Besides, the firm ground does not squeak, precisely and perversely, at the very moment that you want no distraction."

Good thinking, I figured, and wholeheartedly agreed, adding that I thought it also enhanced the pleasure of sex. There is something to say for unyielding earth beneath a body, like the time outdoors in Solan. Granted, we now did not have the delightful touch of green grass on naked skin; or the fragrance of pine forests; or the haunting rustling of the wind; but man, in his quest for perfection, had provided many a perfume, essences extracted from Nature's own bounty. Preeti was welcome to try them on as long as they impassioned; and that was no problem, intoxicated as I was even *sans parfum.* Somewhere in the complexities of love, iodine and methylated spirit had been overcome; in fact, completely forgotten.

If I had had my way, Beeji would have been persuaded to go easy with the sarees and spend her time and money on the intimate enhancement of Preeti's already considerable beauty, with fragrances and jewels. But sarees won. Preeti was not merely a bedroom person; she liked to flaunt her figure; and even I could not deny that a saree well tied, and carried well, had few equals.

But I did extract a concession. Preeti agreed to buy jewelry with an eye as much for its enhancement of her nude body as for beautification of her clothed exterior. You should try it one of these days; I mean making love to a beautiful, bejeweled, and naked woman. Imagine Cleopatra; isn't it an insult to envision her totally bare in the company of Mark Antony? A beautiful woman should not be treated thus; she has a right to a modicum of modesty. A discerning man would clothe her in jewels; cover her nudity with splendor.

It was one of those days when she was modeling in the drawing room for my mother and I, trying on one saree after another, that a thought crossed my mind. I kept quiet, but later, when we were alone, I broached the subject. "Preeti," I asked, "how would you like to be a model?"

"You wouldn't mind?" she asked, her enthusiasm clearly showing.

"Why should I mind?"

"You would not feel jealous seeing me using my charms on others?"

"No, Preeti," I replied, "in fact, if I could have my way, I would show you off to the entire world."

"Beeji is not going to like it, you know. And think of Papaji; it may be just a bit too much for him."

But her expressions betrayed her, for her eyes had lighted up at the prospect. Her apparent reservations were merely to provoke me into providing reasons why it would be acceptable, such as 'if her husband approves, a wife does not need to worry about her in-laws.'

"Preeti," I explained, "I can see no better way to live life than by doing everything you can with what you have, so long as it pleases you. I can tell by the glow on your face every time you model that you love it."

"Yes, I do," she agreed; "may be I am a little bit of an exhibitionist. Doesn't that bother you, just a wee bit?"

"You mean because exhibitionist is a bad word?"

"It certainly has that connotation of depravity," she replied.

"No, I can live with it. You are an artist. Just think of what all the great artists throughout history have done. Their most beautiful paintings are of nude women. I don't see what's wrong with you posing with clothes on," I replied.

"But don't you see?" she said. "A model isn't just modeling clothes. She is using her charms to enhance the value of the clothes, trying to persuade people that they are being offered something better than they really are. They are encouraged to imagine that their woman, if she wore the same, would, in some magical way on which they should not dwell, become one with the model they see within the clothes. You are trying to make them fall in love with you, in the hope that they will transfer the love over to the woman for whom they are buying what you are modeling. It is not a completely honest game, for the model is very much using her wiles on the public, even though only as a surrogate for other women.

"But Preeti," I objected, "it is this way with everything. I would be doing the same if I were writing a novel, asking, even imploring the reader, to imagine himself and his lady-love as the fictional characters that I portray. I certainly imagine myself in the same mold. My method is indirect, requiring the readers to make a greater effort and to create the scene in their imagination. Granted it is with the help of my suggestive words and sequences, the creation still has to be their own. Yours is more direct, dispensing as it does with the more difficult self-creation of visual images."

"But what do you think of the fact that I must use equivalent movements of my body to do the work of your 'suggestive words and sequences?" she asked.

"Don't we all do that every day?" I countered.

"But then we really mean it," she said. "We want the suggestions to be taken literally. It is for our own sake."

I was not sure if she was aware of it, but she was using suggestive movements on me right then, and my imagination was running riot. But I had to supply her with every last nuance, every which way to look on this subtle but acceptable form of seduction, so I reined in my thoughts and continued: "Look, Preeti, I don't see where the problem is. If you don't really mean those suggestive things when you are modeling, why should it bother you?"

"Because what you are saying is almost impossible to do. An actress has to be the part, has to actually feel that what she is doing is genuine, even feel the appropriate emotions, else her performance will be pallid. It will neither convince nor move anyone. So what I am saying, husband dear, is that when I will be modeling, I will, to a large extent, be really trying to seduce."

"Oh! Are you afraid that you will succeed?" I asked, trying to anticipate what she was driving at.

"There's always the possibility," she answered coquettishly, "honesty is a difficult virtue to shed. An honest response to an honest 'come hither' look cannot be easily dismissed.

"I will take my chances with that," I replied. "If I am to have you, it will not be because I have in any way restricted you. Right now, I have you because you want me to. It is not my objections that you will have to fight, it will be your own much more potent ones, your own desire to have this 'boy;' and if those desires were in some measure to wane, my demands that they must not would be futile, even improper. The dilemma is yours, not mine, if dilemma it is."

"Do you care so little for me that you would so willingly give me up, even without a fight?" she objected.

"Preeti, I would be devastated if you left me! You would have destroyed my frame of reference to reality. It would be brought home to me with numbing certainty that all I had assumed before was wrong; that when you looked at me with loving eyes, and I saw your pupils darken, you were not welling with desire, but merely pretending it; that when you trembled in my arms, it was not because of an ecstasy that was unbearable, but because you were making a conscious effort to please; that you loved me not because I was the kind of man you admired and hungered for, but because you felt sorry for me. Preeti, if you left me, all that I believed about you would be proven wrong, not because of any deception on your part, but because I had read you and reality wrong, so utterly wrong. My love would be shown to be an enormous, aberrant affliction or wishful thinking on my part. It is this way whenever a loved one does anything which violates and negates everything you thought you knew about her.

"Dying does much the same thing," I continued, "except that it is a great deal more confusing. The guilt is similar. Why, for instance, did you not understand enough to forestall her death? Why did you not move Heaven and Earth to find a way? It is irrelevant that death is out of our hands; it is only what your mind believes that matters; and your mind is so firmly rooted in the Law of Causality that it insists on finding a cause. You know the proximate cause of death, but causality forces you to imagine a moral cause, an ethical failing that led to it. After all, the separation we call death is like a punishment, Nature's retribution; and since you are the one being punished, it is your deeds or thoughts that must have evoked the punitive response. And worse, the separation seems in some enigmatic way willed by her; in essence a desertion, rejection, beyond any other. It rends your heart, destroying as it does the underpinnings of your existence, and your reference to reality; the only difference being that death, unlike desertion, gives you no second chance. But even that difference between death and desertion is not important. If you had loved someone for the wrong reasons, is there any chance you could love her after you discovered the truth? Slim indeed, I'd say. She would be a different woman, and you'd have to be quite a chameleon to find her just as attractive."

Preeti was moved by the magnitude of what she meant to me; of the centrality with which she affected my being. "Amrik," she asked, trying to delve deeper into our relationship, "do you think of me as your lover or as your wife?"

"My lover," I replied unhesitatingly. "The wife bit is for society. To me, you are a most desirable woman, who I want never to leave me; one over whom I have the right of love. But I cannot conceive of having any legal rights over you, whatever the law says. Any rights I have must be willingly given and ever afresh. If you wanted to leave me, I would be demolished, but I would neither beg for your return nor demand a divorce. I would simply fight to get a hold of myself, to get a grasp of this world I had so badly misunderstood. If I succeeded and subsequently fell in love with someone else, and the law refused me permission to remarry, I would then simply live with her— to hell with the law! Only her permission, and mine, would matter."

"I'm sure it doesn't surprise you that I feel the same way," Preeti observed, "but I would feel anger if you left me. I have been hurt before, and I don't think I'm ready to let myself be hurt again, though, as you say, what use is an attempt to hold the unwilling, the one who no longer loves? I could not live with you for security alone."

We had explored all the possibilities, strengthening and cementing our love in the process. More to the point, we saw no reason why Preeti should not try to be a model. It would please her, help boost my ego, and certainly make a big difference in our finances. The next ten days were spent going through the formalities of securing admission to college, and driving around New Delhi trying to find an apartment at reasonable rent. We were willing to pay up to three hundred rupees a month for a two-room apartment with a kitchen and bathroom in a reasonably good section of the city. Preeti's pension from her late husband brought in about three hundred rupees a month, and my work would bring in another two hundred. We had about a thousand rupees dropped into her lap by nosy, but generous, neighbors as she sat demurely on exhibit the day we arrived in Delhi. My mother had given us another three thousand as a wedding gift, and we hoped to make some more if Preeti could model. My mother had also insisted that we allow her to pay for our college fees, which in India were minimal anyway. Finally, there was a certain amount of income—a few thousand per year—that came in from Preeti's land that was being managed by Harbaksh. All in all, there would not be a money crunch if we spent wisely.

By the end of the month, we had found a place in Defence Colony. It was vacant and for immediate occupancy. It was the annexe to a house owned by a couple. The husband was a colonel; they had one daughter, six years old, and were still trying to have a son. Their plans were very long-term, implicitly based on the assumption that when their putativee son grew up, he would marry, raise a family, and live in the main house. They, the aging parents, would then move to the small, but comfortable, annexe. Renting it out over the next twenty plus years would bring them in more than enough money towards marrying off their daughter, while leaving some over for their old age, in addition to his pension.

Preeti had little difficulty at the modeling agency. She was hired the very first time she went there. To begin with, she would model salwaar-kameezes and sarees, mostly for publication in magazines, and if she was successful, then later for commercials in the cinema world. There was as yet no television in India.

Two weeks after coming to Delhi, with our financial future on reasonably certain grounds, we moved into our new apartment. My parents bought us furniture: a double bed with a wooden board and a Dunlopillo mattress; a small dining table with four chairs; and a desk table with a chair for my typewriter. We had already brought with us Preeti's easel, painting and drawing materials from Solan. Our bedroom served as my office and Preeti's studio. Preeti's dressing table and sofa set were still in Shimla, but we had bought a Godrej steel almirah to keep her clothes and valuables in. Most of the jewelry, though, was kept in Karole Bagh with Beeji, where it was safer. We would get the dressing table and sofas later when we were on better terms with Preeti's mother; more accurately, when her mother's ire and her feeling of being jilted, so to say, had subsided. As far as we were concerned, there were no hard feelings between us and Mummy so long as she was resigned to the fact that we were going to do with our lives more or less exactly what we wished. Kitchen utensils, provided by Beeji, included an oil stove, pots and pans, other cooking utensils, and enough silverware, glasses and plates for us and a half-dozen guests. One thousand rupees of the money gifted by Beeji went into acquiring a second-hand refrigerator from an American who lived nearby and was now headed back to the States. All in all, we were comfortably provided for, and the only thing we needed now was a servant. This did not take long. Govind had his cousin Gopaal come down from his home in the hills so that, in a week's time, we were all set. We had no place for Gopaal to stay, but he had a brother who worked in a house two streets away with servants' quarters where he would spend the nights. A servant would ordinarily have cost us fifty rupees a month, but we agreed to add another twenty for accommodations. Cheating at buying groceries, we figured, would net Gopaal another ten or twenty, so he was well taken care of.

You may wonder why a servant is so essential. It is not because Indian housewives are lazy; in fact, they are usually overworked; but because of two major reasons. One is for buying groceries and doing the cooking. Groceries have to be bought fresh every day because there are no such things as supermarkets or frozen foods. Since most Indians do not have a refrigerator, that means daily shopping. If the wife were not working, one could imagine that she would do the cooking. That is possible and is done in the poor and lower middle class households, though in the absence of ovens, gas ranges and dishwashers, it is a lot more work than for an American housewife. Cooking often has to be done over a coal fire, which is never easy to start; and given the design of most kitchens—there are no exhaust fans—smoke is a major problem. If your wife is working or a student, you are asking too much of her. Besides, the dust that gathers so easily in Indian houses, given the climate and the fact that, for similar reasons, the doors are not airtight, requires a daily cleaning, with brooms, since vacuum cleaners are unheard of. The second and even more important reason for having a servant is that his presence ensures that you do not get burglarized. If both husband and wife intend to be out of the house most of the day, you would be wiped out in less than a week without a servant; and going on vacation would be even riskier.

College opened some time in July. On weekdays, Preeti and I drove together to her Polytechnic, where she kept the car because her classes often finished early. I continued on to the University by bus, which I also took on the way back home. Some days I kept the car and picked her up from the Polytechnic on the way back.

I met two old Cottonians, Ravi Chopra and Suneel Kapoor, the very first day at St. Stephens. Both were former class-fellows of mine. Ravi was planning to become a chartered accountant. His father was a banker, and they were a wealthy and respected family. He was also an excellent cricket player. Suneel was planning to become an engineer. He had always been good at math and science, and was by aptitude a scientist. I remember how in school, at the age of thirteen, without help from anybody, he had built an induction coil—and it worked. He had shown scant interest in other subjects, so I had been able to best him every time in the exams. Nonetheless, I had great respect for his intelligence and ability. He also thought like me. No, he was not a philosopher, but he gave short shrift to tradition. I therefore had no qualms telling him that I was now married. By the end of the day, Ravi too knew. My other class-fellows, though, did not come to know for almost a week. By then, I had made many friends.

The knowledge of my marital status evoked a change in attitude towards me, primarily because the interests of bachelors and married men do not often coincide. But one day Preeti came to pick me up after class because she had finished early. I introduced her to my closest friends and we invited them over for dinner on Saturday night. There were eight of us that evening: Suneel, Jaspaal and Romesh from St. Stephens—Ravi could not come because he had to attend the wedding of a cousin— and Nimmi, Chanchal and Vinona, all girls from Preeti's class. These girls were from relatively well-educated families living in and around Defence Colony, so getting permission from their parents was not difficult. Anyway, we had offered to drop them home after the party. Our landlord lent us some extra chairs, and Suneel's record player served for music and entertainment.

By the time preliminaries were over, everyone was feeling quite at ease. Except for Suneel, none of our guests knew how to dance, so Preeti and he demonstrated the technique for the rest of us. Very soon, we were all dancing the foxtrot and the rumba, but when it came to the waltz, Suneel had to sit down while Preeti and I showed the others how it was really done. Almost all the boys had a crush on Preeti, but none more than Suneel. It led to a certain tension in the beginning but, as the evening wore on, things began to get better. What we missed most was a rug to sit on. In the absence of sofas, that would have been the best way to seat everybody. Suneel came up with the brilliant idea of inviting in the colonel and his wife. We did, and it gave us an excuse to borrow a durree. This way, there would be place for everyone to sit down.

The colonel and his wife arrived, we spread out the durree in the middle of the room, covered it with bedsheets, and all ten of us sat down to dinner, Karole Bagh style. Dinner over, Gopaal was sent home. Then I brought out two of my grandfather's decks of cards, gifted by him to me when I had last visited Dagshai, and the Colonel and I proceeded to teach everyone Bridge. This was followed by Rummy, finally ending on a high note with Bhabo, that most hilarious and rowdy of Indian card games. By the time the party was over, it was a roaring success, and everybody was exchanging telephone numbers. It was agreed we would all go to the movies the following Saturday, the Colonel and his wife included. This way the parents of the girls would not feel they were unchaperoned. Visions of hand-holding, I'm sure, were in everyone's mind, the kind of romantic subversion Preeti and I were dreaming of.

Monday morning, I discovered that I was no longer a stranger in my class. In fact, there were more people trying to befriend me than ever before in my life. I was indeed a celebrity. Once a loner, my life had changed ever since I met Preeti, so that the attention I was getting was quite welcome; indeed, it was very positive reinforcement. Two days later, the first *My Troubled Land* column came out in the National Express. It was titled *"Arranging a Marriage."* Next morning, many of my fellow students were talking about it, both pro and con, sometimes quite hotly and for the most part favorably.

Romesh came up to me after lunch. "Amrik," he said, "you have an illustrious namesake."

"What do you mean?" I asked, intrigued.

"Don't you read the newspapers?" he asked.

"Sometimes," I replied, having realized what he meant, but pretending ignorance.

"Well, you should read the National Express. "There's a guy in there with your name who has written something really hot about arranged marriages. It's worth reading. Our parents and, I'm sure some of our teachers, will be furious."

"Why do you say that?" I asked.

"Why?" he repeated with amazement. "You've got to read that article, yaar (friend); the guy certainly doesn't hold back any punches."

I smiled calmly and said with deliberation: "I've read it."

"Why didn't you say so at the beginning?" he asked, puzzled but suspicious.

"I just wanted to know what you thought."

"I see, so you wrote it, didn't you?" he said, convinced.

I had to come out and tell him: "Yes, Romesh, I wrote that piece."

He was beaming with delight and disbelief. His own friend a celebrity, and such a controversial one at that. He held out a congratulatory hand and shook mine vigorously. "It was good of you; damned good! Look, I know you can take care of yourself, but if you ever need help, I'll always be there for you. You're my kind of fellow."

Then he turned reflective. "You and Preeti; it figures. Did you write this article before or after you were married?"

"After. The inspiration was not there before. She means everything to me and my world is alive as never before."

His admiration knew no bounds, and he was genuinely touched by the way I talked of Preeti. Starved for love, young Indians show great warmth and admiration, occasionally envy, for anyone who succeeds. Among friends, the reaction is invariably positive.

It did not take long for me to be famous, and notorious, in the college. Students unknown to me would come up and shake my hand. "Congratulations!" "Good show!" "It's about time." All sorts of compliments kept pouring in. But I was not used to hero-worship, and I had expected a lot more controversy. That did come later, but mostly from the teachers.

My literature teacher, Professor Karmarkar, was elated, but Professor Pant, my history teacher, was grudgingly complementary of the grasp of knowledge implicit in my article, and sarcastically critical of the views expressed therein. He even went so far as to make a point of it in one of his lectures.

"Notwithstanding the views of some members of this class," he proclaimed, "I will attempt to show you during the course of the next six months that our land is one with a heroic cultural heritage to be proud of, one rivaling that of ancient Greece. I am certain, by the time you are done studying this course, that you will agree with me that Indian culture does not lend itself to analysis by Western norms; and that it is inappropriate and unfair to judge it by alien standards. We were an advanced civilization at a time many millennia ago when the ancestors of Europeans were still wearing bearskins and living at a subsistence level little better than cavemen. They lived in tents and hunter-gatherer-type encampments, while our ancestors lived in cities with centralized sanitation, roads, bath-houses, temples, gardens and palaces. We already had some of the greatest poetry and philosophy in the world, great scientific achievements and even a written language (here I knew he was taking credit for both the ancient Indus Valley civilization, which did have a written language, and the later Aryan invaders who came from Central Asia and destroyed the former, and with them the written word. The Aryans themselves did not have writing for another thousand years, being forced to carry their voluminous compositions, the stunning Sanskrit poetry of the Vaids and other works, by rote down the generations), while the Europeans chased herds of animals, trying to extract a precarious survival. Our institutions have survived millennia and will survive many millennia more, though their ignorant detractors will not."

I was incensed. His criticism was a distortion. My article never belittled the achievements of Indian civilization. It said nothing of Western ethics or standards of judgment—I had merely subjected our marriage traditions to the test of logic, which was by no means a Western concept. My article purported to show the injustices and unnecessary sorrow and grief caused by the institution of arranged marriage; and what to me was its underlying cause, the caste system. Indians had as much right to happiness as anyone else, and my article implied just that. But I was not about to stand up in class and criticize the professor for his bigotry. The student-teacher relationship, unfortunately, is one that can be used unfairly to the teacher's advantage. However, I would instead welcome a letter to the Editor from him, if he dared, and then answer him in the proper public forum where he could not attack me with innuendo and recourse to misguided patriotism without letting it be exposed for what it was. On an equal footing, I would make him eat his words. So I held my peace.

Over the next few weeks, I put my mind to my studies, particularly history. I did not want Professor Pant to have a chance to belittle me in any way. He did respect scholarship, so even if he hated my guts, I would force him to recognize my abilities. In any case, his criticism could make little difference to me. What I believed in was not based on popularity polls, though I daresay I could have won those as well in the University, even if perhaps not in the country at large. My thesis rested on a firm acceptance of reality and logical analysis, twin virtues that had never failed anyone.

Preeti was pleased with her teachers at the Polytechnic, but relations with some of her class-fellows were not faring too well. Several of them had made timid passes at her and, failing to get a response, had descended to making unsavory remarks, the typical kind of hooliganism that is the norm among Indian youth—eve-teasing, they call it. Preeti ignored it initially, but its persistence was beginning to get to her. Fortunately, though, except for a few of the girls, no one in the class had connected her to my article in the National Express. The remarks would otherwise have been nastier.

One day, Romesh and I got off the bus at the Polytechnic to hitch a ride with Preeti. She was coming out to us when one of her tormentors remarked, as an aside but loud enough for her to hear and, unfortunately for him, for me as well: "Oho yaar, look how they sway!"

So saying, he fell forwards on the ground in Preeti's way as if he had been struck dead by Kaam's (Cupid's) arrow. She, of course, was in tears, and running towards the car. This was too much for me. Ordinarily a peaceful man by nature, my mind was now seized by searing flames. Moments later, I stood there, a cut on my knuckles, looking down on my wife's tormentor, his nose bleeding, lips swollen, and fear screaming from his eyes. Romesh was by my side, fists clenched. Daunted by our anger, the frustrated cowards slunk away like vermin, followed by my shouted warning at the one with the smashed nose: "Next time, I will kill you, so stay away from my wife."

The episode had been watched by many and, in subsequent days, Preeti had a lot more friends in her class to take her side. The eve-teasers stayed away, hiding themselves in the sewers from which they had come. Our ancient culture, my foot! All it bred now were hooligans like these, taking out their frustrations on anyone who dared to challenge tradition; in dress, behavior, or what have you. I was not going to let this country be delivered into the hands of cowards, mean self-righteous beasts driven to hatred by envy of anyone who succeeded or was happy; driven by forces that proclaimed them patriots; yet they were no more than venomous bigots.

When we got home, Preeti sent home the servant, giving him the rest of the evening off, put on her jewelry on her nude body, gave me a come-hither look, and invited me to make love. In the arms of my beloved, and in the warmth of her body, the pains of the day, the hypocrisy of our culture, all were forgotten. Only the good remained; just beauty and perfection.

XXII

College was much easier than expected, so that I had time to study whatever I wished; and I had access to the excellent Delhi University library. BCS had taught me little about India; what understanding I had of the country's soul and its people had been gleaned from Harbaksh's philosophy books and the vicissitudes of my childhood. But philosophy, except in the hands of genius, is at heart heavy and didactic, because most treatises are written with more devotion to scholarship than a flair for drama. Aware of this, the creators of mythology, in their earthy wisdom, had peopled the universe with epic characters that millenia of cheerless philosophic commentaries had failed to wrest of their charm. The Mahabhaarat and Raamayan flowed through the waiting soil of my intellect like summer rain, greening the parched plains of Indian philosophy with their larger than life, but often richly human, characters. Their tales were not burdened with mystical paradoxes, and the intricacies of philosophy lay revealed in choices, actions and destinies. It seemed irrelevant at the time whether I approved of their moral assumptions; what mattered was an absence of duplicity.

India's philosophic creations were born in an era lost in the mists of antiquity, and were largely untouched by the hand of history; but much creative fiction, even though poorly datable at best, has survived from similarly olden times; and to that fiction I applied myself. *Shakuntala,* the hauntingly beautiful play by Kaalidas about the love between the captivating daughter of an apsara and a king; the *Toy Cart* by King Shudraka, in which a city's rich and lovely courtesan falls in love with and marries a philanthropic, and consequently poor, Brahmin. Another play, the *Signet Ring of Rakshas*, about Chanakya, India's Machiavelli, and the *Dream of Vasvadatta,* where a queen who loves and is loved by a king acquiesces in the surreptitious marriage of her husband to another princess so that his power may grow. All these I read, and more. I learned that Death must never be represented on the stage; that tragedy was unacceptable. The characters were larger than life, and there was wit and humor, both sophisticated and slapstick. There were also poignancy, charm, moving love scenes handled with delicacy, heart-rending twists of fate, and compassion. In short, it was a culture both vibrant and charming.

Contemporary India had little in that class, except Tagore and a handful of others. The substance had shrunk, but claims of greatness had been much inflated. Not a day passed without someone loudly proclaiming, across the ether courtesy of All India Radio, in the columns of newspapers, or from political pulpits, our ancient heritage, as if virtue was acquired with one's genes. How easy it was to usurp. All you needed was to be born Indian, and the totality of ancient India's greatness would fall into your lap, yours to inherit, effortlessly. Imbeciles claimed to have received the brilliance of Kaalidas, and cowards the courage of Arjun. Historic kinship absolved them of the necessity of achieving, striving, and proving their worth. It was an automatic graduation to greatness, heedless as they were, in the heady intoxication of easy, but fake, superiority, to the knowledge that morons do get born in the houses of brahmins and the powerful, and genius does arise in the hovels of untouchables and the socially abused. They were forgetting too that you are what you make yourself, not what your father was, that your claims are valid only for your achievements, not for those of others, ancestors or otherwise. It was little wonder that many of the congenitally brave and superior today were of the same ilk as Preeti's eve-teasers, and their ranks comprised the legions of communal mobs that ran riot on frenzies of

religious fervor, slaughtering unarmed innocents by the
thousands for the inherited color of their soul, Muslim, Hindu,
or Sikh. Ethical beliefs were invisible and of no consequence
to them; only genetic inheritance mattered, as if something as
avowedly intellectual as religion could be received through the
genes. May be, they figured, if caste could, why not this?

With all this eruditon tucked away in my brain, I looked
afresh at India, in its totality, contradictions and all. The ancient
playwrights, I noticed, seldom violated restrictions of caste, or
the divine right of kings. But they were human, and every now
and then there would be a dig at the expense of the ruler, or his
minister, or a brahmin. I often wondered whether they really
believed in the rigid class code laid down for Hindus, or they
simply went along, because to behave otherwise was social
and economic suicide. Sometimes, their efforts at circumvention
were heartwarming and touching, evoking my silent cheers, as
in the *Toy Cart.* Indeed, women and love were usually treated
with charm and respect. Whether fiction paralleled reality was
difficult to say, knowing that death and tragedy, and the hardship
that is the lot of many an Indian today would have been barred
from the stage, if they existed then.

When I applied my imagination to see what would happen
if anyone were to actually live by the philosophic precepts
propounded by the scriptures, via games that I played with
myself or with Preeti, in which we mentally applied these
teachings to real life, the result, given all the contradictions the
precepts embodied, was often hilarious. But beneath the mirth,
I could sense an existence that could not be laughed away, like
in Tagore's *Binodini,* in which Binodini, beautiful, talented, witty,
charming and young, but a widow, is dragged through a life of
misery because she refuses to accept what Indian societal
institutions demanded of her, that she had no right to love and
happiness. I could laugh at the imaginary, but reality demanded
sobriety. The demoralizing message would not go away.

Steeped in Violence, the second of my literary submissions,
was now in print. Among other things, it had the salutary effect

of alerting my landlord to my literary aspirations and talent. His discovery that Preeti was the daughter of a decorated war hero also tilted him favorably in our direction. He envisioned me now as more than just a student; in fact, I was desirable company. Accordingly, we were invited to his home for a party for his army friends, many of whom lived in the neighborhood. By the end of the party, two of the guests had expressed interest in having me tutor their sons. Preeti and I had already told our hosts that we were willing and able, and would appreciate any new income that could come our way in this manner. A week later, Preeti too had a pupil. One of the army wives in the neighborhood had been visiting the colonel's wife when the latter happened to mention that my wife was a budding artist. Preeti showed the visitor some of her work, and it was agreed that she would give the woman's fourteen-year-old daughter lessons in drawing and painting. I was to teach English every day except Saturday and Sunday to two boys, thirteen and fourteen years old, respectively, and Preeti art twice a week to the young lady. The lessons were to be at our place, in the evenings, mine for an hour with both the boys together, and Preeti's for two hours because in her field little could be accomplished in one.

Many a night we lay in bed planning our strategy. We lacked formal teaching experience and, anyway, my desire for innovation ruled the usual methods out of the question. What went by the name of teaching in most schools was, to my mind, a caricature of that noble activity. I needed a superior way. It was decided that we would devise something innovative, appealing, and highly motivating, because we felt that motivation was the key to the unlocking of a child's mind.

Next evening, Ajay and Shiv, the two boys, arrived at our apartment. Preeti had bought some samosas and gulaab jaamans to make them feel at home, on the premise that a full stomach has a warming, and thawing, effect. In the course of the ten minutes that we spent eating, it became clear that the boys were extremely reticent and, though they did have some grasp of English and its grammar, their pronunciation was atrocious, the vocabulary depressingly deficient, and expressive ability minimal. I explained my plan to them. During the lessons, we would all speak only English, unless it was absolutely necessary for them to use the vernacular to explain an idea that they could not at all express in English. The coming Sunday, Preeti and I would take them to a Hollywood movie, and the Sunday thereafter, all of us, including Preeti, and hopefully her pupil, would go on a picnic to Lodi Gardens. These ploys, unorthodox though they were, produced effects that left no doubt that the boys were now firmly in favor of learning. Who wouldn't be, given such incentives?

The next question was: what should I teach? One way would be to just talk about everything under the sun, whatever came to mind, aiming at as wide an exposure of their minds to the wonders of human knowledge as I could muster. For homework, I would assign them a romantic novel to read, one with both quality and a powerful plot. It would be intellectually elevating, but not skittish about reality—I didn't want my pupils handled with kid gloves. They must learn, along with the English language, values, and both the sorrows and joys of life. As they were post-pubertal, goody-goody fairytales would no longer do, and conservative, 'proper' fare was anathema to me. So I picked, after much deliberation, my favorite novel, Charlotte Bronte's *Jane Eyre*, a book that had the added advantage of being readily available in book stores.

For the first lesson, I simply talked with the boys, inquiring about their life, insisting that they answer everything in English, while making efforts to emulate me in pronunciation as much as possible. Preeti sat with us because I wanted them to feel at home; what better way to do that than attractive female company? I made it clear that they were free to make as many blunders as they wished, but not free to hesitate or act shy as Indian youngsters were wont to do. My plan was a quick success. By the end of the first week, they were both much more talkative and less reticent in expressing an opinion than when the classes started.

The Sunday movie was a huge success. It was *The Three Musketeers*. I paid for the tickets, deeming it unwise to ask the boys' parents to do so until my teaching methods had been vindicated and proven superior to the conventional ways of instruction. The movie had the desired effect in that they were both in love with Constance, and excited. All the way back, they couldn't stop talking, and that too in English, because all else was forbidden. It mattered little that the dashing swordplay eclipsed everything in their minds save the beautiful Constance, but then they were but boys; and anyway, my purpose was to inspire, which the movie did in ample measure. It made them dream brave dreams; hinted that the impossible was possible, and awakened romantic desires in the context of dashing heroism. Preeti and I exchanged knowing glances. Excitement was in the air, and there was no question in our minds that the kids were motivated; and we had adroitly, and wisely, taken advantage of both hormones and innate curiosity.

Preeti's pupil, Sapna, which in Hindi means 'dream,' was a bright little girl who already was motivated. For her first lesson, she had brought along her drawings to Preeti. The perspective in them was often flawed, but there was no lack of imagination. Everything was in pencil, and in outline form. Clearly, she still needed to learn the use of shading, charcoal and paint, but her efforts were promising. Preeti concluded that the precious ore was there, and it only awaited refining. Nurtured with care, she could some day create objects of great wonder. After her first lesson, Preeti and I decided that it may be a good idea to combine the two projects. Supna, with Preeti's help, would make imaginative illustrations of scenes from *Jane Eyre,* learning in the process ideas of balance and perspective, and the myriad little tricks that make a work of art express without verbal explanation what the artist wishes to portray. Art was like music, directly apprehended, bypassing the critical faculty, at least initially. In this sense, it was subjective, but yet sufficiently structured to know what appealed to the human mind and what did not, and that what it expressed could be controlled. For the purposes of the project, Ajay and Shiv would describe to Supna and Preeti the sequence and details of scenes as they appeared in *Jane Eyre*; in English, of course, aided by me whenever necessary. They were also free to make any critical comments about the artwork, if they felt there was any deviation from the spirit of the book. Critiquing, I reasoned, is an activity requiring intellectual analysis and a certain degree of responsibility. Making such efforts also forces one to understand the subtle nuances of artistic expression, and requires a level of conceptualization that would tax their minds and their vocabulary. I would always be there to ensure that it did not overwhelm their as yet immature intellects, but the idea was for me to hold back as much as possible, and to maximize their participation.

The following weeks made it abundantly clear that the boys were spending a lot of time on *Jane Eyre,* to the point that I was worried that they might be neglecting their other schoolwork. Accordingly, I asked them about how they were faring in math, history and geography. It was a relief to hear that they were doing fine, perhaps actually better, for the newfound enthusiasm and their rapidly improving English were having a salutary effect all around.

In the lessons, we spent most of the time discussing *Jane Eyre,* but I interspersed this didactic material with stories of my school and childhood, and eventually had them talk of their own experiences as well, to ensure that they did at least one-third of the talking, if not more. They told me of holiday trips with their parents, about their friends in school, their teachers and how they taught. I was keen to know about the teachers, but had decided that direct questioning was not wise and that this information should come spontaneously from them. The answer to my unasked question came in the form of a question. "Why," they asked, "were classes in school so tedious and boring when they could be so much fun?"

It was clear Preeti and I had the pros licked hands down. I thought back of the ancient custom of tutors, and how much more rewarding it was. Imagine Aristotle tutoring the young Alexander. By comparison, mass education was a pale imitation, weak for lack of energy, the logistics and limitations of the effort detracting from the motivation of the teacher and the taught. Granted I was no Aristotle, yet I could attempt to emulate an activity no teacher in school would dare to contemplate.

The picnic was like no other I had known; a family affair, yes, but much more so than the ones I was accustomed to. This was my own intimate family. I felt like an elder brother to our charges, and Preeti somewhere between a big sister and a mother. It was a combination of work, fun and games. There were jokes combined with lively discussions in English between the boys and me. Preeti and Sapna, meanwhile, made sketches of us in pencil and charcoal. In subsequent weeks, they would work on these and the scenes imagined out of *Jane Eyre.* I remember listening one day to Preeti explaining to Supna the interplay of mood and color: dull blues, greys and browns personified bleakness and sorrow. They were gloomy, enervating, the colors of depression and failure. In contrast, yellows, oranges and reds were warm, fired with increasing energy the redder they got. Clear blues, pinks and even greens were the color of serenity, clarity, dispassionate thought. Then there were the pastels, the shades the Impressionists used, mixing white with color as if to capture light itself. These spoke of joy and happiness, the kind of feeling I had at the picnic. Finally, there were the bright, intense reds and greens, and yellows and oranges, colors powerful and jarring, discordant, immiscible, smacking of the angry and artificial, insulting Nature with their loudness. I had been using these concepts without knowing that there is an invariance in the way the psyche responds to color. Writers had known it always—whence phrases such as 'feeling blue,' 'red with rage,' 'green with envy,' and so on.

As my understanding grew, and as my world continued to make increasing sense, everything was falling together little by little. Our small dwelling was slowly, but surely, becoming a cozy oasis of warmth, extending ever outwards, spilling its love to others. My mind was filled with varying shades of orange and soft red, the kind of skin tone you get when you break all the rules and use daylight film with tungsten light. At the time, I did not own a camera, but in later years, I learned that if you want a woman to look warm and irresistible, snap her portrait in the light of the setting sun or with candlelight, or even a bedside lamp, but never with a flash or tube-light, because such glare would never do. It was a matter of color permeating the soul, the soft glow of love enveloping it in warm oranges and soft reds.

Later that evening, Preeti and I lay in bed, I on my back, she resting comfortably on top, both nude, as always when in bed. I remember thinking at the time about whether there were many Indians who slept like us; nude, I mean. Ours was a conservative society, and I did not personally know of any among my relatives who did not wear clothes to bed. Perhaps others of my generation were like us. I was happy the way things were. Under the single sheet that covered us, my hands cupped the rising roundness of her buttocks with satisfaction, and my manliness emanated its warmth to her. "Preeti," I said, not knowing how else to express my profound feelings, "I love you."

In reply, she softly pressed herself closer and murmured her intimation of like affection.

"My heart is full, Preeti; I have everything I will ever need," I continued.

She simply kissed me on the side of my neck, a gently traveling caress, designed to arouse and to weed out alien thoughts. I sensed her intentions, but they were as languid and subdued as mine. We made love light-heartedly, too happy to take anything seriously. I played with her body, not trying at all, just doing what came effortlessly. "Preet," I said, my mind striving to find words to express the completeness of my enrapture, "I am so happy and grateful that I want to thank someone, everyone, for what I have; for you, and the boys, and Supna. Thanks are bubbling up in me, but I don't know for whom."

"For me, you could thank my father, and Mummy too. I am half her, you know, but who would believe it?" she mused.

"You are her only child; why cannot she feel one with your happiness?" Why does she want to use you as a pawn?" I asked rhetorically, for I expected no answer. It was not a new thought, but something recurring. People continued to amaze me with their desire for the discordant, with their inability to know that what violates our nature can never please. Why are some so afraid of accepting reality? Why are they always wishing for things the way they cannot be, imagining a metaphysics that goes against the grain of every sensation, instinct, reason? What do they expect to gain?

I put my arms around my woman and pressed her close. Why couldn't people be happy with each other's love, I wondered? There was nothing that even came close to the all-consuming fulfillment of a romantic bond, yet people constantly hungered after counterfeit pleasure. Perhaps the demands of true love are severe. You not only must love the person, but also that about her. To accept her, you have to accept Nature, the setting, of which she is but a part. You have to accept what is and is not, what can be and what cannot. You could call it a game, this living, but its rules were unalterable and could not be wished away. Nature's generosity was immense, but it did not tolerate the sullen ingratitude with which many people viewed their blessings. The rules required that you sow your own rewards. Ingrates were unrequited, or so they thought, but in reality, they were paid back in the same coin. Causality was never suspended; tit for tat, it could be no other way.

The interactions with the children had redoubled the joy of life that we always felt when together. As we made love, taking from each other whatever we wished, we reminisced about the past months, about the movie and the picnic, about the excitement of the boys, about the talent of the girl, even about the way Ajay and Shiv were mesmerized by Preeti's beauty. And it showed in the imaginative ways we touched each other. They used to tell us in BCS about team spirit, but this was way beyond anything I had imagined. We were the ultimate team; unique, united in every way possible, players, cheerleaders, spectators, all in one; and the way we played, there were no losers. The more pleasure you gave the other, the more you won, and the best way to give more pleasure was to do whatever gave you more pleasure. What a game! And yet people complained. The sages, the ascetics, the ones who were Negation Incarnate, what could they know of love? It was a game where you were granted your greatest wish, your own pleasure; it was even demanded that you accept it, for if you declined, then you could not please either. When you sacrificed your own desires, you inevitably sacrificed the happiness of the one you loved. The coldness in your heart was imparted to your hands, and their touch could evoke no responding warmth. You could neither give nor obtain by giving up. And yet they said true happiness lay in sacrifice, in negation, in the way of the ascetic, in the denial of Reality, in ingratitude to Nature. What utter fools; deluded beyond redemption, beyond any possibility of attainment. Love was a celebration of life; its opposite had to be a mourning, an absence, a lack of life, Death.

Is that what the ascetics hungered for? Nature had laid down the rules; they could have their desire, but the result would be death, not life eternal. Perhaps that is why they invented God, to have someone who would help them violate the rules, and still get what they wished. But they forgot that God was their own invention, unreal beyond imagining, a will-o'-the-wisp.

And then I thought of meditation—Samadhi— transcendental meditation—a focus on that which did not exist. Nature had given us this most wonderful of machines, this that we call the Mind. It sparkles in glory with the thoughts that fill it, but here were those who wished it empty, eliminated of all thought. Why? Because thoughts jarred? But why should they? In a man-made power plant, you know all is well when you hear the soothing hum of the generators. Why then is the functioning of the mind as so much noise? Noise to be eliminated and replaced by what? The emptiness of opposites; things that

can never be such as the infinite that is at once finite, the soul
that has all the properties of the universe, yet none that are
apprehensible; the giver who is all love yet plays mean games,
offering a world that is but an illusion, giving you matchless
means for pleasure, yet rewarding only their abandonment, and
punishing their use, devising a system of torture unequalled by
non-meditating man, the eternal cycle of reincarnation, of
Heavenly rewards and retributions, where you are punished
for obeying the rules of Nature, and rewarded for denying them,
an inquisition beyond any earthly inquisitions, where you are
guilty because you are of the flesh and will not deny it, where
God wills what you do and punishes you for that, punishes
your soul because it is what reincarnates; yet the soul is but a
part of Him, and its ever-changing face is never really changing.
It is Him, eternally unchanging, the only Truth; or the greatest
Lie?

I had decided what is and what is not. I had made my bed
and in it I would lie, with Preeti; and in my heart, with the rest of
humanity. Reality was real, just like the word said, and there was
no other. To me, the quenching of the humming of the mind was
the snuffing out of life. The peace of meditation was the silence
of Death; those who wished for it were welcome to it. They may,
in the ignorance of their self-righteousness, call themselves the
wise, but to me they were just ingrates insulting Nature's bounty;
mechanisms gone awry; the minuses; the less than zeros.

Time was passing, and our little dwelling was changing. It
now had a rug in the living room and another in the bedroom.
The walls were decorated with Preeti's paintings—the two
picnics: one at Suproon, and the other at Lodi Gardens. There
was also the portrait of the hill-woman by which Harbaksh had
been so taken, and there was a portrait of me in the making,
still on the easel. Adding the joy of sound to our lives was a
record player. Our home was now illumined by the radiance of
paintings, the happy strains of music, and the awakening sounds
of growing children. I was beginning to dance with greater
ease, and all was now set for teaching the children that man is

a magnificent whole; that is, you cultivate the mind, but must never forget that there is a body too. If your mind knows how to command it, the body will do whatever you wish. We called such people all-rounders in school, but that is a weak commendation, for it is really true enlightenment, an attainment of maximum potential. Of course, you could make your substance supple with yogic exercises, but that is not what I wish to imply. To dance is to celebrate the freedom of your body, an affirmation of it, the very opposite of denial. Yoga, in its original sense and form, is a spiritual endeavor, an attempt to train the body to gain such control over its involuntary functions as to be able willingly to release the soul from its bondage; to liberate the incorporeal from the corporeal. In polite, God-fearing circles, this release is construed as the way to union with the One, the Eternal; a salvation, moksha, nirvana, what have you. I simply call it death; suicide, if you wish.

We could have had Indian classical dancing. It is beautiful and intellectually elevating, but neither Preeti nor I knew much about it, so the children were introduced to what we knew best, ballroom dancing. Supna was quick to learn, for she was not as distracted by my holding her as the boys were holding Preeti. They were continually trying to please her, and that destroyed their concentration. Well, I figured, they have to get used to the female touch sooner or later, so why not now? Once they are used to the physical presence of a woman, perhaps they will begin to feel at ease and start noticing her intellectual presence as well. On reaching that point, they would have stepped into manhood. Any woman would now be safe with them. They will have learned that to be a man is not a matter of age, of years of existence, but a state of mind, a state attainable well before the age of consent. A true man treats a woman as an equal, different from him in many ways but at par in the intellect. Perhaps, the real mixture of opposites is here, not in the contradictory oppositions of theistic metaphysics. A man and a woman, unlike the imaginary nonmaterial entities and their attributes, can be truly complementary.

My Troubled Land was not going unnoticed. Many angry letters to the Editor poured in after the publication of the article on marriage. They denounced my denigration of our hallowed traditions, and accused me of ignorance. In reality, they were accusing me of keeping my eyes open, I felt, not playing the simian game of 'see-no-evil.' But this was to be expected. The real furor began with the publication of the next article, the one on violence. In the eyes of many of my countrymen, I was trying to destroy India's carefully cultivated image of the land of non-violence. Gandhi, in his wisdom and caring for the downtrodden, had walked the vast expanses of this land, trying to appeal to the humanity of its people. He had had the gall to call the untouchables Harijans (brothers), and had invited them into the sanctity of the temples. Now everybody was pretending that he had succeeded. But had he? The vast majority of Indians mocked his efforts with their actions; in marriage, in communal violence, in their treatment of each other; while simultaneously proclaiming the exact opposite in words. Now here I was laying bare the fraud, a nobody daring to unveil the truth. What rankled was that the truth was not my invention, but something they had known all along. I was a spoilsport ruining their precious fun and games by reminding them of their ugly secret.

The forces of 'non-violence' were furious. Arraigned in strength outside the offices of the National Express, they screamed: "Death to the atheist (it later changed to the 'Sikh atheist' as my identity became better known); may his soul rot in Hell." The vision of my soul rotting in Hell did not bother me. The problems of the nonmaterial in a nonmaterial torture chamber were the stuff of mystical nightmares, but for those who had expelled the mystical from their mind, they held no fear. But death, that did scare me. The whole farce was an incredible irony; the defence of non-violence, the sacred code of *ahimsa,* by recourse to death threats. And what about the preposterous label, 'Sikh atheist?' Could they see no contradiction in proclaiming me both a Sikh and an atheist in the same breath. Verily, I was a Sikh by birth, but an atheist by choice. I was being accused of both, surely an incompatible combination. But what of the reaction of the Sikhs? What would they have to say to all this? Perhaps they would renounce my membership in their religion, something that would be for the better because I knew of no way to opt out of it. The creators of religion had made no provision for such a possibility. In their enormous leaps of faith, in their total divorce from credibility, such a likelihood stretched the very same bonds of credibility that they had so haughtily ignored. Anyway, the reaction of the Hindus might derail all that. After all, the Sikhs are not merely a religion; they are also a community with moral and ethical traditions, many of which I heartily endorsed. Who knows, a kind of community patriotism might come to my aid. But I did not really want all that. In my mind, the true conflict was between the rational and irrational, not between one religion and another; and I had no desire to see it degenerate into the latter.

Angrier letters flowed in now, many demanding that if I was so upset with Indian traditions, why did I not leave the country to go and stay with my atheistic brethren in the West? India would get along fine without me, they suggested; 'good riddance,' as one prig put it. They had no desire to see their purity sullied by intemperate people like me who had not learned the 'discipline of tolerance.' Here I had written two long masterpieces on the intolerance of the rights of individuals in India, and I was being accused of intolerance!? It was preposterous. What did they want of me, a blanket endorsement of their bigotry. They would never have it! Not one letter addressed itself to the points made in my articles. It was all a dung-heap of innuendo and outrage, viciously venomous. I was glad Mr. Gopalan published them all; for it would let him off the hook. I liked him and had no desire to see him suffer for my views, but it also illumined for me the intellectual bankruptcy of the opposition.

But what about Professor Srivastava? There was as yet no word from him. While all Delhi held its angry breath, the professor had asked Mr. Gopalan for more time for his next piece. He had failed to meet the deadline agreed upon so that now he was faced with refuting both my articles. On the surface, the two columns were not viewed as platforms for a debate, but in practice I was sure that would be the way it would turn out, even though each of us was not permitted to refer directly to the other in his writings. Dr. Srivastava's problem was, as I saw it, to defend the institution of arranged marriage and also justify the caste system, if he could. They were related problems, which certainly went to the heart of the malady in India's social fabric. All I could do now was wait.

But other concerns were also coming to the fore. Preeti's modeling was becoming an increasing success. Demands for her time were constantly increasing. We had to be careful because neither one of us wanted her studies to be adversely affected. Modeling was good for her ego, and provided us much-needed cash, but painting was her very life. Then one evening, Preeti came in with the news that her sponsors wanted her to go to Bombay for a week to model a variety of clothes, both Indian and Western, for ads in the movies. I asked her how she felt about it, but she was ambivalent. She felt guilty about the time that would be lost from college. There was no problem with Sapna, for we could easily schedule make-up lessons for her; yet she did not wish to miss the experience of big-time modeling. "I've got to try it once," she said finally, and that decided it. She would go to Bombay. We did manage to strike a compromise with those managing the production. They scheduled it for a week when college was closed three of the weekdays.

Preeti left for Bombay by plane. Her departure was our first separation, and both of us showed it in our eyes. At the last moment, she hugged me and said: "Honey, it's only for a week."

"Yes," I said, "but I'll miss you."

"I will too, but don't talk like that," she admonished, "I am not good at this sort of thing."

And then she was gone.

XXIII

It was a first for Preeti; she had never flown before. The plane, a Dakota, the American-made workhorse of air travel in the forties, was a child of the heavens. It bumped with the clouds, blew with the wind, and sank with the air-pockets. The end of the monsoon was unsettled weather, and Preeti's mind, like the plane, was unsettled too. As she sat back in her seat, she thought of home and the days ahead, alone by herself. The idea of going to Bombay was exciting; it was the glamor capital of the country; but there was also dread, a fear of the unknown. The big city was no place for innocents, for a girl alone; and as her mind wandered up and down with the plane, she found herself, willy-nilly, humming a popular refrain:

> To live is not easy.
> Not easy, my love.
> *This is Bombay,*
> *This is Bombay,*
> *This is Bombay, oh my love.*
>
> Some spec'late, some gamble,
> Some rob, and some cheat,
> There are holdups and muggings,
> And jiltings; what a treat!
> The jobless have lots
> Of jobs over here.
> Have a care, beware,
> This is Bombay, oh my dear.
> *This is Bombay . . . etc*

Black is white, Dark is bright,
Sex Is love, Naught is right,
Have a care, beware,
This is Bombay, my delight.

Oh, the world is so bad,
You say; but, oh there!
You're innocent? Not so simple
As to have not a care.
You get what you give,
That is Bombay, I declare.
This is Bombay . . . etc

Oh love! It is easy
To live over here.
Listen mister, listen comrade
This Is Bombay, yes my dear.
This is Bombay . . . etc.

Santa Cruz airport was hot and muggy. Walking around puddles of water on the tarmac, the three of them, Preeti, Rita and Dinesh, their agent and photographer, threaded their way to the terminal. The hotel was near Juhu beach. In those days, Bombay was clean, and walking on the sand was a pleasure. While Dinesh made phone calls, Rita and Preeti strolled along the water's edge. Both wore shirts and slacks. For Rita, an Anglo-Indian, it was normal wear; for Preeti, too, it was normal, but a matter more of personal comfort and taste; and certainly untraditional. Neither of them had ever seen the sea.

Preeti's first impression was the smell of fish. That it would be so had never crossed her mind. She had painted many a scene, one notable one of a storm at sea, with a sailing ship tossed about, cavernous dark waves threatening to devour it, dark clouds blowing above, and lightning crackling as the waters raged; but it had never entered her mind that the sea would smell. There was also the intermittent murmur of the waves as they rushed in, dying in little tongues of water that licked their feet, leaving fragments of seashells between their toes. Preeti gazed out over the water, as far as the eye could see. There were boats there, bobbing up and down with the waves, and then a dark grey line where sky met sea. It was an artist's delight. One day she would sit there on the sand and sketch, make a painting for our living room, a memento of her visit to Mumbeyi, the Marathi name for Bombay that most Indians had forgotten.

Dinesh came out with his camera, and Rita and Preeti posed for him; for fun, not part of the assignment. Preeti let down her hair, and she imagined herself on some high, windy cliff, her dark tresses blowing in the wind, lovelorn eyes searching the sea for signs of a lover returning. Dinesh, a sensitive man, knew how to capture beauty on film. Unobtrusive, such that his subject seldom felt that he was even there, he had that special knack of putting her at ease. It was difficult not to be fond of him. As the loving caress of the camera followed her around, Preeti dreamed of far-away places, romantic isles where it was warm, and soft breezes blew, with coconut palms and white sands, and turquoise blue, still water; and all that Dinesh captured in his camera.

Having experimented with my brother's camera, I knew the feeling well. A special bond unites a subject with the cameraman. Unaided, the eye sees her as part of a vast background, a single person alone, owned by that around her; but with the camera, she is framed, emphasized, the background cut to proportion, no longer drowning, but enhancing. It is hers now, to own, wear as an ornament, a tale to weave her spell of fancy. A photographer who knows his art always makes love to his subject, expressed in the way he takes her pictures. The hard lenses soften as the rays of light, warmed by the touch of beauty, come speeding through, to be captured for ever in the warm tones of film. How many photographers have gazed at their product, admiring the perfection of what was achieved, a moment in time captured for ever; and as they gazed, fallen in love with the girl they saw there, forever smiling, or gazing with loving eyes; or dreaming of a love far away.

So it was with Dinesh. He had fallen in love with Preeti a long time ago, but knowing that she was married, had never dared to express it. But now they were alone, far away from Delhi and a husband; perhaps she would look on him with favor. A warmth like hers must yearn for on echoing warmth. I knew her well from gazing into her eyes and her soul, but he knew her too. He had gazed into her soul as well, as she abandoned distance, and brazenly dreamed romantic dreams; now smiling, now thinking, now pensive, now hopeful; all there before his eyes. He knew her moods; she lived them for him. It mattered not that it was for money. For him, it was for love.

Rita was slightly taller than Preeti, her skin fairer, but with occasional freckles. She had green eyes and auburn hair. But to Dinesh she was not the same. She penciled her eyebrows, shadowed her eyes, reddened her cheeks, and darkened her lips; but the hardness of marble was about her. Her hair was cut short about her head, her long neck giving her that special touch of elegance that made her such a wonderful model. Slick with her poses, she could be regal or vampish; chic or coy; but she was not the stuff of dreams. No soft longing touched her. She had too much of the learned art; never lost herself; her soul for ever hidden. A gay socializer, accomplished, worldly, she lacked the touch of innocence, the unabashed sincerity, that wounds a sensitive heart. She was one of Dinesh's most successful models, but she never touched him where it mattered. He had never seen her real self, how could he be moved? May be there was much to hide, but whatever it was, he assumed for her the same detached air of proficient coolness to capture her the way she wished to be seen; and fortunately, the way the world wished to see her.

Later that afternoon, they went over to the movie studio where it had been arranged that they would model for the movie cameras. That day was a session with sarees and salwaar-kameezes. Western dresses were for stills in the magazines, or for the screen in places like Bombay where there was a market for them, but that would be another day. Dinesh planned to take them both out to dinner that evening, but Rita had other plans with one of the men at the studio. So Dinesh and Preeti were by themselves. It was one of the elegant restaurants of which Bombay has many. Their table was tucked away in one corner, secluded from roving eyes by an assortment of plants. A live band played dance music, and many couples were on the floor. Preeti wondered if Dinesh would ask her to dance, but he preferred to talk. "Preeti," he asked, "what made you take up modeling?"

"My husband, Amrik, and I are both in college, and we need all the money we can make to afford to live in the little apartment we rent."

"But you seem to enjoy what you're doing?"

"Oh, yes? I love the work, if you could call it that. It was all Amrik's idea. You know, he has that knack of knowing what I want, and the courage to allow me to go ahead and do it."

"I know what you mean. I could think of few Indian husbands who would let their wives model for the masses."

"Oh! I never thought of it that way—I mean modeling for the masses, though now that you've put it in those words, I have to agree. I am modeling for the masses."

"Why? Does it bother you?"

"A little. I am at heart a private person, and my relationship with Amrik is the same way. You could call it intense; better still, intensely personal. Neither of us cares for popular favor, but we do relish very much the wonderful things there are in life, like living, and loving, and being true, to ourselves, and to our natures."

He looked down at his drink for a while, then raising his eyes to hers, he announced with feeling: "You are my favorite model; I'm sure you know that."

Preeti took it in stride. "I can't say I know, but I've known you are partial to me. I've known it for a long time; and I'd like to thank you for it. It makes my work so much easier knowing that I have a friend."

"You don't have to thank me. You must thank yourself, because you have so much talent."

"I don't know about that; all I know is that I enjoy it."

"You know, Preeti," he said, relishing the taste of her name on his tongue, "on days that I'm not working, I often go out of the city, or on to the wooded ridge in Delhi, to take pictures of scenery, and birds and animals, and sometimes of villagers. Many a time, my thoughts turn to you. I imagine you as part of the scene before me, and say to myself how much more perfect it would be with you in it."

Preeti could sense the drift in the conversation, but Dinesh was sincere, and she had not the heart to stop him. Besides, she was fond of him too. Like me, he had been transplanted to Delhi with his family, parents and a younger sister, from West Punjab, now Pakistan. His father was a small businessman, but they were not wealthy. Dinesh had made a name for himself as a photographer by dint of hard work and talent. He loved his work, just as Preeti loved hers, and she could feel that affinity.

"Dinesh, do you know that modeling is not my first love."

"You surprise me," he said, "I thought nothing could be more important to you than modeling."

"Oh, no! There are many other things I crave for; my husband for one, and painting for another."

He took the reference to me in stride too.

"A kindred spirit, I see. I'm afraid I'm not much at drawing or painting, but I have the same regard for it as I have for creations on celluloid."

"A thought occurred to me this afternoon, Dinesh. I hope you won't mind. Would you permit me to sketch you? Will you pose for me?"

He smiled with relish. "The artist wishes to sketch the artist. Preeti, I would do anything for you."

That won't be necessary," she replied, trying to keep things in a semblance of control, "merely model for me."

"That is easily done. When would you wish it?"

"May be tomorrow afternoon; somewhere on the beach."

"I'm afraid that won't be possible. Tomorrow, we are supposed to be at the movie magnate's house to model swim-suits by his pool. How about the following afternoon?"

"Okay, that will be fine."

The ride in the cab back to the hotel was a little tense. Preeti was afraid he might want to hold her hand, and that she might let him, so she just kept both hands in her lap, out of harm's way. When he wished her good night at her door, there was both sadness and hope in it. She wished him back warmly, and then quickly entered the room, afraid that if she delayed, things might get out of hand.

Next day by the pool was a fun affair. It was sunny, but not too warm. White puffs of clouds dotted the clean blue of the sky as kites sailed about and seagulls occasionally winged their way across. There were many girls here, most of them models from Bombay. At least half were Anglos, with names like Doris and Louisa, and Helen. Some were Parsees, but there were no North Indians except for Preeti. They walked around the pool, lounged about, or stretched out in beach chairs, or simply lay on towels by the side of the pool. There were poses on the diving boards, and by the metal ladders that dipped into the water. Last of all, there were pictures of the girls playing, or pretending to play, with a beach-ball in the water.

Men in gaudy bush-shirts, with loud-colored flowers, walked around among the girls. One of them was a film star, the movie producer's son. Everyone called him Romeo, short for Romesh Mehta. He was a handsome man, quite conscious of his beauty, with dark brown hair, a high forehead, grey eyes flecked with brown, a well-chiseled nose, voluptuous lips, and a sculptured chin. His skin was fairer than Preeti's and certainly fairer than mine. All in all, he was the epitome of Punjabi beauty. His features reminded one of Persian princes. While he walked in their midst, the girls from Bombay gave him knowing glances, and flocked around him when the shooting was over. But he was interested in newer conquests, so he strolled over with his gold-banded swagger stick up to where Preeti was standing drying herself with a towel. Giving her the once-over with his eyes, he smiled his most winning smile and asked: "And who do we have here? I don't believe I've had the pleasure of meeting you before."

Preeti just looked back at him inquiringly, but did not answer.

"Perhaps I should first introduce myself," he went on, "I am Romesh Mehta. My friends and fans prefer to call me Romeo. I am honored to make your acquaintance."

"Likewise, Mr. Mehta," Preeti replied blandly.

"Come now, you don't have to be formal; you can call me Romeo."

"If that is what you prefer, Mr. Mehta, its fine with me. Now what can I do for you?"

"You could honor me with your company for the afternoon," he said, "do permit me to show you around the house. This is where I live, you know."

"Oh! I did not realize. You must be Mr. Mehta's son."

"Young lady," he corrected himself, controlling his irritation, "are you trying to say you don't know of me."

"I don't usually make it a point to know every stranger I meet," she replied.

"Come now, we should be friends. I apologize for my abrupt manner. Would you at least do me the favor of telling me your name?"

"Preeti, if you must," she said, "and now, if you'll please excuse me, I have other things to do."

He caught her by the arm. "Now look here, you don't have to be rude! But if you must, I guess I can't stop you."

He let go of her arm, and assuming his most persuasive, remorseful, film-actor style, he continued: "If I have erred, please forgive me. The offer to show you the house still remains."

Preeti stopped, turned to look him straight in the eye. "Very well," she said, "I will be back in ten minutes. Will you still be here?"

"Yes, I shall be waiting for you."

Preeti changed into her shirt and slacks, and found him still standing there by the pool, but now surrounded by a bevy of beauties. On seeing her, he excused himself from the others, and walked up to greet her

"I believe compliments are in order. You are most becoming."

"Thank you," Preeti replied, correctly.

"Before we start our tour, just answer me one question, if you will. Did you ever see the movie, *Love in Naini Tal?*"

"No," said Preeti, "I have not had the privilege."

"Did you not happen to glance at the last issue of *Filmfare,* or the previous issue of *FilmIndia?*"

"No. I have been too busy for such things. I am sure you will forgive a working girl a lapse like that," Preeti replied, humoring him, but knowing that she was deflating him as well.

Preeti was one of those women not easily affected by physical perfection unless accompanied by a charming mind. If all that his lovely head of hair contained was solid cement, she would be willing to place it in a museum, but not among her living interests. One thing she could not stand was pomposity, and that she detected here in ample measure. She was not going to acknowledge that he was a movie idol, even though she knew he was. She wanted him to inform her of that himself.

"You are a most strange person for someone with such beauty," he said, "but since you are that way, let me then tell you about myself. I am, as they say, one of the most dashing prospects the film industry has seen in many a decade." Then, realizing that she was unimpressed with self-glorification, he changed his tune. "I am really your humble servant," he continued, "and I would not deign to use such words as I have just done, except to say that they are not mine; they are the words of Filmfare's most famous, most discerning movie critic."

"I am glad to know that I am in such illustrious company, Mr. Mehta."

"Tch! Teh! You must not do that. All my friends are free to call me Romeo."

"Yes, you told me that before. I'll try to remember, Mr. Mehta," she replied.

This was going to be no easy conquest, he thought.

I wonder if he has the staying power, thought Preeti.

They went up the marble staircase with the carved mahogany balustrade. From the balcony above, he showed her the ample grounds; with lawns, flowerbeds, and shade trees; and with the peanut-shaped swimming pool on the end next to the house.

"When I finish my current film," he informed her, "I plan to build a house with grounds twice as big as these. There will be fountains in the lawns, flowerbeds and fruit trees; and songs and dancing girls at the parties I'll throw there. They will glitter with Bombay's beauty. Of course, I would expect you to be the most honored of the honored guests."

"I would certainly consider it, if I am in Bombay at the time, and if I am invited."

"Of course you'll be invited. Consider yourself invited directly from my lips as of now. Your beauty must grace my celebrations. But did I hear you suggest that you're not from Bombay?"

"Yes, Mr. Mehta, I'm from Delhi."

"There you go again. Romeo, please! I cannot understand why the most beautiful of my fellow Indians must be so formal. You must promise never to do that again."

"Yes, Mr . . . ." Preeti pretended to correct herself, "Romeo."

"There now! See how nice it sounds, how good it feels in the mouth. I cannot tell you how wonderful it is to my ears."

They continued on with the tour. The last place was the bedroom. Preeti stopped on the threshold as he walked in.

Noticing her hanging back, he urged: "Come on in, there is much to see."

"No. I'll look at it from here. The privacy of a bedroom should be respected, don't you think so?"

"Well, if you must know, I keep no secrets from those I care for. I like my friends to feel at home in my bedroom. It is as much for their comfort as for mine."

"That is most generous of you, Mr. Romeo Mehta, but I think I have seen enough."

Frustration covered his face. Never before rebuffed by a beautiful woman, he was beginning to lose his cool. The facial lines of a spoilt childhood, and a dissolute adult life, were beginning to show underneath the suave exterior. He gave up all pretense. Walking up to Preeti as she stood outside the bedroom door, and placing his hands on her shoulders, he said: "You are most old-fashioned, but I forgive you for that; one cannot always outgrow one's roots. But think of it this way: we are both adults, in the prime of our lives. Nature has smiled with favor on both of us. Beauty was given us for a reason. Who are we to deny what we can avail of each other? I assure you that there is no pleasure greater than that between a beautiful woman and a handsome man."

So saying, he lifted his right hand off her shoulder, and caressed her cheek with it. Preeti caught both his hands firmly in hers, slowly lowered them till they were by his side; then, deliberately playing with her diamond ring, in a way he could not help notice, told him in an icy tone: "Mr. Mehta, I am afraid my husband will not approve of the way you have been treating me. And now I bid you good-day, but a word of advice, stay with women of your own kind, and don't ever touch me again."

So saying, she walked down the marble staircase, out the brass-embellished heavy wooden front door, and back to the swimming pool, looking for Dinesh. Finding him, she cried: "Dinesh, I wish to leave now, if you don't mind."

"What's up, Preeti. Mr. Mehta, the producer, is expecting us to stay for tea."

"Do we have to stay?"

"I think it is in our interest. After all, he is a powerful man, and our main contract in Bombay is with him."

"I will stay under one condition. Keep that son of his, that stupid lust-bitten Romeo, away from me."

"Why, Preeti, has he insulted you?"

"Look, Dinesh, I don't want you to get into a fight with him over me, please! If he has insulted me, he has been paid back in kind many times over. Just don't let him near me."

"That will be done;" assured Dinesh, "If he so much as looks at you, I will smash that pretty face of his."

Preeti smiled, amused and pleased at the way Dinesh felt so protective of her. That evening, perhaps because Dinesh had talked to Romeo or his father, it was a fact that the movie idol kept his distance and stayed as far away from Preeti as he could. His ego was so badly damaged that he was sulking, letting his groupies nurse it back for him.

Dinner was again with Dinesh, but in a different restaurant this time. "Do you think you would like to tell me what happened with Romeo, Preeti?" he asked.

She debated what to tell him, if anything. Finally, she decided, some sort of explanation was in order, since he did have to deal with the elder Mr. Mehta.

"Romeo mistook me for one of his groupies," she informed him, "and I disabused him of some notions he had of himself. To me, men like him are repulsive, if you know what I mean."

Dinesh was quiet, so she continued: "If a man wants a woman, he has to live up to her expectations, else he should have the good sense to keep his distance. That Romeo is such a pompous ass, I wonder what any woman finds in him. Is he a good actor, Dinesh?"

Dinesh smiled: "You would be the better judge. Did he act well with you?"

"The buffoon, yes; but more like slime. Shallow as a puddle, he doesn't know the first thing about charm. He is vain like a peacock, though I daresay those lovely birds would disown him if he tried applying to their flock. I had a desire to slap him when he laid his perfumed, ring-covered, soft hands on me; but then I thought the better of it. I was alone with him, and he was the stronger. Yet he was a coward, so I decided I could risk giving him a tongue-lashing, which I did."

Preeti smiled at that, reflecting with enjoyment at the tinge of fear which she saw in Romeo's eyes as she played with her wedding ring before him.

"Dinesh," she said, "I feel a little guilty because I enjoyed his discomfiture, in a way."

Dinesh was quiet most of the time, probably weighing in his mind how much he could safely say to Preeti. He knew now that she was something fierce when riled, but it was still not clear what she would tolerate and what not.

"Preeti," he finally said, "I've never known you like this. You are a proud woman, and I admire you."

Preeti's eyes softened. Dinesh knew how to touch her heartstrings, so she had to be careful, but she could not let down a real friend. "Tell me about yourself?" she asked, "I know so little about you."

"There's not much to tell," he said. "I had a simple childhood. My family is from the town of Gujraat, in Pakistan. It is a small town, known more for its ancient citadel than for anything else. My father used to own a small factory there, making hockey sticks. We lost it all during partition; but we were lucky that none of the family was killed. I have a younger sister who is twenty, about your age and height; and I daresay she is pretty like you. She never will be a model though, I'm sure, even if she wanted to. My father would never allow it. The school I went to in Delhi is not worth remembering: Lahore Montessori School. I'm sure you've never heard of it. And then Hindu college. I learned little at either place. This photography stuff I learned on my own, courtesy of a camera I received as a birthday present from an uncle of mine when I was eighteen. The rest has been work, and more work."

"I'm going to ask you a rather personal question," warned Preeti, "I hope you won't be offended."

Preeti waited for him to say something. When he indicated that it was okay, she continued: "Is there anyone you love? I mean a woman?"

Dinesh was a handsome man, about twenty-two years old, five nine; about the same complexion as Preeti. He had a heavy head of black hair, and shining, very intelligent, black eyes. There was softness and warmth in them, and sincerity. He was sturdy of both build and character. Self-possessed, and with a sensitive mouth and relaxed lips that were soft and full, he was, all in all, quite an attractive man. So Preeti wondered about his attachments.

"Yes, there is," he said.

"I'd love to hear about her. Do you think you could tell me?"

He just looked at her, not saying anything. Then he lowered his eyes, and said: "I'm afraid that is not possible."

Preeti wasn't about to give up, so she continued: "Do you think you'll ever marry her?"

"No. That won't be possible either."

"Why? How can you say that? If you really want to marry someone, there is no one in the world who can stop you."

"I believe you mean that, but you don't know what you're saying."

"I know what I'm saying because I can tell you from personal experience. I married someone that way."

"Your husband, Amrik?"

"Yes; marrying him was the most courageous thing I ever did, and in some ways the easiest."

"Why do you say easiest?"

"Because, when you're in love, everything is easy. Marriage, and things of that kind, you take them in stride."

"What is he like; Amrik?"

"He is something like you, in character, but different in other ways. About your height, may be a touch shorter; quiet like you, but his mind is always working. He is the most independent thinker I know. Only when you learn to think totally rationally can you anticipate what his attitude to anything will be; and yet he has fooled me many times. May be it's his sense of humor. He can be uproariously funny; and yet he looks at life with all the seriousness of a grave thinker. Dinesh, that is the way to be. Look at everything with eyes wide open; you will then see so much more which others miss; and you will enjoy living every day of it. He says that we deny ourselves too much, that we generally say the world does not permit us this or that, but in reality it is nearly always us, ourselves, who do the denying. We are our own worst censors. May be now you will tell me who this girl of your dreams is?"

"I will tell you, Preeti, but not today."

Next day was a free day. In the morning, Preeti sketched Dinesh. He was quieter than usual, but peaceful, somehow more satisfied than before and unusually content. He was a good subject, and her heart was in it. They sat there perhaps an hour. When it was finished, she signed it: "With love, Preeti"; and gave it to him.

He gazed at it, his eyes a little full; then he bit his lip, and looking up at her, asked: "You want me to have it?"

"Yes, it is a present, a little token of my affection for you."

"I will cherish it," he said; then turned to look away. After a few moments, he turned around, and said, his mood suddenly reckless: "We have the whole day to ourselves; let us go out and sightsee all there is to see."

"A capital idea," cheered Preeti, "let's go."

The rest of the day was spent gazing at the sites of Bombay: Marine Drive, Malabar Hill, the Jeejeebhoy museum, Cuffe Parade, and the Gateway of India. By this time, it was dark and they were standing in front of the Taj Hotel, Bombay's best.

"Do you think we could go in, just to look around?" asked Preeti.

"Sure, I'd love to. I've never been in there myself." Inside the main lobby, they could see the glitter of gold, beautiful shops with jewelry, sarees, brass and other ornamental things, Kashmeeri rugs, and all manner of goods to cheer the heart.

"Preeti," asked Dinesh, "would you like to eat here."

"I don't think you could afford it. On second thought, I will accept if you agree to share the tab with me."

"I couldn't let you do that," he said, "I would not feel right. I have plenty of money, and I'm sure the company will be willing to pay at least part of it."

"Don't say I didn't warn you. My father used to take me to places like this, and they were mighty expensive."

Dinner was by candlelight. At Preeti's suggestion, they ordered red wine to go with the food. By the time they were through the main meal, the wine, the candlelight, the ambience of the place, had permeated them, so that the mood was romantic.

"Would you like to dance, Dinesh," asked Preeti.

"I'd love to; I know I'll never get a better offer than this, but I don't know how to dance."

"When we get back to Delhi, I'm going to invite you over to our place, and I'll personally teach you. Now that is a promise," Preeti said, with emphasis.

"Preeti, I don't think I've ever been so happy in my life."

Preeti looked at him fondly. She was happy too, but a little voice at the back of her mind whispered: 'Careful, be careful.'

"Preeti, you asked me yesterday who I was in love with. I am now ready to tell."

Preeti was excited, though a touch apprehensive too. Dinesh had been showing her a bit much affection. Who knows what he was about to reveal?

"I'm all ears, lover," she said.

"Preeti, its you I love."

So saying, he put his hand over hers. It was warm and sincere. Preeti was loath to pull hers back. She kept looking at him, not evading his eyes; kept looking even when tears welled in her own. She could not move. If she pulled back her hand, or lowered her eyes, he would see her sorrow; and it would hurt. She let him caress her hand.

"Dinesh," she said, "I half expected this, but had hoped it would be someone else; I love you too, but I can never be yours."

Dinesh lowered his eyes and loosened his grip; he was about to pull back his hand, but Preeti stopped him.

"Tell me how not to hurt you," she implored. "Look at me. There is nothing to be ashamed of. You are one of the finest men I know, and I would gladly make love to you if I were free; but there is someone else I have to think of. I don't know if I would be able to face him or myself later, so I have to say no. I have to deny you what I am willing to give. Forgive me; I love you, but I can't love you."

With this, she lowered her head. They kept sitting there, hand in hand, neither one willing to make the first move. Ten minutes passed. Then Dinesh lifted his hand, placed it under her chin, and slowly lifted her face:

"You are telling me not to be ashamed, but look at you! Come on, cheer up. This is not the end of the world."

She smiled at him. "Yes, my love," she said, "if you say so. Let's go back."

After leaving the hotel, they did not take a cab right away, but walked along the seawall in front of the hotel, past the Gateway of India, hand in hand. Once Preeti turned around and said: "Hold me in your arms."

Dinesh embraced her warmly, then she pulled back, and holding his face in her hands, said: "Fate has not been kind to you, has it?"

"No, it has. You could have pulled your hand back."

"Will you come see us back in Delhi, my husband and me? You cannot shun him because you love me. I cannot think of a nicer thing than just the three of us together. Now don't say anything foolish. I know this is unheard of, but I know in my heart that it is right. We have something here; nothing but good went into its making; we cannot just throw it aside as so much deadwood. It cannot be that way."

There was vehemence in Preeti's words and Dinesh could sense it. "Yes, I'll come. May be I'll even get to like your Amrik."

"He is only mine because he loves me. But that does not shut him from the rest of the world's friendship. You don't want to punish me because I can't be your lover, do you? You wouldn't hurt the woman you love, now would you?"

"Shh! Preeti." He placed his fingers on her lips. "Don't worry. Everything will be just fine. Right now my heart is too full. Give me some time, and I will be my normal self again. Now let us go back to our hotel."

At the hotel, Dinesh stopped before her room. He was reluctant to say good-night. Looking at her, he smiled and said: "I've photographed you in all the poses I could think of, wearing the most beautiful clothes that our designers could conceive, and I have gazed at the photographs alone in my studio, admiring the perfection that you have displayed, and that I have captured. But you are an artist. Tell me, what is it that an artist wants to capture above all else?"

"The essence of her model," replied Preeti.

"And what is that essence?"

"The model as he is."

"Or the model as *she* is."

"Yes."

Preeti saw herself being drawn inexorably into a position which was rapidly evolving out of her control. Finally, she came out with it: "What do you want me to do?"

"Let me photograph you in my room. I know I'll never be able to ask you again."

"I am willing, Dinesh. Let's go."

In his room, Dinesh quietly went about the business of setting up the props, the tripod, the cameras, and the lighting. But he had not yet finished when she hegan to disrobe. He stood there, close to her as she slowly took off her shirt and brassiere, and then let her slacks and panties drop to the floor. Finally, she stepped out of them as if Aphrodite was coming out of her seashell. Then she let down her hair and stood there in all her perfection.

Dinesh walked over to his camera and photographed her as she posed for him. She was self-conscious, but only in the way she was when she walked naked in the meadow before me. She was as a woman in her own element, proud and perfect. Dinesh loved her with his camera as he captured what he had never thought he would. Then he walked up to her and handed her back her clothes. She put them on and he escorted her back to her room. They looked at each other as she opened the door and went in. And then the door closed. It was over, and all this time not a single word had been spoken.

XXIV

The day following the call for my death by the militant votaries of nonviolence, a demise of different measure awaited me, namely a note from Shiv's father that my services for his son's tutoring would no longer be needed. As confirmation, it was accompanied by a check for the money owed. That evening, Ajay and I were alone, Preeti was posing in Bombay, and Shiv was never to come again. I felt cheerless, for my sun was in eclipse. But my young pupil was as yet innocently unaware of all that had happened.

"Amrik," he suggested (deliberately, as a matter premeditated, I had requested that the boys address me by my first name. It conferred on me the position of a friend or older brother, which I much preferred to that of formal teacher. Punjabis customarily address an elder brother by adding the suffix 'ji' to his name; or by using Veerji—meaning elder brother—both forms intended to convey respect and a concession of superiority to the addressee; an extension, as you might notice, of the Indian system in which elders automatically are accorded supremacy by virtue of their age. My breast harbored no such desire; and even though my pupils were being offered equality, they felt uncomfortable lest familiarity be misconstrued. Time eased their burden and helped cope), "I think we should wait for Shiv. I saw him in school today, and he said he would come."

"I'm afraid he's not coming, Ajay, and won't be from now on," I replied, preferring to give him the bad news without preamble, because I felt that the quicker I got it over with, the better. "His father sent me a note to that effect."

"But he likes to come to these lessons," Ajay objected, bewildered by this turn of events.

"I know, but his parents pay for them, and if they say no, there is little this teacher can do, now can he?"

Ajay ignored my question as unworthy of a teacher. To the taught, the teacher must have an answer to everything. "I miss him," he complained, demoralized by the news and by my helplessness. Having had his say, he was silent awhile, then observed: "You don't look too happy yourself."

Did melancholy so grip me that a little boy could see? I was setting a bad example, but the truth must out. "Yes," I replied in resignation, "today is not my lucky day."

This was followed by another short interlude, with both of us still wallowing, each in his own sad thoughts. He then asked, now even more apprehensive: "Where is Preeti?"

Who knows, I wondered, what goes on in the mind of a boy who has just hit disappointment? "She went to Bombay on a work assignment," I explained.

"Will she be coming back?"

"Yes, Ajay, she couldn't stay away from you too long," I teased, "I wouldn't give her more than a week."

"I saw her picture in the Illustrated Weekly; she was wearing a very beautiful saree."

"She models clothes," I explained.

"I think she is very beautiful."

"I think so too, but I'll let her know how you feel. She will be delighted."

"Oh no!" he cried out, "don't do that. She may become angry with me."

"Come, Ajay! Why would she be angry? Can you imagine her cross at such a lovely compliment? Look, if you are worried about me, why don't you tell her yourself?"

"No! I can't do that. It would be bad manners. My mother says it is rude to talk like that."

A problem of social etiquette, I realized; but I must find a way out for the aspiring young man. His piquant remarks had awakened my curiosity, focused my mind back on Preeti's charms, giving it solace of a kind. Also, a vague feeling lurked that something spicy may be involved here, so I continued: "Why do you think it would be bad manners?"

He hesitated, unsure, then said: "Preeti is married. May be you won't like it either if I told her she is beautiful."

So that was the problem! Love smote the nascent man, but cruel fate decreed that the woman of his dreams was out of bounds to him, lost in matrimony, or was it just bashfulness? I was his friend and teacher; then too, also a rival. Quite unfair, I thought. Sincere admiration deserved a break. "Do you think a married woman who is beautiful would not like to be admired?" I asked, humoring him and trying to draw him out some more.

"No! She wants to be admired by you."

"But I already admire her. I am in love with her," I protested.

"Oh! Like D'Artagnian with Constance in the Three Musketeers?" he asked.

"Yes, like that; may be even more so."

I feared my answer may have pulled the rug out from under him, for he was silent for quite some time. But he was a plucky little boy. The new information was digested, and a silver lining to the cloud discovered. As if to reassure himself, he asked: "You don't mind if I tell her that she is beautiful?"

"No, not at all. In fact, I am quite proud to have a wife so admired by you."

"Doesn't it make you jealous?"

"Just a little bit, but I'll survive."

A lot of assumptions were biting the dust in his mind, but after the carnage was over, what remained greatly relieved him. He was, however, not quite done, so he continued, now with a different observation: "You are not beautiful like her, but I still like you."

An active mind, I was glad to see; but a left-handed compliment. Was he trying to turn the tables on me? "Why do you think I'm not beautiful?" I asked.

"You have this beard," he said, "and mustache. How can you be beautiful?"

"Preeti thinks I'm good-looking." That, I figured, should give him pause.

"No . . . o!" he said, un-flapped, "she says that because you are nice to her."

"Come now! I know she really thinks that I'm the most wonderful person in the world; why else would she live with me?"

"Because you are married to her."

"And because I am nice."

"I too think you are nice, but men can't be beautiful," he continued objecting.

This was more acceptable, now that it no longer was directed at me personally. "You are right, Ajay, but only if you look at beauty in one way. In English, the word to describe beauty in a man is 'handsome;' but in Indian languages, men can be termed beautiful, just like women. So, being an Indian, a man like me can be beautiful."

"No!" he insisted.

I gave in. "May be you have something else in mind; why do you think men can't be beautiful?

"You are not beautiful because your skin is not smooth like hers."

"So that's it. But let me tell you something. We men may not have silky smooth skin like women, but beauty is in the eyes of the beholder."

"What does that mean?" he asked, perplexed.

"It means that women like us the way we are. We are beautiful when women are the beholders, the ones doing the looking. Likewise, they are beautiful when we are the beholders," I explained.

"Do you think you'll ever shave your beard, or cut the hair on your head?" he asked, changing the subject again. "My father does, but he keeps a mustache like yours."

Ajay's father was a Rajpoot, a member of the martial class of Hindus who hearken from the arid western desert of India, Rajasthan, the abode of kings. They customarily sport full mustaches.

"Why? Don't you like me the way I am?"

"I like you, but I just wanted to know why you want to be different. So! Will you ever cut your hair?"

"I don't know," I replied, "I've never thought deeply on the question."

"My father says that Sikhs don't cut their hair, so you won't cut it; is that it?"

"It is true that Sikhs are not supposed to cut their hair," I agreed, "but a free bird like me cannot be wedded to the idea. If and when the desire comes, my long locks will vanish."

"Then you won't be a Sikh any more," he concluded, putting his finger on the real issue, at the same time derailing my lighthearted, offhand answer to so serious a question.

"That is both right and wrong," I answered.

He laughed. "You are teasing me; how can I be both right and wrong?"

His forthrightness evoked an echoing smile. "You are right," I conceded, knowing that he could not be put off, "give me some time to think an answer to your very difficult question. Would you be willing to wait until tomorrow, or the day after? I promise to answer by then." He nodded his head in approval. "For now," I continued, "we had better be getting back to *Jane Eyre*."

"Could we do that tomorrow?" he pleaded. "I don't want to do *Jane* without Shiv."

"But Ajay," I reminded him, "Shiv is not coming back to these lessons."

He did not like the reminder, but agreed reluctantly. "Alright, but can't we do it tomorrow? Not today, please!"

"Okay, tomorrow. What shall we do today?"

"Can we just talk some more? My father says that Sikhs are very brave fighters. Are you a brave fighter?"

"Yes, Ajay, we are all brave fighters, Sikhs and everyone else. But bravery is not simply something that happens in war; you don't have to fight to kill to prove your courage. After all, war is an unnatural aberration of life; it is not something expected to happen in the natural course of events, but something imposed on humans by demented people."

"Then what kind of fighting do you mean?"

"No fighting at all. I'm referring to the bravery of doing what you believe to be right, something that you're up against every day. It takes courage to stand up for what you believe, especially when most others disagree with you. For one thing, you have to be sure you are right; and once convinced, confident enough not to give in to other opinions. On many an occasion, it seems better to look the other way, to agree with those others, even knowing that they are wrong, rather than insist on acting your way. The brave do not yield to such temptation, preferring instead to live by what we term the 'courage of their convictions.' They will stand up to an injustice, no matter how unpopular their stand, for to them it seems the most important thing in the world to defend what is right. That, in my opinion, is true courage. You don't have to hurt someone to prove that you have it."

"If Shiv was brave, he would come back to the lessons, then. Yes?" Ajay concluded.

"No. Shiv has to listen to his parents because they are his guardians, paying for his food, his clothes, his school, even the lessons with me. If he were earning his own money, then he would be right to do anything he wants, but so long as it is his parents' money that he uses, he should be grateful and do as they ask."

"But that is not fair," Ajay objected, "Shiv is a good boy. Why is his father so cruel to him?"

"They are not punishing him, Ajay," I replied, "he is their son; and I am sure they love him. They care for him, and feel responsible for what happens to him. Perhaps they feel that my lessons are harming him."

"That is not true," he protested angrily, "and you know that."

"All I know, Ajay," I replied, "is that I try to teach you both the truth, as I see it, and the best I can. Whether my teaching is good or not, it is for you two to judge."

Ajay was quite unconvinced. This was his first exposure to the irrationality of adults, and surely not his last. But his persistence was admirable, and earned him my respect. I sincerely wished his parents would not take him away too."

Next day, as I was about to begin his lesson, Ajay cried out: "Look, Shiv is standing out there at the gate! Should I go and get him?"

"No, don't do that. Let me go out and say hello; may be he wants to talk to me. You wait here."

I went to the gate. Shiv was standing there with many books in his hands, including *Jane Eyre*. "Hello there," I shouted, "it's good to see you. I am sorry about your parents not wanting you to take lessons with me. Perhaps they'll find someone else, may be even someone better than me."

He looked glum, and optimistic talk was the least that I could offer to cheer him up. "Amrik," he asked, his expression, which was accompanied by slight evasion of the eyes, suggesting that he was not sure that he should be doing this, "can I still take lessons with you?"

"But your parents won't like it," I tried to explain.

"They won't know. I told them that I was going to a friend's place to do my homework; that is why I have all these," he said, extending the books out in explanation.

"All right," I said, "come on in."

"But, Amrik, I can't pay you. I don't have any money."

"You don't need money; there are other ways to pay," I assured him.

"You'll let me work for you?"

"That won't be necessary. You have more than enough to pay me with. Tell me, does my teaching make you happy?"

He beamed: "Yes!"

"Well, that will be my payment. When you become a teacher one day, you will realize that there is no better payment than a student who is so eager to learn, and enjoys it so much as to defy his parents for it."

"I promise I will work very hard," he said with sincerity.

"I know you will, but try expressing what you'll do differently. 'Hard' is not quite the right word. When your heart is so much into doing something, it never feels hard; it is easy. Perhaps you should make a bargain with me and say that you will promise to attend my lessons only if you enjoy them. Do you think you could live up to a promise like that?"

"That is easy; it's as if I don't have to do anything."

"In a way, that is true. When you love what you're doing, it never seems like work, but more like enjoyment. On such occasions, the question of working hard seems inappropriate," I explained.

And so Shiv and I were back with each other. When I explained to Ajay what the two of us had decided, he observed: "Shiv is brave because he is doing what he believes to be right."

"Yes, it takes a brave man to decide to do what he wants to do, and what he believes to be right, even when others disagree with him," I added in endorsement.

"But Shiv is only a boy," objected Ajay, "you just called him a man."

"He's not a boy any more. When someone makes the kind of decision that he made, he has leapt into manhood. Shiv makes me proud, and I'm sure Preeti will feel the same way," I answered.

"I think you are brave too, Amrik," added Ajay.

"Why do you say that?" I asked.

"Because you agreed to teach him for nothing."

"No, that is not true. I am not offering him charity; he is paying me with happiness and gratitude, and as I told you before, the happiness of a bright student is worth more than all the money in the world, so much so that I am greedy for it."

"I still think you are brave," Ajay insisted.

"Perhaps you are right. Both Shiv and I are standing by our convictions; he because he is willing to do what he believes to be right, and I for doing what gives me the greatest satisfaction." So saying, I hugged the two boys who were so dear to me. But something still remained to clarify. "There is one more thing I would like you to understand. Have you realized that Shiv has lied to his father? Don't you think that is wrong?"

Their faces fell. They shook their heads in affirmation, but sadly.

"Come now, you don't have to be so glum. May be we can find a way out. Shiv is faced here with what we call a moral conflict. On the one hand, he has a conviction, born of experience, that he is benefiting from the lessons; and he also enjoys them. On the other hand, he feels it is important for him to be obedient to his father. What is he to do?"

"I don't know," said Ajay, completely confused.

"I could tell you what a weak man would do. He will say to himself: 'This is too difficult to decide. I better do the safe thing; I'll just obey my father.' On the other hand, a stronger man like Shiv would think in a different way. 'Look,' he would tell himself: 'whatever is going to happen is going to happen to me, not to someone else. What happens cannot matter to others as much. Since it is my life, I should be the one to decide; the responsibility is mine. If I can prove to myself that it is better for me to take lessons from Amrik than to stay away at my father's behest, than I should go ahead with the lessons.'

But this will create another dilemma: 'should I tell my father of my decision or not? If I do tell him, will he allow me to carry it out?' Using this type of reasoning, he decides that the course of least harm to anyone, including his father, is to keep him in the dark. Lying will not hurt him, but telling the truth will destroy the entire endeavor; and who will be hurt the most? Shiv himself. So, reluctantly, he lies to his father about going to study with his friend. Is that what you thought, Shiv."

"No, I did not reason in all that detail. I just wanted so much to learn that I did what I had to do. It was the only way."

"Shiv, you did not reason with words like I did, but you must have thought deep and long, and in the end you must have decided that there was more good to be obtained doing it your way that your father's."

"Yes," he replied, "I spent all day thinking about it, and I did think like you said at the end."

"The decision, of course, is not perfect," I continued, expounding further, "lying is, in essence, giving someone a wrong view of the world. It is as if I were to teach you wrong things about reality. It is not a nice thing to do, to anyone. But the compromise has been forced on you because one of the persons involved, your father, is not being reasonable. The word we use for his behavior is 'irrational'. It means making a decision without looking at all the facts, or allowing them to be presented. Whenever irrationality is involved in a decision, it makes it that much more difficult. Perhaps you can do me a favor, Shiv. It will satisfy my curiosity, besides making it easier for me to understand the reason for your father's decision. Can you ask your father why he does not want you to take lessons with me?"

Next evening, Shiv had the answer. "My father says you are an atheist. Are you?"

"Yes, I am."

"What is an atheist?" Shiv asked.

"An atheist is one who is not a theist."

"What is a theist?"

"A theist is one who believes that there is a God."

"My father says atheists are bad people, but you are a very good man, Amrik."

"Thank you, Shiv. Did your father explain why he thought atheists are bad?"

"He said they are bad because they don't believe in God. But why should someone become bad just because he does not believe in God? If Hindus are good because they believe in their God, and Sikhs don't believe in Hinduism, does that make Sikhs bad?"

"What do you think?" I asked.

"No, I don't think that would make a Sikh bad."

"You're right. You cannot tell whether a person is good or bad simply by knowing whether he is Hindu or Sikh. You have to know what he would do when faced with a moral decision. Would he do the right and just thing, or would he do the wrong thing? Would he be rational, or would he succumb to the irrational? The answers to these questions will tell you whether he is good or bad, not the religion that he belongs to."

"My father says that God is a very loving and good person," continued Shiv, "so why don't you believe in him?"

"Because I don't believe that God is a person, or anything at all. I have tried my very best, but I cannot find any evidence that such a being exists. If you find any, I am willing to listen; and if you can convince me of the truth of the evidence, I will change my opinion."

"I will ask my father," Shiv assured me.

In the meantime, we turned to *Jane Eyre*. There were several passages in the earlier parts pertinent to our discussion. Jane spent years ten to eighteen at the Lowood Institution, a boarding charity school for orphans and those otherwise forsaken by their parents. The first year she was there, it was a dismal place, though it improved somewhat in later years because of a public outcry following an epidemic of typhus which wiped out forty-five of the eighty girls who had, like Jane, the misfortune of being confined there. Soon after arriving, Jane became fast friends with an older girl of fourteen, Helen Burns. Though very fond of each other, there was little else in common between the two. Jane was a fighter, one who would not concede her rights even under extreme duress; Helen, on the other hand, was passive, docile, willing to endure any pain or humiliation. It would not be stretching the truth to compare her to a Christian facing with equanimity the prospect of being fed to the lions. Both girls were strong in their own way: they could endure pain and privation, but one would do it without conceding anyone the right to inflict it, the other with resignation. What interested me was the different sense of life implied by the two attitudes, and the basis that inevitably underlay the difference.

"Shiv," I asked, "who do you think was the braver of the two, Jane or Helen?"

"Jane, I think," he replied.

"Why do you think that?" I asked.

"Because she was willing to fight back against her oppressors," he replied.

"And what about you, Ajay," I asked.

"I agree with Shiv."

"It seems that we are all agreed," I concluded, "but Helen was a brave girl too, though in my view less so than Jane. Why I favor Jane can be best explained by examining the different reasons for their strength." I turned the pages of the book, showing them different quotes by Helen: " . . . the Bible bids us return good for evil." Regarding punishment: " . . . it is weak and silly to say you *cannot bear* what is your fate to be required to bear." When Jane says: "I must dislike those who, whatsoever I do to please them, persist in disliking me; I must resist those who punish me unjustly," Helen replies by quoting from the New Testament: "Love your enemies; bless them that curse you; do good to them that hate you and despitefully use you." And finally a passage in which Helen Burns unveils the deepest layer of belief which is the womb of all the others: "We are, and must be, one and all, burdened with faults in this world; but the time will come when, I trust, we shall put them off in putting off our corruptible bodies; when debasement and sin will fall from us with this cumbrous frame of flesh, and only the spark of the spirit will remain,—the impalpable principle of life and thought, pure as when it left the Creator to inspire the creature."

After explaining to them the new and more difficult words in the passages, I asked: "Now, what do you think of Helen's ideas?"

"I don't understand them," said Ajay, "they don't make sense to me. I cannot see why you should let people hit you and tease you without trying to make them pay for it."

So I explained: "Helen believed that we should love our enemies, the more the worse they treat us. To me, it sanctions the right of evil to do what it does, to ride roughshod over good. It places it at par with the good; in fact, concedes it superiority, granting it permission to overwhelm unresisting good. Only a miracle could make Helen's philosophy work on her tormentors, and miracles, being impossible, as I will explain one day, cannot happen. But the real driving force behind Helen's actions, or the lack of them in response to beating and humiliation, lies in the thoughts expressing the feeling that what happens to us is in the hands of Fate, meaning not in our hands; and those expressed in the last quotation. She believes that our bodies are bad, so what does it matter if they are beaten and disgraced? Anything bad deserves to be treated thus.

"The body, to me," I explained, "is a marvel of perfection, not something to be denigrated or mistreated. As individuals, it behooves us to care for this wonderful thing that we are, our body."

Ajay and Shiv had no quarrel with my concept of the body and the fact that it was our responsibility to defend it from those who wished it harm. If we did not, who would? But they were not clear on what was meant by the spirit. So I explained to them the concept of the soul and other nonmaterial entities, including the Creator. They were still innocent, their minds uncorrupted by exposure to the mystical. The longer that they were exposed to rationality, I reasoned, the less susceptible they would remain to the depredations of religion.

"The problem was," I concluded, after explaining to them the irrationality of things such as the soul, and the belief in Fate or a Creator, "that she refused to accept reality for what it was. She gave credence to that which could not be perceived, for which no evidence could be adduced, while at the same time ignoring that for which an abundance of evidence was at hand, and for whose protection Nature had provided us with feelings, such as pain, sorrow, hunger, to warn us of danger so that we may take care of ourselves. For Nature, as for Jane, there was only one imperative: our survival as living beings. Any compromise with the defense of life would result in its annihilation. Fortunately, all through the ages, there have been more Janes than Helens; that is why the human race is still around. Hopefully, things will stay that way.

"Now, coming back to why I think Jane was braver than Helen. The ultimate essence of bravery is the refusal to deny the evidence of our senses, or to accept that for which no evidence exists; even in the face of threats of damnation. On that basis, Jane was way ahead; she had her feet firmly grounded in reality."

"But why did Helen believe all these things if you think they are not true? She was not a liar; and you yourself said that she was brave?" asked Shiv.

"What I have been teaching you so far is what I call a philosophy of Life. It deals with how to live life, because it believes that that is all that matters, and all that is. Helen's philosophy, her way of thinking, focuses on Death. But think of it this way. Life is long, seventy, eighty, even a hundred years; Death is but a moment or two at its end. Why should we give so much importance to the latter, and so little to the former? It is as if an ending were more important than the living of all that comes before it. If Death is on your mind constantly, then you will invent fairy tales, all manner of imaginary beliefs, that will make it more bearable; even make it attractive. You will build in your fancy a Heaven, where you will live for ever and ever, and in never-ending happiness; where no one will hurt you; no one will be mean; no one will be sick; in short, a place which is nothing like anything we know. And with time, you will forget that it was all an invention; you will minimize the importance of life as we know it, and think only of a 'Life after Death,' never once trying to ascertain whether there is at all any life after death. You will invent a spirit that leaves the body to go to Heaven, and lives there, because no one will believe you if you said that the body itself goes to Heaven; anybody who has dug up a grave to see what happens to a body after death knows that there is no way it could go anywhere. With us Indians, of course, the body is cremated and becomes smoke and ashes; here again, there is no sense in pretending that it could be reincarnated or make it to union with God, the Universal Spirit. This, Shiv, is why I am an atheist. You don't have to accept my views, but think about what I've said, talk to your father about his beliefs, and then decide what makes the most sense to you."

There was nothing more that I planned to discuss that day, but Ajay had not forgotten. "You promised to tell me whether you would cut your hair, and whether that means you will no longer be a Sikh," he cried.

I had thought about it and had come to a decision. "Ajay," I replied, "one day I will cut it. But I have to make sure that it will not hurt those that I care for. For their sake, I am willing to accept a little discomfort. Preeti is used to my long hair; I must ask her first to make sure that she does not object. Her happiness is very important to me. Then there are my parents; they would be far more upset than her. But the person who really matters is still her. If she says it's okay, I will cut my hair; if she objects, I won't; after all, it is only a small sacrifice. So, Ajay, you will just have to wait till next week when Preeti comes back."

"Yes, I can't wait to see her. I have to tell her about that other thing, remember?"

"Yes, I remember, that other thing," I agreed.

"But you still have not answered my question: can you still be a Sikh if you cut your hair?"

"A Sikh, Ajay, means a pupil; that is what the word means; somebody who learns from the teacher, here a religious teacher. Tradition has it that Sikhs had ten such teachers; gurus, we call them. What the first nine taught is what is in the holy book of the Sikhs, the Guru Granth Sahib. There are some things in it I agree with, and some not. Firstly, it is a theistic philosophy, meaning that many of its teachings are dependent on a belief in God; then there are long passages which do nothing but praise God, trying as it were to extol him to the point that sheer weight of scripture will sway a nonbeliever. For an atheist like me, who has reasoned his way to his beliefs, it is like flogging a dead horse, a waste of breath and effort. In my own eyes, calling me a Sikh, even while I still have my hair, doesn't make any sense. I would much prefer to be called just a human being;

or if people insist on knowing what I believe, a Rational Human Being.

"But it is not so easy. People claim you are what religion you are born into. If, later, you reject that religion, you are supposed to give it up because you prefer another. If a Sikh becomes a Muslim, he would be hated by his fellow Sikhs, but the change would be considered acceptable and comprehensible; after all, he is still within the theistic fold; but to give up religion entirely, that is inconceivable to them. It is like being set adrift in a sea of evil, with no sail, or rudder, or oar, or guidance. It is the ultimate horror. How could a man like that know what to do? He has denied himself access to all the wisdom of the scriptures. They fail to realize that wisdom is not a monopoly of their religious tomes; in fact, may be largely absent there; but something that comes from observing Nature, discovering its rules and its causes, the Laws of Causality and Identity, and many others; the very laws that all religions deny by their very essence, the belief in God; and learning to manipulate and use them in the interests of survival, of survival as whole human beings, not half-deluded ones. Science, which you are just beginning to learn, is part of this quest; but the larger part is that other philosophy, secular philosophy, which religions would have us deny as evil. All lands have had it, but none more than ancient Greece. One day, when you are a little more grown up, I will teach you about Aristotle and Plato, and all the other great thinkers that lived there. Religious movements that followed them historically, particularly the Christians, destroyed a lot of what was then written, afraid that those who partook of such knowledge would desert the fold of Christianity as irrational; but much has survived, and every time you read the thoughts of those ancient men, you wonder with admiration at their enlightenment, and cringe at the present state of our thinking. We have the same caliber of intellect, but look at what we have allowed the irrationality of theism to drag us down into. Does this answer your question, Ajay?"

"Yes, I would like to be called a Rational Human Being too, even though I am proud of some of the traditions of the Rajpoots that I have learned growing up in my family, just like you are proud of some of the traditions of the Sikhs that you have learned from yours."

"So you keep your hair because you are afraid that people you are fond of may be upset if you cut them?" asked Shiv.

"Yes," I replied.

"But they are being irrational, just like my father. Why do you submit to irrationality?"

"Shiv, one has sometimes to bear the burden of others' irrationality. No man is an island. May be one day I will be strong enough to do things on my own, but right now I still need the affection of others. But that does not change what I think of long hair. There is nothing wrong with hair; after all, we are given them by Nature. There is no reason we must cut them; I simply object to giving up my property rights over them. If they are my own, like nails, I should be the only one to decide what I wish to do with them. I object, on principle, to the stricture against cutting the hair, not because I have any great desire to cut them."

"I like the way you think, Amrik," said Shiv; "I would like to be called a Rational Human Being too."

XXV

Preeti **woke** up early next day, quickly bathed and dressed, and came down to the hotel lobby to browse in the magazine shop till Dinesh came down and they could go in for breakfast. While there, she noticed that day's copy of the National Express. She seldom read newspapers, but something, perhaps curiosity, perhaps the fancy that another of her husband's creations had been published, or even the possibility of letters to the editor denouncing or, hoping against hope, praising him, tantalized her mind. She bought a copy. To her surprise, Professor Srivastava's column, *Our Ancient Heritage,* was in print for the first time since Amrik's column had started. She settled down in a chair and started reading. It was the first of two installments on the subject "The Goal of Life." She sat there, oblivious to all else but the article. The contents were familiar, awash with *déjà vu,* though not ever before experienced in such detail. Amrik had anticipated it all, and the two of them had gone over the ground many times, but never before had she seen the ideas spelled out by a proponent. Their discussions had been based on what they knew of Indian society by having lived in it, or from Amrik's readings, but not from anything she herself had read. Now she read with an interest and enthusiasm that had not existed a bare six months ago.

The pros and cons were not difficult to see, including the one fundamental flaw, the postulate of the nonmaterial. And as she thought of it, a heaviness descended upon her; a feeling of being all alone. She thought of Amrik, and how he too was in like manner alone. Was it probable that anyone would understand? Why had no one questioned it before, questioned the basis of what the Professor was asserting. Were people just an inertial mass, dull and immovable, or did they really believe all this? Perhaps the answer was brainwashing. But, she mused, thinking of herself and Amrik, you cannot brainwash a person who thinks. Those only could be brainwashed who had little brain to wash. Yet almost everyone she knew, except for a very few, countable on her fingertips, acquiesced in the beliefs expounded here; and she was convinced that the thoughts expressed in the article made no sense. 'Why,' she asked herself, 'why did people believe all this nonsense?'

Dinesh had come down to the lobby and had been standing there a while watching Preeti. She was engrossed in the paper, and had not felt his thoughtful gaze, a confusing mixture of love and pain. He had not slept well; all night long, he had gone over and over all his options, all that had happened, only to see every time that he had no options at all; it was a dead end. She had done more than any woman in her position could have done for him, but he still felt empty, for where was the fulfillment in denial and failure? Though she avowed her love for him, which he did not doubt, and had posed for him in the nude, what good was it? Every time she let go and responded to him, he could sense the touch of pain, pain for another, cross her face. She who had never shown doubt or unhappiness was now in a position much like him; she had no answers. The problem, he realized, was in the question that underlay the dilemma: can you love two people, giving of yourself to both, or is there something inherent in human nature that will not permit it, at least for long? Never having been so in love before, he could not answer the question. Well, life must go on, he observed philosophically, arming himself with a resolution not to give in to despair and demoralization; and with that he walked up to her.

"Good morning," he said cheerfully.

Preeti looked up. The words were cheerful, but his face and eyes looked tired. "You have not slept well," she said, half stating, half asking.

"Is it so obvious?" he asked.

"Yes, Dinesh, but perhaps my company will cheer you up."

"It has already," he replied, knowing it to be true. "You were quite engrossed in the paper, I noticed. What piece of news could be so important that a beautiful young girl would ignore the presence of an attractive young man who has been watching her shamelessly without a pause for the past ten minutes.?"

Preeti smiled back at him, amused at the way he claimed the right to intimacy. He had earned it, and she was not averse to it either. "I was reading an article on the goal of life by Professor Srivastava of Benares Hindu University," she explained.

Dinesh could barely believe that he had heard right. "Let me look at it," he said, taking the newspaper from Preeti, and briefly reading the first couple of paragraphs. "This is heavy stuff," he said, "I cannot believe that it would interest you. Even I find it forbidding."

"Come on, let's eat. We can talk about it over breakfast. I am famished," she replied.

Having seated themselves and placed their orders, Dinesh came back to the topic. "Okay, now explain to me the unexplainable: a beautiful girl like you reading about salvation. From the way you're doing in this world, I would say you have already achieved it. What more could you want?"

"To be two women at the same time. It would solve all my remaining problems," she answered philosophically, then chuckled at the succinct cleverness with which she had defined the predicament that beset him.

"And the Professor is going to show you the way?"

"Not quite; he seems to be more lost than me."

"Oh! So you were reading as a critic! But that simply adds to the mystery. If he has nothing to offer, why spend your time on him?"

"I'll give you two guesses," Preeti said playfully.

"You could give me a hundred; there is no way that I could even dream of an explanation."

"Well, it is actually quite simple." Then Preeti went on to explain to him that her husband was a writer, and had written a couple of columns in the newspaper with the opposite viewpoint. This was the first time she had seen the opposition's point of view.

"Don't get me wrong, Preeti," added Dinesh, "it sounds to me that your husband is some sort of professor, but I distinctly remember you telling me that he was a student. Perhaps I misunderstood; you probably meant a student in the sense of a professor immersed in the study of something of major interest to him. I had been imagining him as an undergraduate like you."

"You are not mistaken," she replied, "he is just an undergrad student."

Dinesh was even more perplexed. "How old is he?" he asked.

"Eighteen going on nineteen."

"You're not joking, are you? That would make you older than him. Forgive me, but I happen to know your age, being your agent."

"Does my age show?"

"Beautifully."

"Yes, he's younger than me."

Dinesh thought awhile, then asked: "If you two were not married, but you loved him as you do now, would your behavior towards me be different?"

"No," she replied without hesitation, "it would be the same."

"So it is not marriage that stands in the way?"

"No."

Dinesh was silent a moment. "Would it be too presumptuous of me to ask how you two came to be married?"

"Not at all; you have more rights on me than that. I have been wanting to tell you about it anyway, ever since we came to Bombay, but the time never seemed appropriate." Then she told him of how she met Amrik, and they fell in love. She left out the really intimate details; those could not be revealed to anybody. She went on to explain how they had decided that they were going to live with only one aim, to achieve their highest the best way they knew how, and how they had determined that the only way that could be done was to do what gave them the most happiness. He gave up the idea of becoming a doctor for what he really wanted to be, a writer, and she gave up moping and crying over spilt milk to do what she most loved, painting. "We have been at it only a short while, but we both know we made the right choice. Life is so full that there is no time in the twenty-four hours of the day for us to do all that we wish to do. It is like photography is to you. Writing for him and painting for me are like that."

"I don't understand one thing. You suggested that you were unhappy before you met him, something about spilt milk. What was that all about? It is difficult to imagine you listless and unhappy, for you are the most motivated person I know."

Preeti was silent, just as she had been once before; with head lowered. It was a matter of shame to her, her unhappy first marriage. It reminded her of her time of weakness. She raised her head, bit her lip, then lowered it again. Then she raised it again, and opened her mouth as if to speak, but gave up, lowering her head again. Dinesh just looked at her, wondering what could be so difficult to say, but he kept quiet. She obviously wished to answer truthfully, else she would have simply given him some easy, plausible explanation, instead of going through all this heart-rending. "I was a widow, Dinesh, of an unhappy marriage. That is why I was without desire."

"Was that a love marriage too, one gone wrong?"

"No. He was not a Romeo Mehta, though I daresay he was almost as handsome. He was an honest and good man, but we were as different as fire and water. It was an utter failure. The marriage ended when he died in an accident."

This was more than Dinesh had expected. Such details are not usually divulged, not in this country. But now he respected her all the more; and unfortunately, loved her even more hopelessly. "Thank you for telling me this, Preeti. I think I understand you better knowing all you have just told me. Would it be very wrong of me to feel jealous of your husband?"

"Your being jealous, I believe, is a compliment to him; at least that is the way he would take it."

"Sitting here listening to you I can believe that. How much do you love him?"

"He is everything to me. I could say more than life itself, but I know he would not approve."

"And why not? What could be a higher expression of love than a willingness to give one's life for it?"

"He believes, and I agree, that life is an ultimate goal. To sacrifice it is to accept utter failure. How could the one you love ever accept the giving up of your life. He could accept your sorrow; he could accept unbelievable grief; but he could not accept your total destruction. He would want to see you rise again; perhaps find another love, and be happy again the way you were destined to be; for if you love someone, you cannot but imagine that her destiny is happiness."

Dinesh could not agree more, about the destiny part. "But can't you think of the possibility where you may save his life by giving up yours?"

"That is the ethics of emergencies. To think in such terms is ridiculous. You cannot base, as an ultimate test, right and wrong on something whose likelihood of happening approaches zero. Suppose he were dying, and the only way he could be saved was by my donating to him an organ vital for survival, meaning that I would die of the donation and he would live. Could he ever approve of that? Could he ever accept the sacrifice of my life for him? He thinks not, and I agree. We reason it something like this: it is only when you love your life to the maximum that you can love anyone else's life to the maximum. The ultimate self-sacrifice is the ultimate denial of your worth. It is your death. How could anyone love you when you have proclaimed yourself so worthless? I know what you are thinking; that this is the opposite of what the Professor says here in the newspaper. When you read the whole article, you will agree with that assessment. It is the opposite of what we are all taught from birth. Who is right is not a matter of opinion polls, but of what appeals to reason, so that one person can be right and many millions wrong. The Professor here condemns the use of reason as impotent; and he uses reason to convince us of that. Why then should anyone accept him?"

Dinesh could not believe his ears, or his eyes. A beautiful philosopher, that's what she was. But who ever heard of a beautiful philosopher? And to top it all, a model and an artist to boot. The more he came to know of her, the more certain he was that he would pine for her for ever; but sitting here in her presence, he also felt happy; and his pain was stilled. For his own happiness, he had to remain a part of her life; and why not? She herself had invited him. He would not turn down the invitation. He would visit her, and her husband, as often as she would permit him. It was resolved; it would be done.

The rest of the week passed swiftly. The modeling of western dresses was a big success. Preeti had never worn evening gowns; now she was delighted trying them on. There was a black one she particularly liked. It was sleeveless and had only thin shoulder straps, leaving much of her upper body totally uncovered. The rest hugged her, leaving little to the imagination. Dinesh noticed her feeling of elation as she modeled it. There and then he resolved that he would buy her that as a present. He talked to the designer, and it was done. The last day that they went out to dinner, he extended a package to her. "I would like you to accept this present from me," he stated.

"Thank you," she said, accepting with delight, "may I open it?"

"No. Wait till you are back in your room. It is a dress which I would like you to wear when you call me home to dinner." Dinesh knew that it would not be possible for her to wear it out, given the attitude of Indians towards western dress for Indian women; but in the privacy of her home, she could indulge herself as she wished.

Back at the hotel, Preeti opened the package. She had not expected this; and it was obvious Dinesh knew her better than she had suspected. He had read her heart; and her heart went out to him. Her eyes shed a tear; love, pain, beauty, sorrow, they were all there together, and she let her mind be that way; how else could she come to terms with this but for experiencing it all; she must let her feelings fill her. And as she lay in bed, she thought of the two men in her life, Amrik and Dinesh. They came and went, met and fused, then drifted apart; and so it went on till sleep closed her lids, and the peace of impossible dreams soothed her mind.

XXVI

"Renunciation is the essence of life, and the ideal man is the perfect embodiment of that renunciation. This message was brought to us by God incarnate himself, in the guise of Lord Krishna, on the battlefield of Kurukshetra. Arjun, the most accomplished warrior of the Paandavs, stood there in his chariot betwixt the forces of Good and Evil, gazing with dismay at the opposing armies of the Kauravs and Paandavs arrayed for battle. Peaceful dawn illuminated with its soft light a nightmarish specter: visible there before him in the ranks of the enemy, glittering in their armor, were his kith and kin— cousins, uncles, grand-uncles, nephews, friends, and teachers. An unenviable task lay before him; an opportunity, indeed, to fight for the right, but also one heavy with responsibility so awesome he would fain not have it; and whose execution entailed death at his hands of those he had known to love, those who were dearer than life itself, but in exchange for what? A kingdom? Power? What if his cause was just; could anything be worth attaining that demanded such heinous deeds? Was there no better way? His mind, unable to conceive of another, recoiled in horror; his strength ebbed; his knees weakened; he sat down, paralyzed by a moral impasse which had no answer. "I will not fight," he said. Right and wrong fled from his mind, vanquished by loathing of an act beyond contemplation, the mind denying room for a purpose so dread. Man, even the great Arjun, could go no further. The barriers of attachment, of *Maya*, would permit no more.

"Lord Krishna, Arjun's charioteer, now stepped in so that right may be done. With divine words of eternal wisdom he nursed the despondent warrior, guiding him through what had once seemed insuperable obstacles, to the path of righteousness, slowly coaxing him back into the coming battle; giving him the strength to do his duty. The message was eternal, and though it seemed he spoke to Arjun, he spoke to all mankind; to all those who were wrapped in the cobwebs, the traps of Maya; to all who mistook illusion for reality."

Thus began Professor Srivastava. But I must here interrupt, for an introduction is in order, one which the professor himself would have approved and proudly given, had he the space. Welcome, then, to the field of Hindu cosmology. Imagine, if you will, a totality: all, everything, the source, the substance, the cause, the effect, the Godhead. Call it Brahman. It is the central, the only reality. It cannot be defined in terms of attributes, for it is everything. In secular thought, one defines existence by a slow, turning movement of the body with arms outstretched, indicating all that is. Existence is an axiomatic concept, a self-evident truth, a given that cannot be defined in terms of anything else, because all such are but its parts; nor ever questioned. But Brahman is more. It is also that which cannot be conceived or expressed, even by a spreading of the arms. It is the totality of the nonmaterial. It is the Absolute of everything; but not everything as we perceive it. It is not of the phenomenal world. If you were to eliminate all that is phenomenal, that is, that defined by an axiomatic spread of the arms, and amenable to the senses, directly or indirectly, then Brahman alone would remain. The phenomenal, in this view, can be questioned, but not Brahman, because it is the only true Reality. This is the Godhead you must imagine. But words, mere mortal creations, are hopelessly inadequate for this task; yet they must suffice, with the hope that they will hint, at least, at what is truly impossible to define. With that we must be satisfied.

Brahman is within everything, whether animate or inanimate, matter or energy. It is the divine spark, the Aatman that is within us all, our essence, the only part of us that represents true Reality. But Aatman is not distinct from Brahman It is identical with it. Beyond all action, it can neither be created nor destroyed. Brahman is also the creator of the phenomenal universe. This attribute of him, the active and personal aspect, can be termed God, or Ishwar (pronounced Eeshwar). In this form, Brahman creates, preserves, and destroys the phenomenal universe. Brahman, in the absolute sense, cannot possibly be known by the conscious mind, but Ishwar can. ('To know' here means to have substantive, direct, personal knowledge of the entity).

In order to comprehend what the Professor says, imagine, if you will, a Divine Unity. It is all there is; all of existence. Let us call it the Divine Ground *a la* Aldous Huxley. View us—you and me, and the phenomenal world of matter and energy, the myriad individual consciousnesses with which we sense it, and all the gods we can imagine, in one sense as inseparable from this Divine Ground and hence not separately identified, but in another sense, at the same time, as partial realities within this Unity.

Now this partial reality, which is us, individualized human beings, may come to know of the Divine Ground through force of reason, but weakly. Much more potent a path to such realization is the process of super-rational direct intuition. But what is this direct intuition? To understand it, you have to realize that we are organized in a complex manner. First, there is the body; next is the ego, the phenomenal ego with which we sense, and which we often refer to as the self (mistakenly, says the Professor). This ego is perishable, as is the body. The Real Self is not. But what is this Real Self? It is the divine spark in us, the spirit of like nature with the Divine Ground.

The spell of the body, which is Maya, demands its comfort, so we use reason to discover means to achieve this end. But, the Hindu cosmologists complain, we should be practicing self-abnegation instead of this folly where a delusion, which is what we sense with our mind, is proclaimed as happiness, and a path of eternal bliss, which is known by direct intuition only, is termed suffering. Happiness, in our eyes, results from successfully gaining knowledge of the universe by rational analysis based on a focus on the phenomenal world, the world that we apprehend with our senses, and then using it for our benefit. However, in Hindu theology, this is folly because, they claim, the phenomenal world is non-real. Instead, they urge an intuitive, non-rational focus on the nonmaterial world, what they call the Real World, the one all evidence screams to us does not exist. The evidence we have, the evidence of the senses, they claim is an illusion of Maya; how then could we lend credence to it? You would imagine that, to back such a statement, they had some trump card up their sleeve. But no, all they have going for them is their assertion, which they insist is superior to any proof offered to the contrary by reason. All their evidence is but a blatant assertion, in the face of reality, in the face of all evidence to the contrary. They have won by force of obstinacy; by claiming continually and shrilly that they know what they are talking about, and we don't. They have threatened force, and damnation, and Hell-fire. I am here referring to the world's religions in general, since it is obvious that they have a common base of which Hindu philosophy gives the clearest exposition. Armies of soldiers have fought under the banner of these religions, and dark hordes of inquisitors have tortured and torched the living who claimed reason as their judge; even the innocent whom Nature had maligned with deformities, both physical and mental, all these in the name of that which is beyond reason, beyond the senses, beyond evidence, the so-called True Reality, the Truth. If it sickens you, that is my intention, for men need to ponder on this cruelty.

It is an ethics of elitism that they flourish before our eyes, an ethics in which all knowledge as we know it is denigrated, and all not verifiable acclaimed. To the question "how do you know?" they answer "because it is given to the likes of us, persons with a particular kind of mental constitution—an evil constitution, I think—to know. We know it to be so, they say, because we have the inherent ability to know it to be so. No evidence can be demanded of us nor given. Our mode of knowledge is beyond discursive reasoning, and outside the sphere where reasons are demanded and given."

This philosophical stance is a veritable womb for the origin of dictators, autocrats, fanatics, and masters. Spurning the necessity of justifying a claim, they are arbitrarily placing themselves above and beyond others. It is only a matter of time before they proclaim the right to exercise, in action, the superiority thus claimed, and later justify the injustices perpetrated by refuting the accusers with the argument that theirs is an ethical system born of the same knowledge, so-called super-rational direct intuition, which exists only in those *with a particular kind of mental constitution.* Most of mankind, except for a rational few, has conceded to them, under threat, through exhaustion, or ignorance, the title of the Good. Unreason has thus defeated reason.

It was Saturday night. I lay in bed brooding on the Professor's cheerless article. Preeti was coming home Sunday morning. Till then, my counsel was my thoughts alone. The Geeta lay by my bedside, for I too had been studying the Hindu scriptures. The origin of the Professor's ideas was no longer a mystery to me. He wrote with charm and passion, and a seemingly total belief in what he said. But, I thought, if he has half the intelligence that I and the general run of mankind have, he could not possibly insist on the correctness of what he states. His command of language alone suggests the obvious presence of intelligence, so what gives? It was a mystery, so I covered the whole territory over again, as dispassionately as I could.

The Professor's article continued: " . . . the Aatman is changeless, untouched by anything, immune to harm. It being the only reality, what could Arjun do to it? Nothing. He could slay all he wished in battle, he could yet not be a killer. There was hence no cause for him to sorrow. Death of the body that housed was no reason to grieve when the dweller within remained untouched. Caste-duty enjoined every individual, including Arjun, to act according to his station in life, which is the God-given caste he is born in. For a warrior, then, there is nothing nobler than a righteous war, for it opens a door to Heaven; but turning aside from one's given duty is sinful and a disgrace, and to be thus dishonored is surely worse than death."

He goes on: "Caste-mixture must, at all costs, be shunned, because wrong duties cannot possibly lead to the ultimate Truth, or even to a movement towards it. It will, instead, lead into greater spiritual danger. From sense-object to senses, mind, intelligent will, and Aatman, there exists an ascending hierarchy; and the duty proper to each stage is different. The purpose of the caste-system is simply to ensure that such is not lost sight of, because different men are in different stages, evidenced by their caste at birth. Think of it not as an accident (of birth), but something ordained, a message from Ishwar as to where a man stands in relation to the *gunas,* for was it not Ishwar himself who established the four-caste system to correspond to the different types of gunas and karms that exist among men?"

Let me explain. The basis of the phenomenal world is Prakriti, or Maya (these are interchangeable words). Maya is comprised of three forces or *gunas*—sattwa, tamas and rajas. The universe recycles between cosmic night and day, destruction and creation. The creative function of Ishwar is conceived of as Brahma, the preserving aspect Vishnu, and the destroyer aspect Shiv. During the night of Brahma, which is the potential phase of the universe, the three gunas are in perfect equilibrium, but with Creation they begin to differentiate. Their various combinations result in the myriad aspects of mind, matter and energy; and all are subject to psychic perception. Sattwa is perceived as tranquility, purity, calmness; tamas as stupidity, laziness, inertia; and rajas as aggressive activity, passion, restlessness. A man's mood and character varies with which guna is dominant in him at the time. By cultivating rajas, tamas can be overcome; and by cultivating sattwa, rajas too can be overcome. This is not enough, for the three gunas are the bonds that bind the Aatman to the body. Only when they are overcome can you achieve realization. For this you need Yoga, which is both a philosophic and physical discipline, to overcome sattwa, and thus ascend to the ideal of union of the Aatman and Brahman.

The Professor states: "The Self in us is the Aatman, the divine spark that is of a piece with Brahman." That is easily refuted—no such evidence exists.

"It being the only Reality," he continues. This is mischievous, calling that which exists 'unreal,' and that which does not, 'real.' With one stroke of the pen, he has eliminated all knowledge as we know it, because our knowledge only pertains to what he calls the unreal.

"He could slay all he wished in battle, he could not be a killer; . . . death of the body that housed was no reason to grieve when the dweller within remained untouched." This was straight out of the Geeta, where Krishna attempts to persuade Arjun to join the battle, even though it would involve the slaying of many of his close relatives. But what else is this if not a license to kill? Granted Arjun's cause was just. A kingdom, their's by right, had been denied him and his brothers, with no alternative left but to fight, yet to pretend that killing was somehow not killing opened up a Pandora's box. Many a modern-day ogre, the likes of Hitler and Stalin, would have welcomed with glee such an interpretation, eliminating as it did any possible censure by the conventional view of killing, for their dastardly acts. That Hitler sought mystical advice is well known; and the Aryan connection with Hindu religious doctrine was not lost on the Nazis. When you make light of reality as we know it, you make light of existence as we know it; why then cringe at its snuffing out? The Professor claims another existence, but it is a fatuous claim, for there is nothing to back it.

"Life's goal is the achievement of knowledge of Brahman by knowing the Aatman." But the Aatman and Brahman, once eliminated from consideration for lack of evidence, cannot be used to justify any further claims.

"Work for work's sake, not for its fruits." How otherworldly! We are asked to work without motivation. The Professor wants us to work for nothing; at least nothing in the worldly sense. He merely states that if you will be a good boy, and do what he tells you to do, you will not be punished.

And what is the punishment? "The undesirable cycles of never-ending reincarnation." His concept of being in the world is a concept of misery. Perhaps that is exactly what life was like when the philosophy he expounds was conceived. Yet there must have been hope, there always was, in the workings of the mind, and the inventiveness of man. But that route the Professor condemns, with all the cunning of a snake. (Sorry for that metaphor. It had momentarily slipped my mind that it is unacceptable in our country. My lapse could be blamed on the influence of English and its long relationship with Christianity. The snake—Naag—you see, is an object of worship in India). This is how he does it:

Imagine that you have a problem of survival. Normally, you would try to think of a solution such as a course of action whose end-result would be removal of the hardship. The motivation here is your survival, or survival with more comfort and satisfaction. That, after all, is the reason for the advances made by civilization. The means is the use of rational analysis based on the Law of Causality, knowing from prior knowledge gained by the senses that 'if you do this, that will happen . . . and so on.' Life is, in essence, a continual series of such experiments, relating cause to effect, whose end-result is knowledge. This knowledge is used to devise a solution to your problem, and if the knowledge is sound, you will have the solution, assuming that all else remains the same.

"But," the Professor says, "to achieve true knowledge, act selflessly . . . work for work's sake, not for its fruits. Renounce the latter. Permit not success or failure to sway you."

Try that in real life and see what happens. If you paid no mind to the results of your myriad experiments with Nature's ways, you would most certainly end up destroying yourself. Perhaps that is what the Professor has in mind. The union of Aatman and Brahman occurs only when you have renounced everything, reason most of all.

When "you have reached the ultimate truth, action is uncalled for." Surely he speaks the truth here. The cosmological assumptions proclaim that you have reached the ultimate truth when your Aatman, which is a reluctant guest, has been released from the body that houses it. The Professor may quibble over this interpretation, but this release, to me, is Death. Here he and I agree: once you are dead, "action is uncalled for."

But what was all this about justifying the caste system?

"Think not of it as an accident (of birth), but something ordained." Sure! Delude yourself if you are discriminated against because of your birth, do not fight back for your rights against those who have invented the nefarious system, but resign yourself to their discrimination " . . . for it was Ishwar himself who established the four-caste system." But Ishwar (God) is that which does not exist. It then comes down to 'accept your misfortune as causeless.' This way you will have forgiven those who have caused you the misery, and you will have accepted what they term your caste-duty, which is willful surrender to coercion, or the defeat of right by wrong. Given such an acceptance, you will slave for their sake.

Notwithstanding their avowed contempt for the phenomenal world, even the proponents of this philosophy want to survive; and you as a member of an organized society, are a cog in their survival machine. If you refuse to fit in with their other cogs, and many others follow your example, where would they be? In Heaven, in Aatman-Brahman unity? But they would rather have your world, till the day it is time to go anyway. Then they will don (or un-don . . . after all, dress is an illusion too. In India, we do have a bunch of ascetics, the Naangas, who disdain clothes, but not in the sense of Preeti. They do not love the body, but condemn it as Maya or illusion. Fain would they be rid of it, but shed it they won't) the dress of an ascetic, meditate and achieve Salvation. The best of both worlds, isn't it? The only catch is that there is no other world; and the scoundrels know it. That is why they hold on so tenaciously to the caste-system and the rewards it offers them. They, the Brahmins, the literate, are the authors and the recipients of the benefits; and yet the Professor claims that he is teaching you right, not wrong. When reality itself is turned on its head, why not justice? It all makes sense.

Next morning, at ten o'clock, I was at the airport to meet Preeti. Accompanying her was another attractive woman, and a handsome man. A tinge of jealousy stabbed me, but then she smiled and it was all gone.

"Amrik, let me introduce you," she said. "This is Rita, a co-model; and this is Dinesh, my agent and an accomplished photographer. "And this," she turned to the others, "is my very own, my husband Amrik."

There was a shaking of hands all around. Dinesh's grip was firm and warm, and I reciprocated in kind. As I looked into his eyes, he did not evade mine, but looked straight back. It was friendly, that gaze, but there was also an element of sizing me up; and he seemed to know something that would have been impossible with this simple introduction. Preeti must have talked of me.

We celebrated Preeti's return by going out for lunch to a restaurant. We normally avoided that for financial reasons, but now we had more than enough cash; and besides, there was reason to celebrate: we were together again. I told Preeti what Shiv's father had done, and what Shiv had done in return. She was proud of both my pupil and me. I told her about how Ajay had a crush on her. She smiled at that, inwardly, but remained silent. Then I told her about the Professor's article. She said she had read it.

"What do you think of it?" I asked.

"You know what I think," she replied. True enough, I knew; there had been no need to ask.

"So tell me about Bombay," I said.

"I'll tell you about it when we are alone together; tonight."

"But we are alone."

"Not the way I want it."

So I just had to wait. But I had noticed a solemn, far-away look cross her face; the kind that tells you that more than just a narration of events is involved here; there is emotion too in the experience.

That night, as we lay in bed, she opened her heart to me. She told me all about the modeling, about Romeo, and about Dinesh. She asked me to hold her tight as she talked. It made her feel closer, and it was easier to confide. When she was finished, I knew all that had passed through her mind. She was not one to hold back anything from me. We had conceded that right to each other, and happily it was turning out to be the easiest, most natural way to be. What was there to hide? Love knows no secrets. That which is dearest to the heart must needs be shared. When she told me of how she posed in the nude, I was a little dismayed, but she held me close and soon I had forgotten. Thinking back on it, I could sense how a beautiful woman might want to be the subject of a piece of art, like all the nudes of famous paintings; or it may simply be a way to see what it is about her that men find so beautiful. Far from destroying my desire for her, the thought of her nude in front of another man who truly loved her was more erotic than I could imagine. She was lying on top of me with her face in the side of my neck. When she lifted up her head and asked me to make love to her, I knew what she had in mind; and by her response I could tell that she had truly missed me. There were times when I forgot that she was another person; it was as if she was a part of me. What happened to her, in that sense, happened to me.

While we played with each other, Preeti turned to me. "Darling," she said, "I love you so much, even as much as I love myself; yet he keeps coming into my thoughts. Is something wrong with me? I should be able to forget him in your arms."

"Don't fight it, love," I answered; "just let it be. If you love him, what is there to be ashamed of?"

"I don't want you to feel hurt."

"Do I look hurt?"

She lay on top of me. There was longing in her eyes as she gazed into mine; and a playfulness. "Do you know what I'm thinking right now?" she asked.

"No," I said. This was dangerous territory; it was not smart to hazard a guess. Anyway, she wasn't looking for an answer.

"I am wondering how it would feel having two men making love to me at the same time."

"I have never thought of another man in our bed, Preeti, but I have often thought of a woman."

"Who?"

"Aasha."

"Oh! How could you?" She pretended to be outraged, but I could tell that she wanted to hear more.

"With one woman, Preeti, I can control myself. I can see into her eyes and tell what she is thinking; so then I know how to respond. But with two, their plans would be beyond my ken, and what they do would be beyond my anticipation. It will be truly heaven; attended and loved hand and feet, literally, by women."

"Let's make love," she said, too aroused to wait any longer.

Lying there on top of her, happily inside, breathing my warm breath into the side of her neck, I could feel her mind. "Preeti, I love you," I said.

"Shh," she replied softly.

"Preeti, are you thinking of him?"

"I don't know. I can't tell who is in my mind. You or he; you come and go. I see you in him, and him in you; but you are both mine, and making love to me together."

And when she came, she clung to me, her heart full, satisfied that she had given of her love to all who loved her; that she had not slighted any man who truly cared for her. I could not fault her, for I loved her all the more. It took courage to admit that she owed my rival something more than just words, and I have always been putty in the hands of those with courage. But reality sorts it all out, making it acceptable. Some acts are simply that, acts. Others must, by force of that which we cannot change, remain symbolic; and so it was with her. Even as I enveloped and possessed her, I knew she was not mine, nor anyone else's. She was a free spirit, independent like me; and like all who truly love, giving what she owed, and taking what she was owed. She preferred to make love to me, I knew. It was my good fortune and my right, but only so long as she desired it that way. And it was no different for her. Love was a right she or I could never have against the other's will. Love believes in this truth, and there is no room for jealousy.

As we lay in bed, she told me about the kind of man Dinesh was, about his mind and his talents, everything she knew. And then she said: "I want you two to be friends. I could not accept it any other way."

I caressed her as she lay in my arms, and answered with complete sincerity: "I cannot not love someone whom you love. What happens to you, happens to me too. Of course he will be my friend; he will be welcome to this house any time he wants, and without invitation."

And as I was fondling her hair and feeling the warmth of her body, I found she had fallen asleep; the sleep of the happy, of one who loved and was loved, fully and honestly. I kept holding her close, till I too was asleep.

XXVII

Two weeks after the first, the second installment of Professor Srivastava's article was out in print. He continued: "Knowing that your Aatman is the same in all beings, you will think: 'The senses sense; the mind and body act, for they are the instruments. I, the Aatman, stand aloof, not acting, dreaming no dreams, suffering no delusions.' When the darkness that hides the Aatman is driven out, you will see a sun in splendor—Brahman. Your mind will be dead to the call of the world; and the pleasures of the senses will not trouble you. In place of their evanescence will be lasting bliss—Nirvana.

"Retire to a solitary place far from the madding crowd. There meditate ceaselessly on the Aatman and Brahman. Practice yoga constantly. Even if you falter, all is not lost. You will still attain to the heaven of the doers of good, where you dwell awhile among the immortals, the phenomenal Gods, before you are reborn into the world.

"The three gunas delude the doers of evil, dragging ever lower, destroying their judgment, blackening their heart. But those who seek Brahman; those weary of the world; the knowledge-seekers; and those with spiritual discrimination, the noblest of all, their bad karm ebbs away, and they are free.

"Keep your thoughts ever on Brahman. As you master the yoga, your vital force will rise from its sacral dwelling up the *sushumna* (spinal canal) to that part of the brain deep between the eyebrows. Close firmly now the doors of the senses, so that when death comes, the Aatman is free to leave through that aperture which is in the center of the brain. Utter the sacred symbol, 'OM' (pronounced ome; oam), all the while meditating on Brahman. Then you will achieve the ultimate union.

"From Brahman pour forth all the creatures of the universe, and when the cosmic day is over, they are gathered back into him, there to stay dormant till the dawn of another day. Maya is the lord of the creatures of creation, but Brahman is the lord of Maya. Those who obey the triple Vedas, they gain entry into the realm of the immortals. There they live awhile, but ultimately are drawn back to the world of endless returnings. It is a cycle where you beget what you sow: if you dwell on Brahman to the exclusion of all else, you will achieve union with him. This is the ultimate goal, Nirvana.

"The actions of the gunas makes it a weightier task for those who have saddled themselves with bad karms in past existences. These are born into the lowest castes: Vaishyas (merchants, artisans, producers), Shudras (servants), and women. So think not of the caste-system as man's inhumanity to man, but as divine justice; a reaping of that which was sown.

"Then there are the Godless, the atheists, who say the scriptures are a lie; that the universe is not backed by a moral law. To them, it is conceived in lust and created in copulation, knowing no other cause. Such creatures are steeped in tamas, deluded through and through. Some others, driven by rajas, are arrogant beyond belief, lusting endlessly, believing that the aim of life is the gratification of the senses. Their acts are not selfless, given that they are full of egotism, vanity, wrath and the intoxication of power. They have crossed all the doors into Hell, which are the doors of lust, rage and greed.

"Shed the delusion of 'I' and 'mine'. Be unswayed by emotions. Hold steadfast to your goal. It is in the nature of Aatman to be united with Brahman; for the two, though seemingly separate, are as one. This union must be your goal; there can be no other. It is in the nature of Truth for that which truly exists, that which is Truth itself, to be united with itself. OM! OM! OM!"

It was now a week later. There was a knock on the door. Preeti was standing next to me, radiant in her black evening gown. I walked up to the door and opened it. There was Dinesh with a long-stemmed red rose in his hand, and two large packages. I smiled him a welcome, then asked: "Surely these are not for me?"

"Not the rose," he replied, "but the packages are."

Preeti walked up to us, kissed him on his cheek, and accepted the rose. Placing it in our prettiest vase, she turned to the larger package. The wrapping paper crackled as she deftly removed it. Beneath it was a large, framed portrait in black and white. I picked it up and placed it on the sofa. It was Preeti, her hair blowing in the sea breeze, dark monsoon clouds threatening in the background. The three of us stood there looking at it, barely able to take our eyes off except when Dinesh and I looked up at the person herself and admired that lovely head, and the spirit that dwelt therein.

"Dinesh," said Preeti, "you know where I must keep it. It will be in our bedroom, for Amrik and me."

"I know," he said. But I could sense the unspoken. He could live with it; there would be one iu his bedroom too.

When Preeti turned to the second package, he requested that she wait until he had left. She therefore put it aside. A bottle of champagne was opened, and the three of us sat there, sipping the sweet bubbly slowly. Few words were said. Then I got up, excusing myself for a while. There was something I had to fetch, I told them; I wouldn't be gone more than ten minutes. With that, I left them alone. Preeti had known nothing of this. Fifteen minutes later, I was back from the local market with a package of hot samosas, and some burfee. I never asked Preeti what, if anything, had transpired while I was away. It was not my intention ever to know; but when I returned, the ice had been broken, and our home was full of gay laughter. Dinesh was a likeable person. It even occurred to me that I could introduce him to one of Preeti's girl-friends—some of them were quite pretty and bright. But then I thought the better of it; better to let Preeti and him sort it out; they would find a way. In the meantime, I would have the love of a woman, and the friendship and respect of a good man. When Dinseh left, we opened the second package. It was prints of the nude photographs, and all the negatives. Obviously, he had decided that they were Preeti's property, and she should be the judge of what to do with them. We placed the prints in an album, and put away the negatives in a safe place till the day that she might want to display herself as a work of art in a photography magazine, if and when we migrated to the United States.

In subsequent months, Dinesh was always at our parties; and many a photograph by him came to decorate our little home. As the days went by, he began to pay increasing attention to Vinona, Preeti's friend. In fact, he confided to us one day that he had begun to take her out, and that he was very fond of her.

"Do you love her?" asked Preeti.

"What would you want me to say?" he replied rhetorically.

He had Preeti at a disadvantage, but not for long. She cupped his handsome face in both her hands, and said slowly, and softly: "I want you to tell me that you love her." She let go his face, stepped back and continued: "Now, Dinesh, you can be as happy as Amrik and I."

"Yes, we will need you at the wedding," came his unexpected reply.

"You never told us that you had proposed to her?" said Preeti.

"I haven't, but I will. The marriage is a foregone conclusion. I remember you telling me a long time ago that 'once you have love, there is nothing earthshaking about marriage.' I'm sure you're right."

"Dinesh, those words were not mine. Those were the words that Amrik spoke to me when he proposed; and I know he was right."

"I can see now why you would sit alone in a hotel lobby reading what a certain professor of theology had to say about salvation, about his goal of life. But I much prefer our own professor." He looked at me as he said these words. As we had come to know each other better, I had taught him what I knew of philosophy, and he had taught me what I know about photography. Both had been excellent pupils, both having produced on occasion creations that rivaled those of the teacher. Thanks to him, I now owned a camera.

The marriage was set for November. It was the time when Harbaksh and Mohini were here for the wedding of Preeti's cousin. They and Veena stayed with us, sleeping on the carpet in the living room. We had offered them our bedroom, being much too embarrassed at offering nothing better than a carpet for them, but they would not hear of it.

Dinesh already knew a lot about them. It had been friendship at first glance. Harbaksh and Dinesh really hit it off. They sat apart in one corner of the room the first time they met, talking I know not what. It had been barely a matter of fifteen minutes, and they were laughing away like old friends. Every now and then, they would sneak a glance at Preeti and me, and then break out guffawing. From the way they were going, I figured they would soon be exhausted. "What's all the laughter about?" I asked finally, unable to hold back my curiosity.

"I was just telling him how you and Preeti broke to us the news of your proposed marriage," replied Harbaksh. "I have not had occasion to tell you before, but Mohini and I still sometimes think back on it; and every time we do, we remember how funny it was—us sitting there posing as if for a family portrait, and the two of you acting out a well-rehearsed play."

"But it was not rehearsed. We swear it; it just came out that way, spontaneously," I replied.

There were smiles all around while we sat back thinking of the good old times in Solan.

"Harbaksh," said Dinesh, "I would like you and your family to come to my wedding."

This is going to be fun, I thought, and Preeti smiled as I looked at her. Her sentiments were the same as mine.

Dinesh had been converted to atheism, but Vinona wanted a conventional religious wedding, not because she disagreed with his ideas, but because she liked the pomp and show that went along with it. So that was the way it was. Ajay and Shiv were with us too. They were part of my family, along with Harbaksh, Mohini and Veena. Shiv had, in addition, a direct invitation from Vinona so his parents would not object. There was much crying at the wedding, of course, but with tears of happiness in anticipation of good times to come. The newlyweds moved into a house near us in Defence Colony. We had convinced them by our example that people are sometimes better off taking their cues from the birds, that is, leave the parental nest, and make a nest of your own. Solitude is fertile ground for love to grow and flourish. Company is all very well, at times, but it should be of your own choosing, and only when you wish for it, which is not all that often when you have just been married; in fact, may not be for years. The joint family system does not make allowance for such a possibility. In my way of thinking, it is preferable to have the in-laws as guests in your house, than for the wife to be a guest in theirs. It is psychologically much healthier all around.

XXVIII

It was well over a year since our coming to Delhi. Life had been wonderful. College was proceeding at its own slow pace, and I had come to the conclusion that there was far more to be learned outside it than within its classrooms. Anyway, knowledge was something acquired by each person individually, with his or her own mind and efforts; sometimes unassisted, as it was with me mostly, except in the company of Preeti; and sometimes with guidance, as college was supposed to be. But in philosophy, at least, I found little to learn there. There was far more in Harbaksh's books, in the university library, and in the process of living itself.

Professor Karmarkar's lectures were enjoyable. There was Shakespeare, and Jane Austen, and many other literary figures for me to familiarize with; but it was not outstanding. Professor Pant continued to harbor antipathy for me, though, except for my articles, I gave him little cause. But, on the whole, he was a good teacher, and I learned much history.

The real enjoyment of life, though, was with my pupils, Shiv and Ajay. Lately, one more had been added to the group: Beena, a girl who has just turned fourteen. She was from Shiv's school, and had been so impressed by all he had told her about me that she approached her father about the tuition. It had been quite easy convincing him because Shiv had shown remarkable progress in his grades in school. But it was not just his grades that had impressed her; it was far more his maturity. He had an attitude to life that bore little resemblance to that of his class-fellows. Whatever he talked of, there was an intensity and a profundity to it that was unusual for one his age; and why not? Here he had been for over a year debating the characters and motivations of *Jane Eyre;* discussing things, important and not-so-important in life; and even metaphysics, with its questions broad as existence itself, and deep as the meaning of life. There was no question in my mind that she was attracted to him.

We had, by now, finished going though *Jane Eyre,* and used to spend our time analyzing characters and motivations, and the writer's philosophic views. I remember one such memorable session. "Shiv," I had asked, "what do you think of Jane's religious views. Do you think she was an atheist like me, or do you think she was religious, like your father?"

"She was religious, but not like my father; and she was like you, but not an atheist," he replied.

"I'd give you an 'A' for that answer, if I was to grade you, but I will explain to you how you could have got an A-plus. Do you like her?"

"Yes, greatly."

"And why?"

"Because she had courage; and because what was right to her appeals to me. I found myself always cheering for her to win."

"Yes," I added, "I like her for the same reasons. She was willing to suffer a lot for the sake of God; she even agreed to go with Mr. Rivers to India as a missionary; but in the things that mattered most, she went her own way. You could say that she believed in a God who would approve of what she did. That is evident particularly if you contrast her belief with that of Mr. Rivers. His God was a demanding one, demanding self-sacrifice even at the expense of his pleasure and happiness; and even to the point that love was but a duty rather than the spontaneous motivating passion it should be. For Mr. Rivers, love, in the human sense, was an inferior emotion, not worthy of him who would be nearer God; and the act of love was even more demeaning, to be dispensed with if possible; and indulged in only with guilt, as a necessary evil."

I had, over the previous weeks and months, with the help of Preeti, given my three pupils, and Sapna as well, our version of sex education, modeled to some degree on Mr. White's version that I had received in BCS, except that it was even more liberated after our own experiences. I wanted my pupils to feel that both the spiritual and physical aspects of love were among the most profound and uplifting experiences available to man; and shame should have no play in it at all. The technical aspects of love were explained with reference to how Preeti and I dealt with it, and only in the context of love. I made it pretty clear that in any other context, shame becomes unavoidable, and it leaves a bad aftertaste. We also talked about clothes and nudity, and beauty not just of nature, the clouds and scenes and animals, but of human beauty as well; of man and woman. We talked of motivation and inspiration; comradeship; and love; above all, the love of man and woman. And I know they understood.

"What meant most to Jane" I continued, "was the love of Mr. Rochester. He was now disfigured, having lost a hand; and was scarred on his face from burns; and blind so he could no longer gaze into her eyes and her heart with his piercing eyes the way she had found so irresistible before; yet she loved him. She no longer needed him for money; she had enough of her own. But she needed him because her heart and mind demanded it; the power of his words and thoughts, and the intensity of his caring for her, of his desire to possess her, all these evoked an answering call in her. Being with him was no sacrifice for her. Some people would say it was.

"Look," they would claim, "she could have had many a handsome man. She was well off, intelligent, even brilliant. She had no reason to settle for a cripple. She owed him nothing so great. His misfortune was not of her making; it was of his own. Her debt to him was little; perhaps a little gratitude and sympathy; but not her whole life." Yes, that could be said, but it would miss the whole meaning, the drive of that which we call love. She did not eventually marry him because she felt sympathy for him; no more did she as an obligation for past kindnesses done her on his part. She married him because she found him the most attractive man in the world, and because she would give of her own body and soul only to him whom she loved, and who loved her in return.

"It is for that very reason that she refused Mr. Rivers' proposal of marriage. She neither loved him, nor was she ever loved by him. The marriage was conceived by Mr. Rivers as a duty to God, and Jane could not ever conceive of marriage in those terms. In the things that mattered most to her, there was no duty owed God; simply a duty to oneself and one's happiness. If you think of it deeply, God mattered little to her. Even going to India on a mission of God was really to go there on a mission of hope; to remove illiteracy and ignorance; and to nurse the sick. Whether the reason should have been ascribed to God, or to the joy such activities would give her of their own, I will leave for you to decide, but clearly God was not a prime necessity.

"Jane was a self-made woman. She hung in with her vision of reality all through the trying years of her childhood at Lowood School. At Thornfield, with Mr. Rochester, she felt the first challenge to her mind, and to her heart. The man was intellectually powerful; he seemed as if to play with her, both with her heart and her mind. Yet, under his gruff exterior and his seemingly unpredictable, whimsical ways, she could see that he was a man of steady purpose, who knew what was good and bad, right and wrong. He could charm the most beautiful of women, such as Blanche, but he disdained them, giving himself instead to the outwardly plain, but inwardly intense and beautiful, Jane. It has been said that Charlotte Bronte deliberately used a plain-looking heroine rather than one who was beautiful. It was a challenge she set herself to show her talented sisters, Emile and Anne, that such could be achieved successfully. Not only did she achieve it, but she arrived at a universal truth, that the beauty of the mind outweighs that of the body. It is, of course, best to have both, but where a choice exists, the mind, the most pre-eminent of human characteristics, has no better."

One day, at Sapna's insistence, Preeti decided to model for us. She wore salwaar-kameezes, and then some of the sarees my mother had bought for her; and some she had received in her previous marriage; but the crowning glory of the display was the black evening gown.

"Oh . . . Oh!" cried Ajay, "You are beautiful."

"Come to me, you charmer," said Preeti; and as he came to her, she grabbed him in her arms and kissed him passionately on the lips. Then she hugged him close, and held him there for a long, long time. When she let him go, she said: "This is what you get for telling a woman she is beautiful."

Ajay was crimson, blushing all over. "Thank you," he said.

"Unh Unh. Don't ever thank a woman for a kiss. You are a handsome man; she owes you just as much as you owe her. Do you want another kiss?"

"No!" He ran and hid himself among us.

"Are you sure, Ajay?" she asked.

He turned around and looked at her. Slowly building up courage, he said: "May be one more."

"Then come and get it."

This time she let him kiss her. It was soft and gentle, more in keeping with a boy who has been awed by the beauty of a woman, but there was much warmth in it. I would not have to teach my pupils any more of love. They were now forever in its grip; the question of arranged marriages for them did not arise; they would never permit them. I had at last accomplished something, and without much effort. Yes, I had spent long hours teaching them, but they were as much a pleasure for me as for them. And I had my fun too: the movies together, the picnics, the outings to the museum and the zoo; and even to places of historical interest. Life was so much fun, I could not understand why it had not always been so.

Towards the end of January, Mr. Gopalan gave a party at the Gymkhana Club, inviting personal friends, members of the press, and people like me. Also invited was Professor Srivastava. Till now, I had only read his columns, never seen him. He was consistent in his philosophy, and it had evoked a grudging respect in me, though tinged with sorrow that an intellect of his caliber should have let itself be led astray along the classical dead-end street. Now I would get to solve the mystery firsthand. Mr. Gopalan made the introductions and walked away with Preeti, leaving the Professor and me alone.

"Tell me," the Professor began, "what sort of books do you read?"

"The sort of books I would like to write one day."

"So you wish to be a writer. Fiction or non-fiction?"

"Fiction, I think. I wish to dramatize in my books an ideal the way I see it," I explained.

"In that case, you must read my kind of book; like the Geeta or the Vedas. Have you read them?"

"Yes, occasionally."

"And what do you have in mind when you read them? Knowledge? Enjoyment? Enlightenment?"

"I read them not so much for enjoyment as for understanding what moves you and people like you, what you all think, and why."

"And have you understood?"

"Not completely. Several possibilities have occurred to me, but I'm still hoping that there is something missing in my analysis. You see, the thoughts that keep crossing my mind while I read these books are not what one would call charitable, if you know what I mean."

"It is not charitable of you to say that, but let us hope that today I can dispel them."

"I have my doubts," I replied, "but I am willing to listen and be persuaded. As to being uncharitable, I am one of those who prefer not to bend the truth. That is the only reason I have those feelings."

The Professor continued: "That is nice to know. Now where were we? Ah yes, I was going to dispel the uncharitable thoughts from your mind. So let me begin. The way I look at life, I believe a man should have love, and only love in his heart."

"Love for whom?"

"Love for his fellowmen."

"All of them?"

"Yes, all."

"But are all deserving of our love?" I questioned.

"I know what you are thinking. You are still young, but I see the mark of intelligence on your brow. Your guru, Guru Nanak, did he not preach that we should love everyone?"

"I could say yes, but to answer truthfully, I would have to say that I am not fully conversant with his philosophy. I have never read it personally, only listened to what people have said."

"Well then, how about Christ? Surely, with your educational background . . ." Here he glanced at my blazer—I was dressed in my school blues, the light blue blazer that was yours when you won the blues, that is, made the school team in any sport. It was hockey for me. He finished his sentence: "you are familiar with his teachings?"

"Yes, you could say that."

"And how would you characterize them?"

"I would say that, in many respects, they are much like the Geeta. There are differences, but there are also major similarities."

"How true! How true! I see you have a perceptive mind. Now, do you not see how love is everything?"

"Mr. Srivastava, . . ."

"Call me Panditji," he interrupted, "I much prefer that. It is Indian and has the ring of authenticity that makes me feel one with my land."

"Punditji," I continued, "why should I love those who are not worthy of my love?"

"My child, do not look on people with a clouded eye. Him who you believe to be a scoundrel; or the one who is a thief; or even him who has murdered, have pity on them, for they have been deluded by Maya. Their Aatman, like the Aatman in the rest of us, is pure and bright. What you do to them, you do to their Aatman; for that only in them is real. They are as much a representation of God, to use a term more familiar to you than Brahman, as you and I. So why should we hold them in contempt? You must shed the veil of illusion that blinds your sight to the beauty within, and see them for what they really are, creations of God himself, with God dwelling within them, as pure and untouched by time or travail as distant mountain snow."

"Punditji," I interjected, trying to bring a semblance of definition to his terms, "why do you have such contempt for reality?"

"You are mistaken, my son. Reality to me is all there is. I pine for it."

"I do not understand. Here, just a minute ago, you were willing to overlook one of its major aspects, crime, and now you say reality means everything to you. Could you explain?"

"Son, if you wish to see reality, you must use the inward eye. Look inside you; that is where reality is. The real you lies there hidden from your eyes."

"Are you trying to tell me that this person standing here in this blazer before you is not me, and the person I am talking to is not you? What are we then?"

"You and I, I and you, these are concepts of delusion. We are in the grip of a malady so powerful that our minds deceive us."

"Then, Panditji, who is doing the talking if not us?"

"That is the marvel of God's Maya. He has created a magic shadow-show where characters come and go . . ."

I interrupted his words with verse:

> "For in and out, above, about, below,
> 'Tis nothing but a Magic Shadow-show
> Play'd in a box whose candle is the Sun,
> Round which we Phantom Figures come and go."

"Yes, yes! That's it! I like your words."

"I wish they were mine, Punditji, but they are not. They belong to a Persian poet by the name of Omar Khayyam, who lived about eight centuries ago."

"A man of much wisdom, I see."

"Yes, I think so too, but I'm not sure you would approve of him. You see, he is one of my type of writers."

"In what way?"

"He writes of Love and Fate."

"But that is what I write too."

"Yes, but he writes of earthly love, the love between man and woman, not between the God in man and the God without, as you do."

"I see. Then he has not seen the light. There is and can only be one type of love, that which you feel in unity with the One. It is bliss beyond any that can be conceived of in earthly endeavors. The love between man and woman is momentary, and the fleeting joy is tinged with the pain of separation; but the blissful union with the One is eternal."

At about this time, Preeti joined us. Seeing that our table was empty, she offered to bring us drinks. I protested that I should be the one getting the drinks, but she pointed out that I must keep the Professor company; she would fetch the drinks. Whereupon, I asked her for a glass of red wine. The Professor declined alcohol. "Daughter," he said, "such things are not for me. Intoxication scatters the mind; but I live for God. A nimboo-paani will be more than enough."

When she left, he observed: "I am surprised that you drink, and at so young an age."

"Age, Panditji, has little to do with it. You are of age when you take full responsibility for your life. I did that over a year ago. As far as drink is concerned, I know alcohol loosens the tongue, makes conversation easy, and warms the heart so that the world seems friendlier. Right now, standing here with you, I perhaps don't need any such help, but who knows later. Anyway, drinking is a minor matter; not something I would place in the realm of right and wrong."

"But surely you see that all things have small beginnings. Some day, you may find alcohol irresistible. Then it would become a matter of morality even in your eyes. I see it as another of those traps Maya sets for the unwary."

"Punditji, I don't accept the notion that this around us is unreal, or Maya, as you put it. But let us get back to love for the moment. I love my wife very much. Why should that be considered anything less than lofty?"

"I would say you are fortunate, son; it is not something to object to, but in the larger view of things, you are making yourself vulnerable to ever deeper attachments to this world."

"I believe that to have attachments in this world is proper," I countered.

"But the love of a woman is one of the strongest distractions on the path to Truth. You cannot have divided loyalties. You either love your maker or you love others; you have to make the choice."

"But I see no evidence of a maker."

"How could you say a thing like that? If there was no maker, what are we doing here?"

"Merely because we exist does not mean there has to be a maker," I objected.

"And why not?"

"Because if you believe that there is no beginning to the universe, as you and I both believe, then we can go on regressing *ad infinitum* ascribing our making to a perpetually regressing set of parents, but never having the need of any other maker who lives in something you call a Real Reality."

"He does not live in it, he is it," the Professor corrected.

"But, Panditji," I objected, "don't you think you are overdoing it, making postulates of grander and grander cosmologies when, in fact, you have no evidence of them at all?"

"Of course there is evidence. Who do you think created the universe if not someone of immense power and ability?"

"No one."

"You mean to say it came into existence by itself?"

"Like your real reality? No, I am merely saying that it has existed for ever, without a beginning, and you yourself have conceded that."

"But, son, I meant the maker has existed for ever; we are merely creations within him."

"I only see us, and the universe around us. Where is this maker?"

"Ah, that is the goal of life, to see the maker with your inward eye."

"And have you seen him?" I asked.

"There are few who have, a lucky few. But I am not one of them. I have not dedicated myself enough to the seeking of him. One day in the not too distant future, I will."

"What makes you so sure that there is a maker?"

"Look around you. Look at the perfection of existence; the trees; the flowers, the people. What more evidence do you need?"

"But only a little while ago you dismissed all this as an illusion. If you use this as evidence, then you are conceding it as the True Reality; in which case, you will have to accept my way of thinking, and produce as evidence what is accepted as evidence in this world, evidence amenable to the senses or the rational intellect."

"An illusion this is. What else but a transcendental maker could produce such a wonderful illusion?"

My assessment of the Professor had been right—he would not play by the rules of logic. Rationality was anathema to his thesis. But I wanted to force a concession that his concept was wishful thinking, mere whimsy, though I would grant that it was a very organized one. He and his predecessors had used the past several millennia to perfect it, but how can one perfect that which has no foundation? Like any house made of cards, it would remain just as vulnerable to collapse. So I continued to pursue him. "Punditji," I asked, "how do you know that this is an illusion?"

It was the old game of Liza, Henry and the hole in the bucket. Henry wanted Liza to fetch him some water. She objected that the bucket had a hole:

"There's a hole in the bucket, dear Henry,
          dear Henry, there's a hole>"
"Then plug it, dear Liza, dear Liza, then plug it."
"With what shall I plug it, dear Henry . . . ?"
With straw, dear Liza . . ."
But the straw is too thick, dear Henry . . ."
"Then cut it, dear Liza . . ."
"With what shall I cut it, dear Henry ; ; ; ?"
"With an axe, dear Liza, . . ."
"But the axe is too dull, dear Henry . . ."
"Then sharpen it, dear Liza . . ."
"With what shall I sharpen it, dear Henry . . . ?"
"With a stone, dear Liza, . . ."
But the stone is too dry, dear Henry . . ."
"Then wet it, dear Liza, . . ."
"With what shall I wet it, dear Henry . . . ?"
"With water, dear Liza . . ."
"With what shall I fetch it, dear Henry . . . ?"
"With the bucket, dear Liza . . ."
"But there's a hole in the bucket, . . ."

If he was going to call everything an illusion, then I would, in the manner of Liza, force him to treat it as one too. Before he could answer, Preeti came back with the drinks, and right after her, Mr. Gopalan drifted in. He had a whisky and soda in his hand. I looked at the Professor to see if he would object, but he desisted, though the provocation was grave. Preeti handed us our drinks; she herself had a nimboo-paani.

"It is good to see two of my eminent columnists so deeply engrossed in conversation. Panditji, have you met Mrs. Randhawa?"

"Yes, briefly, before she went to get us some drinks."

"Amrik, that is not nice of you at all; making your wife fetch your drinks. You must change with the times."

I smiled at him. He had inadvertently revealed another flaw in the Professor's thinking, so I thought I would avail of it. "Punditji," I asked, "do you agree with Mr. Gopalan? Do you think men should fetch drinks for women, or do you think it should be the way it was, the woman fetching drinks for the man?"

Preeti glared at me. I could hear her silent thoughts screaming: "You ungrateful wretch!" But I winked at her to calm her nerves. "This is not as it seems," I explained silently as best I could. The Professor was now in a quandary, but he soon had an answer.

"In our culture," he replied, "women take care of the needs of men and children. Men have responsibility for the financial support of the family and its spiritual guidance, but woman is the handmaiden of man."

"And what do you have to say about that, Mrs. Randhawa?" asked Mr. Gopalan.

"You do not have to be so formal, Mr. Gopalan; you can call me Preeti," ahe said."

"I'd be delighted," replied the editor. "What do you have to say to the Professor's observation, Preeti?"

"I believe the Professor is trying to say that we women are second-class citizens." Preeti, as always, was blunt, but with her good looks, she could get away with it.

"Call me Punditji, please! It is more soothing to the ears."

"Punditji," said Preeti.

"Daughter, it is not I who say it. It has been so willed by God."

"That I do not believe, Punditji. Our customs are man-made, by and for the use of man, and only man. Let us not burden God with our faults."

"I believe the lady has a point," Mr. Gopalan remarked. "You and I are old-fashioned, Punditji. The educated women of today cannot be expected to sit in the kitchen and spend the rest of their time massaging our tired feet. They have a point when they say that their feet are tired too; they need a massage just as much. Luckily for me, my wife believes that old is gold, and I live in peace and comfort—guiltily, I grant you, Preeti, but comfort none the less."

Preeti smiled knowingly at the editor, laughing in her mind at his awkward concession to her presence. "Punditjit," she asked, "what is the position of women in your scheme of salvation?"

"Bayti,"—he had momentarily switched to the Indian version of daughter—"the salvation of a woman lies in her man. It is only through him, through care of him in her wifely duties, that she can hope to be born a man in the next incarnation, and then as a man, if she does the caste-duty demanded of him, she may achieve salvation."

Preeti was incensed. No one had ever treated her or women so shabbily. Granted the Professor was soft-spoken and very polite, but his ideas were insulting. "Punditji, I don't believe this salvation stuff, and I think even you merely wish to believe it because it is convenient to your arguments. I think women are every bit as intelligent as men; on occasion more so. We do the cooking; look after the home; and give birth to and look after the babies, just as your mother did for you. We make life worth living for men with our affection, our charms, and our pleasures. You only have to pick up any book of poetry to see how much men owe us; yet this is what we are offered in return? Salvation in another lifetime? It is unjust, too cruel, too unworthy of a man of wisdom like you, Punditji."

"But, bayti, we are all here in this world of illusion, all subject to its captivating influence. You are upset with the way of the Vedas; but that is the guile of Maya. It makes us believe and think this way. You are reading the lines of this illusion; you must try to read between the lines. Ignore what seems to be; think of what is. There is no other way. You mustn't wish to be perpetually plunged in darkness. Fight your way out to the light."

"If your mother had believed that version of reality when

you were a little baby, Punditji," she replied, "you would have been abandoned; and she would now be on her way to reincarnation as a man. Is that it?"

"No, bayti. We all have our duties. It is proper action for a mother to look after her baby."

"Even though it is an illusion?"

"Illusion, reality, these are just words; little toys we have weaved out of the cobwebs of Maya. As words, they do not express anything. Real thinking is not done with the concepts you call words, nor with reasoning as your husband is so fond of believing, but with the will. It can pierce all, and with its inward gaze see directly without the mediation of rationality, logic, and all those other creations of illusion such as science that we hold on to so greedily. Yes, it can see then the real reality, Brahman. There is no comparable splendor. Once you know that, you will disdain what you see here. Your husband had asked me earlier why I disdain what he calls reality. This is my answer: because it is only an illusion."

We were back where we had started—there was a hole in the bucket. Enough was enough, I concluded, so I steered the conversation to other areas, such as the Professor's university, and the type of students who took his course; and when all had become banal and pointless, Preeti and I took our leave and joined the other guests.

XXIX

A year has gone by since the meeting with Professor Srivastava. Much has happened in the interval so that life has been anything but dull. An increasing number of letters have praised my column in the National Express. Most of the topics that I had visualized earlier have been covered, like clothes, free love, generalizations, false and true, a woman's sanctity, public expression of feelings of warmth; and in addition, newer ones such as the needs of a growing mind, eve-teasing, and integrity. Writing is also coming easier to me, and I have started the opening chapters of a novel about life in BCS.

Some four months ago, Preeti won a commendation for her paintings in an exhibit at the School of Fine Arts, and she sold one of her paintings through a gallery in Connaught Place. The price was only fifty rupees, but it was an occasion for much celebration in our home; and it was the opening salvo in what was to become an illustrious career. Modeling, meanwhile, was proceeding apace, though Preeti had restricted her trips to Bombay to only two that year. There was no romance this time, for Vinona went along to keep her husband company, but Preeti enjoyed herself now that they were all such thick friends. Dinesh and Vinona have not been wasting any time either—their first baby is due four months from now.

I still have my three pupils learning the intricacies of the English language from me; and even more so the philosophy of life *a la* Amrik. We have covered *Binodini* and *The Broken Nest* by Rabindra Nath Tagore, and are presently working our way through *The Fountainhead* by Ayn Rand. Ajay is still his delightful self. Shiv and Beena, I believe, have an affair going, though of what depth I do not know. They are wonderful students, the best I could think of. Shiv, in particular, has matured into quite a man, and will soon be starting college. He now drops by my house whenever he wishes, even on Sundays. It is difficult to believe, but he is interested in my philosophy texts. We have together studied Plato and Aristotle, and his understanding is almost as good as mine. My major advantage over him is in language, and perhaps that of a more extended period of study. I also don't have to spend time on math and science like him, but in almost all other respects, he is my equal. With philosophy, Shiv is in his natural element. He is very definitely an Aristotelian, like me, and he wants to become a writer, again like me.

What else? Ah yes, I had completely forgotten. You might be wondering what, if anything, happened to my hair. Did I cut it, or is it still the same. To answer as quickly and briefly as possible so as not to keep you in suspense too long, let me confess that they are still there, long and uncut like a lion's mane; but in wraps, as before, under a turban. Is this the beginning of a compromise of principles, you may well ask. How could I still accept a religious symbol? And what about the steel bangle I still wear on my wrist? Is that not a religious symbol too? As so often happens prior to the rendering of a full explanation, the answer can conceivably be yes and no, but my action, or lack of it, is not a philosophical compromise, no more than it is a religious acceptance.

When I was a young child wearing my turban for the first time, this addition to my attire seemed onerous. The head normally yearns to be free; one instinctively pulls it back if someone tries to place a hand on it. To place a turban, with all its restrictions, was much beyond placing a hand. Then there was also the matter of tying it. The way it is done, at least among the educated, is not a simple processs, but an art. Take a hat, for example; all you do is plop it on the head whenever you wish,

and take it off as and how you like, as many times as you
please; and when you're quite done for the day, you simply
toss it off in the direction of a hat-rack, where it will probably
make the target, given practice. No great harm is done if you
miss. The Sikh turban bears no similarity to it, nor does it to the
ladies' turban that western women wear on occasion as an item
of fashion. It is not ready-wrapped and usable, like instant
coffee. The only item of western dress that even remotely
approaches it is the necktie, since it has to be tied anew every
day; but that is easy. The turban, in contrast, is not, not without
years of practice tying it afresh daily.

A piece of fine muslin, usually six yards long and a yard
wide, it is bought initially as plain white, un-dyed cloth. You
then take it to a *lullari,* a dyer, who will dye it to the color you
wish. Any color is permissible, but I favor light or dark blue
since they match my blazer; or maroon, occasionally peach,
and sometimes cream or navy blue. There are also turbans called
cheeras, uncommon nowadays, that come with printed patterns
such as little flowers or designs on them. These particularly are
tied with a fan-shaped expansion, a *turra,* extending stiffly up
from the back of the turban over the head like a peacock
spreading its tail, an impressive backdrop to a handsome turban
and face in front. You may think it fastidious, but imagine it on
someone with the imposing figure of Harbaksh; it will look
magnificent. Sikhs have always admired class and style; and,
as a group, appearance counts for much among them.

If that is true, what then has happened to the concept of
Maya so rampant among Indians in general? To understand,
you have to take things in a somewhat different perspective.
The Sikh, as a member of the community of Sikhs, and the
religious Sikh, are two different entities. At this point, a few
introductory words on the Sikh religion may be of value. Sikh
cosmology is not as convoluted as the Hindu one; the
ceremonials are few; fewer still are the rituals; there is no
sacrifice, and no multiplicity of Gods. But the concept of Maya,
and what Aldous Huxley terms the Perennial Philosophy, are

very much in evidence. Truth, as with Hinduism, applies only to God; yet there is no equivalent contempt for reality, no urging to asceticism and, of course, there is no system of castes. In the eyes of the scriptures, everyone is equal. In practice, things are not quite so egalitarian; but such differences are not a matter of religious belief; they are rather the offspring of social custom, where Maya is taken as literal reality as in the rest of the world, not as an illusion.

The truly religious Sikh, as with the Hindu, is a sorry specimen. He is not as self-effacing, though; but his motivation, his zeal and commitment, even in the face of great challenge and prodding from reality, is mystical. It owes no allegiance to reason. Yet you have to admire the highly religious Sikh for a history awash with deeds of valor and unwavering commitment to cause and purpose. The Akalis, vanguards of Maharaja Runjeet Singh's army, are an example, but even those of later times have covered themselves with glory. In the final analysis, though, where reason is not the driver, the credit owed must be tempered with that knowledge; and with the likelihood, given time, that catastrophe awaits inexorably down the line. The headlong plunge of unreason is akin to a runaway locomotive; sooner or later, it must crash. In that light, I consider my religious brethren as a lesser breed of human; not in any sense of barbarism or cruelty, or even callousness, but as an unfortunate waste of precious intellect; a mind gone awry. From my vantage point, a religious man is one with an effectively sabotaged intellect, one that is functionally stricken. I can think of no worse calamity this side of insanity. Enclosed in a self-made vise that permits no learning response to the elevating light of reality, and in a state of arrested maturation from the continuing disuse of reason, their minds are the functional counterparts of the shrunken heads so gruesomely displayed as trophies by South American head-hunting tribes.

The non-religious Sikh, on the other hand, knows little of the mystical underpinnings of the Sikh religion, but is steeped in the traditions of the community. He likely looks at the example of the last of the gurus, Gobind Singh (since my early days at Solan, I have learned a little more of the writings of this last Sikh guru; and I am a little disappointed at the degree to which he accepted some of the Hindu religious beliefs; but his actions in the field of reality retain their splendor), and aspires to equivalent courage and integrity in the face of evil; with justice as we know it, where acts are acts with motivation and purpose, and no one is an illusion; where rights belong to individuals, and not to some imaginary, supernatural being; and where the apparent reality is the only reality.

As a member of such a community, could I shed my steel bangle, that stainless symbol of strength and integrity, or my hair and turban, the marks of acceptance with pride of the many acts of compassion and courage that shine in the annals of the community. In India, at least, where all know what a Sikh stands for, the shedding of these symbols would be construed as a denial of ideals that are precious to my persona, and their keeping would not compromise my belief in reason and the existence of only one reality, the reality of the senses and of rational inference. Whether my parents, brother, other relatives, friends, and Sikhs in general, view it as religious acceptance, is irrelevant to me. They could throw me out of the religious fraternity for my writings. I would accept that with equanimity, even pleasure, knowing that my views had been understood, not brushed aside. Yet there is no way they could deny me my secular heritage, of which there is much among the Sikhs. All these I pondered, but the final decision was easy. Preeti's words: "I like you the way you are," said it all.

Retaining the hair does not in any way mean that I consider myself different from any of my Hindu friends who have atheistic ideas similar to mine. In my view, we all belong to the community of man; and as such, we all retain the same options to do with ourselves as we please. Having grown up in the Sikh community, I have come to regard certain symbols such as the turban as imbued with certain secular meanings quite apart from the religious ones. If, for any reason, some time in the future, there was a change in what the Sikhs as a group believed they stand for, and it clashed with my principles, I would feel that the symbols had lost their value, and therefore need not be adhered to. Till then, who is to say whether hair should be left as Nature intended them, or cut as fashion dictates? It is a curious fact that long hair is a sign of beauty among women, but currently has no such implication among men; an observation that, to my mind at least, has received less thought than it deserves.

January 20, 1955 is a memorable day on my calendar of events. This is the day Shiv took part in the annual declamation contest at his school. The school teacher in charge of the contest had asked for volunteers. It had been decided that the ten students who had signed up would be permitted to speak on topics of their own choosing, each for a period of eight minutes. Shiv had discussed a variety of subjects with me prior to making this choice. Finally, he had come up with the most unusual of the ten that were discussed that twentieth of January. He titled his talk "We are what we are." To a casual observer, it was a mere tautology, but for Shiv and I it was the essence of the philosophical dilemma of our land. I helped only in that I discussed with him over again some of the ideas that had given birth to this topic in his mind; but I never helped him write what he was to say, neither the ideas or the language; nor did he rehearse it with me; in fact, I had not even seen what he had written. He wished to demonstrate to me what he had achieved, and I was keen to put my confidence in him to the test. I was not disappointed.

He was the last of the speakers. He began: "I am; you are; we are; they are; or I, you, we, they, are not. Which is the truth? This is not the kind of question that troubles a common man, but we are not common; we are the educated, the thinkers. Our minds are enlightened; they are buoyant, ever rising to a challenge, aspiring to escape the heavy dreariness and sloth of mere survival. They dare to think of what is and what is not, even imagine it proper to frame a question in that manner; a question that has curiously troubled thoughtful man since time immemorial. I say 'curiously' because the choice to me is obvious and self-evident. Of course we are; how could we not be? But there are many who have denied our existence.

"Let us, for the moment, postpone the reasons why, and instead just look at what it means to be. If we are, what then does it imply? It means that I stand here before you, speaking to you. The sounds I make are not just sounds, but words with unambiguous meanings which each of you understands; and these words are concepts, thoughts compressed into audio-visual symbols. The most human of human achievements, these are the symbols of language.

"The senses sense the reality about us; the mind marshals all it knows; the two come together, and lo, we understand what we have sensed. It is seldom the same. Even things we know before are seen afresh each occasion, for the time, the place, the circumstances are different; and the mind knows and remembers, in words. There is a fresh nuance each time; sometimes even a new word to express a thought quite different from the ones we've known before; and so our language grows in its depth and subtlety, grows as we continue to apprehend reality. And as our language grows, so grows our ability to think, for thinking is but a play of thoughts; and words are the bricks of thoughts.

"Every day, every waking moment, we think; we cannot not think; the mind cannot be turned off. Even asleep, thoughts constantly cross our mind; vague admittedly, and perhaps disconnected, but thoughts none the less. Even dreams have stories. And what do we think? We think: "If this, then that: if not this, then not that; if I am, then this; if I am not, then this something else." It is the process of reason and logic. There is no escape; no other way to think.

"Yet there are many among us who would have us believe that all this does not exist. "It is not," they say. And then they try to tell us why it is not, but all through their argument, they reason with us, show us with logic what they mean when they say it is not. The very faculty, reason, that they say is impotent to grasp some other reality they believe in, they use to convince us of its impotence. If they succeed, they have proved that the faculty and process which we call reason is indeed very potent. If they fail, and we are convinced of that, it still proves reason as very potent; only what they were trying to demonstrate was false.

"To denigrate reason without the use of words is impossible; but the use of words without reason is impossible too. The laws of grammar are a process of logic. Words arranged according to these laws express thoughts understandable to all who know the language; words divorced from this discipline of logic which we call grammar are like curry, for the ingredients are forever lost in the mixture, making the end-result merely a succession of sounds with no connection except that of a random sequence. Speech without the use of reason is no longer speech; it is simply the un-understandable babble of a human animal, jungle chatter expressing sounds, but no more.

"To suggest that knowledge can be obtained without the use of reason is a contradiction in terms; to suggest that such knowledge exists is a contradiction of reality. To attempt to demonstrate it is foolhardy. To attempt to concentrate on one thing only to the exclusion of all else is not to evict reason from the mind, but to use it to the most intense degree. "Mind," you say to it, "stop thinking of anything else. Just stay on this thought alone. If you do, I will be able to do what I wish to do." A logical statement has been presented to the mind; if it sounds reasonable, the mind will do what you wish it to do. There is no other way it can be done.

"The mind is programmed to function through the use of reason; it requires no effort; it happens willy-nilly. To make a pretense of abolishing the process is simply another use of the process. This is the reality; there is no escape. You can delude yourself, but only if you reason yourself to delusion. But you might say: "What about the words 'rational' and 'irrational'. Can a man not be irrational?"

"The answer to that is: "Yes, a man can be irrational, but being irrational merely means using wrong reasoning, not not using reason at all." It is said that if you meditate, and if you train yourself at it enough, you will be able to abandon reason, and use a new faculty, super-rational intuition, via which you can apprehend knowledge directly. But the claim is false. Intuition is merely subliminal reasoning. If anything is apprehended at all, the mind will accept that as something sensed; then it will subject it to the test of logic and reason by comparing it to all that had been learned through the senses in one's entire experience. The mind will tell you that you have used much imagination, and come up with a fanciful construct that exists only in your imagination. The only way you can claim it as reality is to deny the verdict of your mind, and lie, first to yourself, and then to the rest of the world. That which is not real cannot become real merely because you wish it to be so.

"Aristotle said that that which is, is, and there are no two ways about it. It is the Law of Identity, implicit within which is the acceptance of the axiomatic concept, "Existence exists." People before him, and people after him, have tried to deny the truth of that statement. But every argument they have used implicitly accepts the statement. If you are trying to convince me that what I see about me is not real, that I am not real, that you are not real; then if I were to accept your statement, you and I would have to be accepted as not existing. If so, who was trying to convince who that the two did not exist? Non-existents cannot talk to non-existents; even the talk cannot exist since somebody has to be doing the talking, and that somebody must exist.

"Ladies and gentlemen, I submit that we are, and if we are, then we are what our senses tell us we are. We are what we are. Thank you."

For a moment there was silence; then there was thunderous applause. Everybody was standing. But Shiv had said nothing that was new to me. We had discussed all these thoughts many times, but I had never realized how well he had understood.

His was an incredible mind. At seventeen going on eighteen, he had grasped what few ever do. It was an overwhelming triumph for him, for me, and for reason.

Shiv accepted the trophy, and as he walked back from the stage, he stopped momentarily and scanned the hall for us. Preeti and I were standing at the back. His eyes met ours, and for a few bright seconds, the world stood still. Smiles of acknowledgment briefly crossed our three faces, and then he stepped down. I could see him hugging his father. They talked for several minutes, his father's face glowing with pride. Then they walked over to us.

"Mr. Randhawa," said Major Sharma, "I owe you an apology. I did not know. I would like to pay you for what you have done for my son; and I would like you to continue his lessons—with pay, of course."

"I cannot accept your money, Major Sharma. Your son has paid me more than was owed, in kind. Shiv will explain that to you. As for lessons, he is now my equal. There is little I could teach him that he does not already know, but as a friend we, my wife and I, would expect him to visit us frequently. The warmth of our home depends on people like him,"

When the Sharmas left, I saw Beena coming away from her parents as they were leaving, and hurrying over to us. She hugged Preeti, emotion overflowing all over her lovely face. "Preeti," she said, "I love him."

"I know," said Preeti; "here is a key to our bedroom. Shiv has one to the front door. We are going away to Solan for a week. We want the two of you to make sure that the plants are watered and that our home is looked after."

Beena kissed Preeti on the cheek, then protested lamely: "But it is cold in Solan this time of year."

"Not for us," replied Preeti. "Amrik will be with me; then there's a fireplace in the bedroom' and you know how the sun shines for lovers."

Beena smiled, hugged her again, gave me a hug too, and hurried off to her waiting parents.

That night, I sat at the typewriter, typing in my next column for the newspaper. "Something happened on the night of January 20 this year that may be a harbinger of good things to come. For a brief spell, my troubled land seemed troubled no more. The occasion was a declamation contest in M . . . School. The last of the speakers was my seventeen-year-old friend, Shiv Sharma. This is what he said: "I am . . ."